I0901174

POSTCARD HISTORY SERIES

Badlands, Gateways, and Ghost Towns

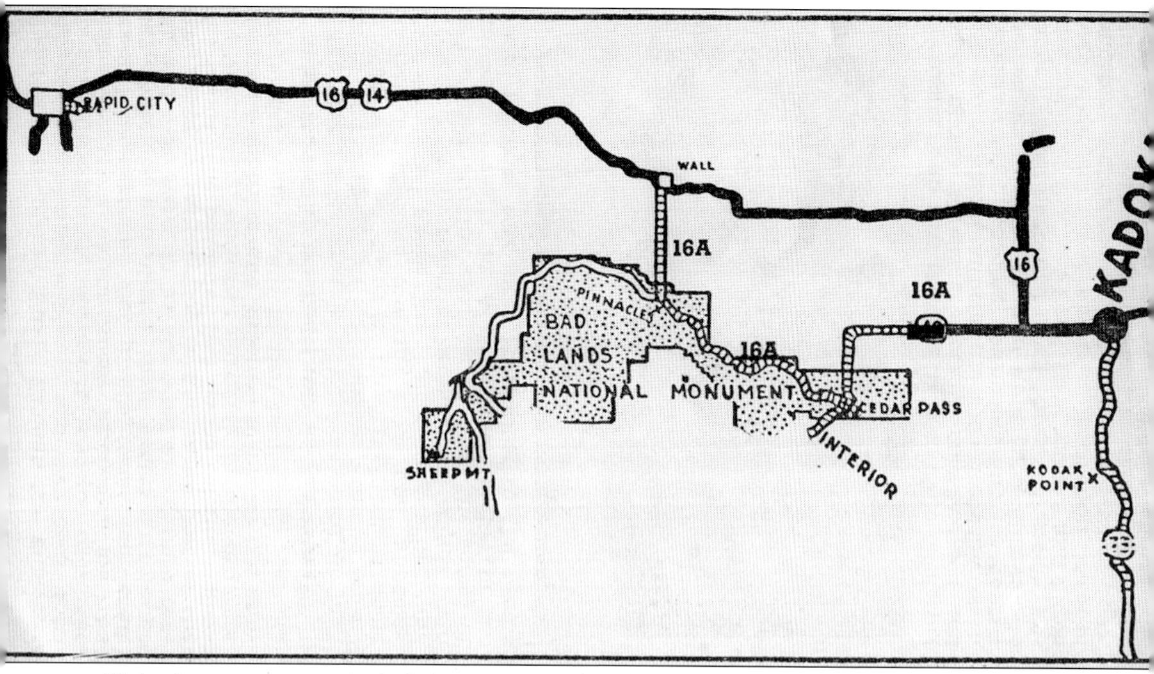

This vintage map was included on a tourist brochure compliments of Camp Joy in Kadoka, South Dakota. The map shows the accessible route through the Badlands at the time. Kodak Point pinpoints the entrance into a Badlands basin on Highway 73. Quiver Hill ascends the basin to the south. (Author's collection.)

On the Front Cover: A group of climbers are using a rope to reach the top of this formation. The loose soil and slick surface often render climbing difficult, especially after a rain. Caution is urged in attempting an ascent. (Author's collection.)

On the Back Cover: An unidentified man rides a bronc in this undated image. Support from the audience is apparent as the men at the chutes cheer him on. Rodeos are still popular in Interior, South Dakota, and are usually held on an annual basis. (Courtesy of Keith Crew.)

Postcard History Series

Badlands, Gateways, and Ghost Towns

Jan Cerney

Arcadia Publishing

ISBN 978-1-4671-2836-0

Published by Arcadia Publishing
Charleston, South Carolina

Printed in the United States of America

Library of Congress Control Number: 2017953049

For all general information contact Arcadia Publishing at:
Telephone 843-853-2070
Fax 843-853-0044
E-mail sales@arcadiapublishing.com
For customer service and orders:
Toll-Free 1-888-313-2665

Visit us on the Internet at www.arcadiapublishing.com

Contents

ACKNOWLEDGMENTS

Unless otherwise noted, all images used for this work come from my private collection that I have accumulated over the past three years. A few images were obtained from other sources. Thank you to Bonnie Riggins, Keith Crew, Bernard and Barbara Herber, Lawrence and Betty Kruse, Only Classics (onlyclassics.com), and Badlands National Park for providing images. A special thanks to Wall Drug Store for giving me permission to publish their postcards, and to the Kadoka Depot Museum for the use of their images. Finding postcards of the old towns was often difficult. In a few cases, photographs have been used. A bibliography is included at the end of the book, crediting the multiple sources I used to research the captions. I am indebted to those who have studied Badlands history extensively in the past, although there is more to glean from local sources.

INTRODUCTION

The White River Badlands presents more to the eye than its eerie scenic beauty. Within each canyon, gorge, and plain, a rich history unfolds. This landform has been many things to its inhabitants and its visitors. First and foremost, the Badlands is an obvious geological and paleontological mystery, evolving for millions of years to become what it is today. It has been a place of vision quests, a paradise for fossil hunters, a cattlemen's domain, a homesteaders' elusive dream, a tourists' destination, and a home for those who have endured its capricious nature. So extraordinary is the Badlands that a portion has been set aside as a national park. The Badlands was once a great shallow inland sea. Fossils of sea life such as the ammonites, a shell-like creature, give evidence to this. Millions of years later, an upheaval of the earth's surface occurred at the same time the Rocky Mountains formed. After millions of more years, a series of turbulent streams and rivers flowing from the west filled the area with sediment deposits that eventually eroded into the fantastic shapes we see today. The process was anything but simple and challenges the imagination to even consider how it all came about.

The first animals that lived in the area we now call the Badlands were the oreodonts, the titanothere, three-toed horses, saber-toothed cats, camels, giant pigs, rhinoceros, and protoceras. They were a unique animal life and survived until the climate changed. After they died, they were naturally interred in the vast sediments.

Fast forward a few more million years, and after more geological evolution, people appeared. Early native people's fire pits, stone tools, flakes from flint knapping, bone fragments, and potsherds validate their early occupation of the Badlands region, dating between 896 and 1187 AD. The Sioux Indians, who called themselves the Dakota, came to the area around 1775. Here, they led a nomadic life, hunted the buffalo, and lived in tepees. They used the Badlands for vision quests and as burial grounds.

When scientists from the East heard from the trappers and fur traders about the great number of fossils lying exposed in the Badlands, they came in great numbers during the 1840s and hauled away wagonloads. The Sioux called the larger fossils thunder-horses and were not happy with the scientists' intrusion. Some of the fine specimens taken are displayed in museums throughout the country.

The Sioux hunted buffalo that grazed in great herds on the prairie, but a series of dry years caused the shaggy beasts to leave. In the late 1800s, the cattlemen moved into the area with their large herds of cattle to graze and thrive on the nutritious grasses as the buffalo had. By then, the Sioux were living on reservations carved out of the Great Sioux Reservation. The leftover land was opened up to public domain. The era of the open range flourished for a time until harsh blizzards killed many cattle, driving great numbers over the precipitous Badlands Wall. When the open range ended in the early 1900s, the homesteaders, clamoring for land, came to the semiarid region of the Badlands and tried their hand at coercing the land to yield to their hard work and agriculture skills. The drought years of 1910–1911 and the Great Depression of the 1930s ended their hopes of conquering the land, causing many homesteaders to leave disappointed. But not all homesteaders left. Instead, they acquired more land and learned to adapt to its demands.

Before the railroad reached the Badlands region, the Lakota Sioux had already labeled the Badlands *mako sica*, difficult to travel across. French trappers referred to the Badlands as *mauvaise terres*, meaning terrible terrain. The rugged and nearly impenetrable Badlands Wall had also made travel difficult for the earliest native inhabitants, the fossil hunters, the cattlemen, and the settlers.

The Chicago, Milwaukee & St. Paul Railroad pushed west from Chamberlain below the Badlands Wall in 1907, bringing homesteaders and settlement with it. The steam engines required water stops about every 10 miles or so. To accommodate this important mode of transportation for goods and services, small towns sprang up, providing water for the train. Since travel was slow and cumbersome, many of these towns grew and established their own trade centers as well as post offices, schools, and churches; others provided only a store and post office. These centers of commerce and socialization dotted the landscape of the desolate and lonely regions along the White and Cheyenne Rivers in the late 19th century and early 20th century. These train stops became shipping points for cattle trailed from ranges to corrals and loading chutes, where they were loaded into boxcars for Eastern markets. Little of anything remains to remind us of those settlements other than a few foundations and memories.

Conversely, the homesteaders living on the upper prairie, north of the Badlands Wall, relied on the Chicago & North Western Railroad, which was building west from Pierre in a race against the Chicago, Milwaukee & St. Paul. The towns rising out of the prairie along this railroad were numerous too.

For 60 miles, this escarpment of rugged Badlands known as the Badlands Wall rimmed its northern edge, preventing travel from the upper prairie to the lower prairie. Early travelers approached the Badlands from other directions. But the homesteaders who were establishing themselves on the northern side of the Badlands were prevented from reaching the basin below unless they traveled miles around it or rode horseback through the precipitous landscape.

The homesteaders who filtered into the upper prairie north of the Badlands desired to penetrate the Badlands Wall to reach the prairie below. Becoming impatient with road-building progress, homesteaders took action and constructed the first crude trails. Eventually, due to organized efforts, roads were constructed in the Badlands in the 1920s and several passes opened for travel, connecting the upper prairie to the lower prairie.

When the trains no longer needed steam to power them and transportation and roads improved, the small railroad towns began to decline, especially during the Depression. Most of these once vital villages, now considered ghost towns, have disappeared; however, a few continue as modest trade centers.

South Dakota was well on its way to establishing an economy based on tourism when the Badlands achieved monument status in 1939 and became a national park in 1978. By then, suitable roads had been constructed through the most scenic portion of the Badlands.

Because of improved motor vehicles enabling people to travel farther distances, the scenic Badlands and Black Hills of South Dakota enticed tourists to explore the state's natural beauty. Towns along the main traveled roads took advantage of the traveling public and provided accommodations to house and feed tourists along the way. Ambitious entrepreneurs built cabins and motels, often with flair to appeal to the traveling public, and others established cafés, serving delicious meals. Several towns in the area advertised themselves as gateways to the Badlands and established businesses to accommodate the tourists.

Today, over a million people visit Badlands National Park every year. Not all the gateways are as busy as they used to be. With the ease of travel, tourists can travel many miles to cities that offer more choices in lodging, dining, and entertainment. Local residents shop in their area towns but also travel to larger cities for their needs and entertainment.

Badlands National Park continues to be a tourist destination during summer months, while the local population maintains their towns, ranches, and farms, supporting the rural communities that they call home.

One

The White River Badlands

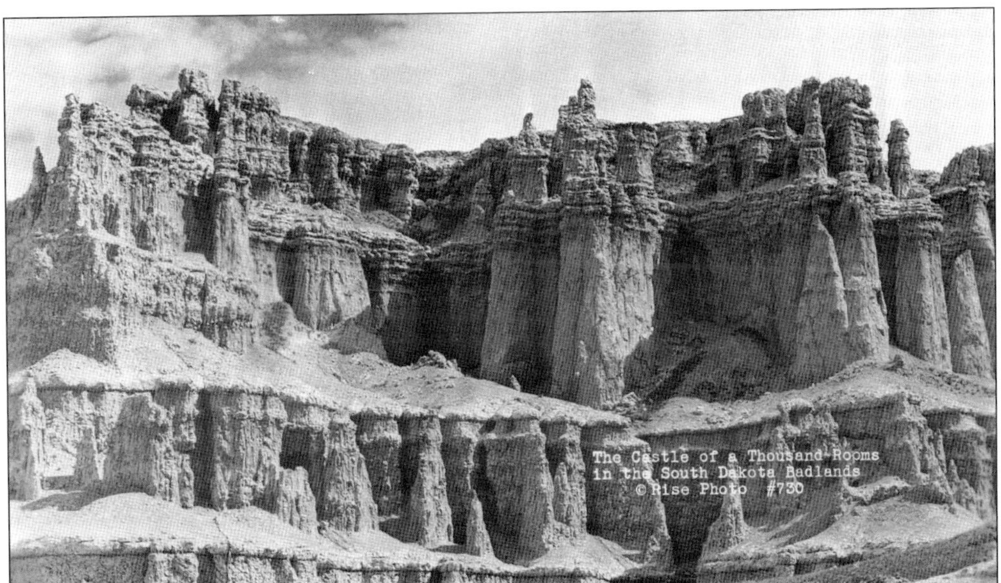

The hand of nature has worked its magic chiseling the magnificent Badlands scenery. Much of the landscape is regal in appearance, such as this formation called Castle of a Thousand Rooms. However, a closer inspection reveals that the structure is fragile and vulnerable to wind and water. The Badlands' scenery subtly changes due to erosion. A knob, a pillar, or an unusual point may disappear or wear away depending on its soil composition.

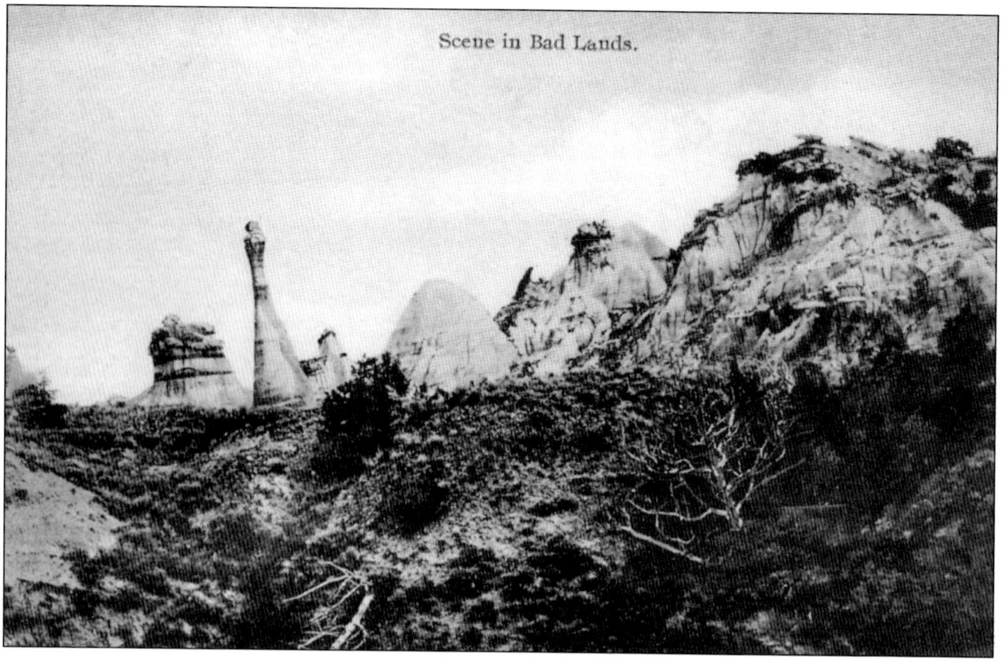

The geologic layers of the Badlands tell an amazing history. The region began as a sea inundating the area known as the Great Plains, about 69 to 75 million years ago. The first layer, called the Pierre Shale, formed when sediment hardened into black shale. Eventually, an upheaval of the earth's surface caused the sea to drain away. As more deposits were laid down by flowing rivers, the underlying black mud that became shale was also subject to erosion, creating—with the help of local streams—a gentle, rolling landscape. Fossils of sea life are found in this layer.

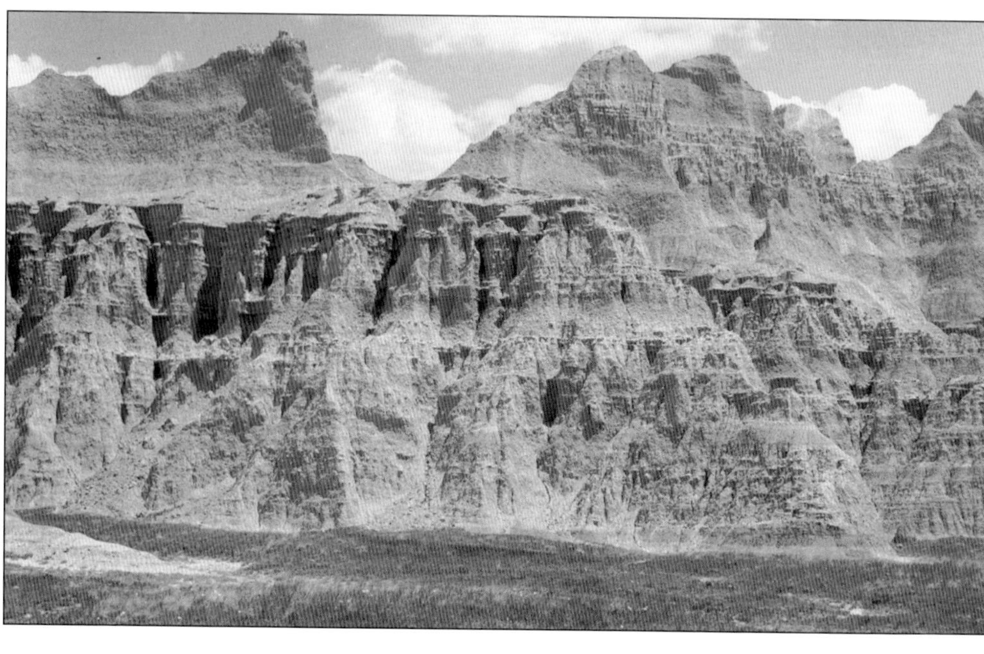

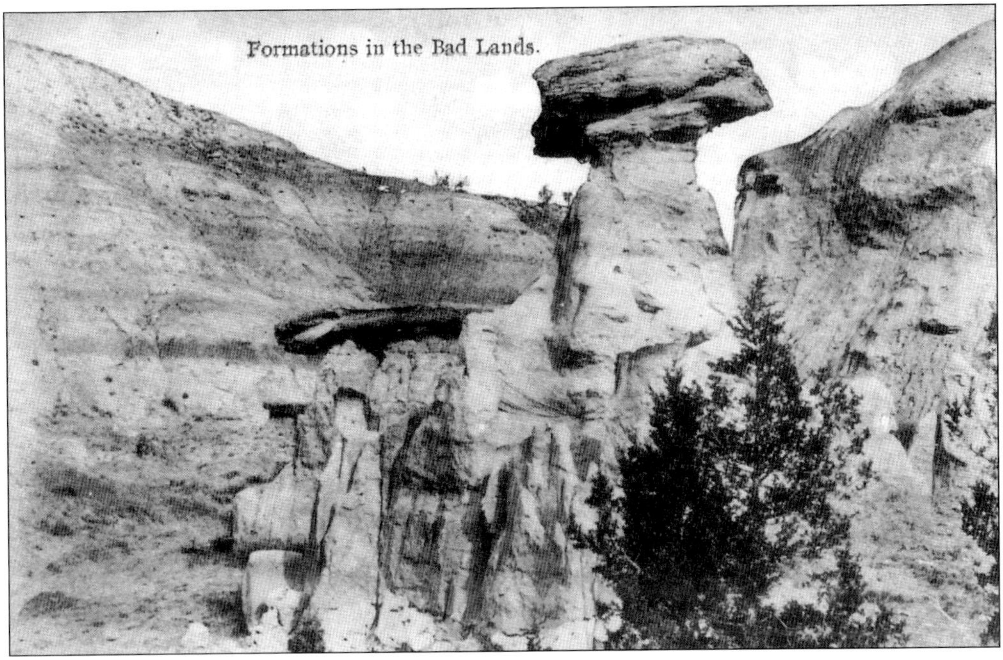

The Chadron and Brule formations formed layers upon the Pierre Shale. Raging rivers from the west deposited more sediment. Winds brought in volcanic ash. It is within these layers that the animal fossils can be found, including alligator, titanothere, oreodont, metamynodon, protoceras, and giant pig. As erosion occurred, fossils were exposed.

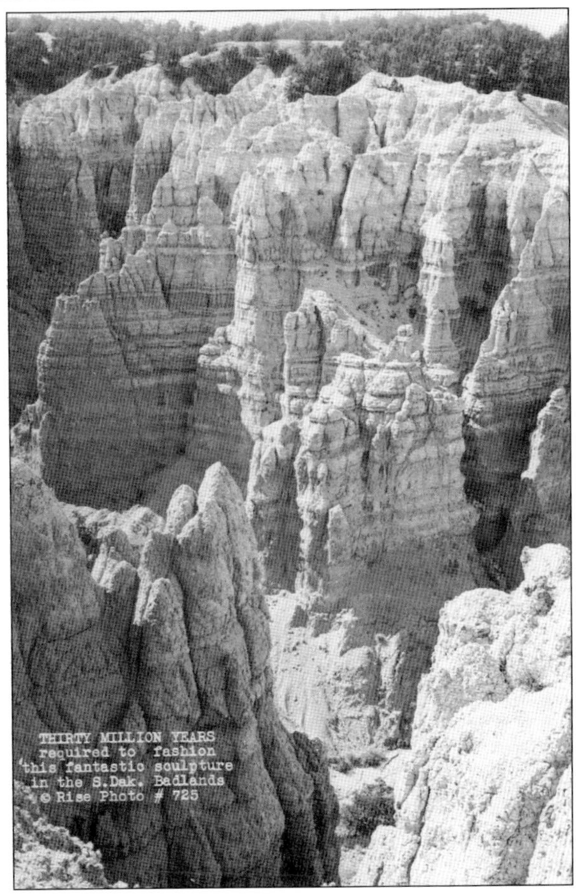

Great rivers from the west had washed in more sediment, which built up for millions of years. Thirty million years ago, wind and rain sculpted these fantastic formations from clay stone, silt stone, and mudstones. From a distance the formations appear as rock, but they disintegrate in water, leaving behind sandstone, limestone, and concretions.

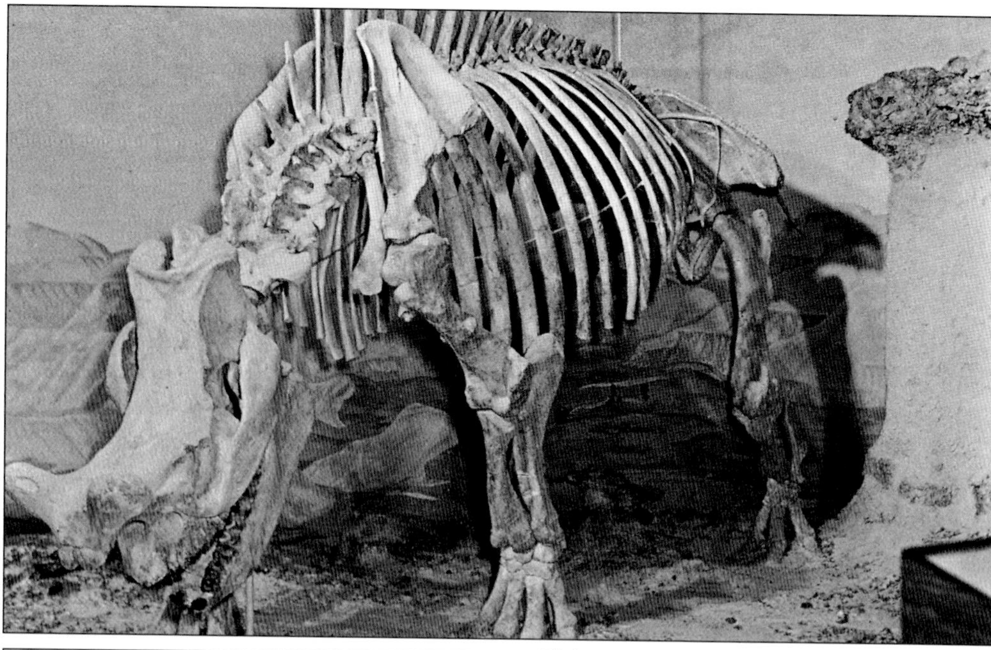

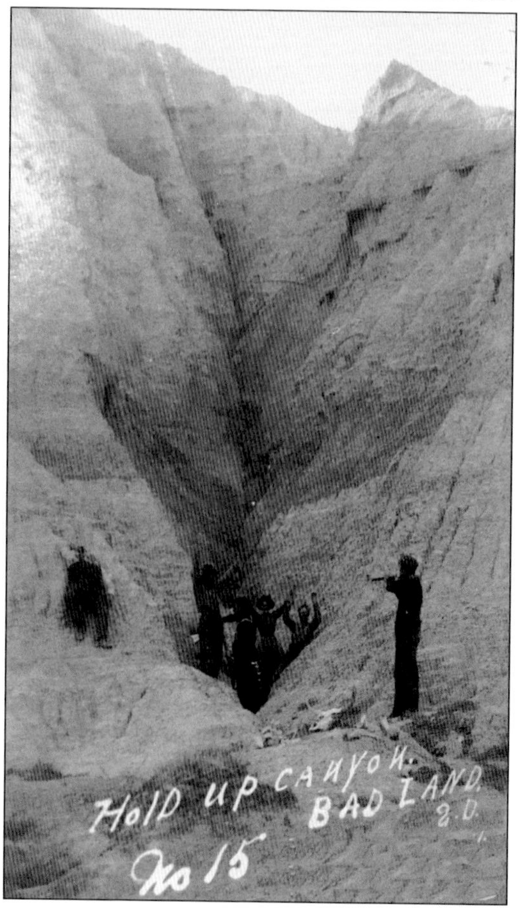

This composite skeleton of a titanothere is the largest known of the Badlands' fossils. Found in the Chadron formations, this animal was smaller than an elephant, about the same size as a rhinoceros. They originated about 50 million years ago as a small animal but evolved larger. The titanothere became extinct about 32 million years ago.

Unusual crevices and formations invite exploration to many visitors. Holdup Canyon could be merely the product of imagination, although actual hideouts have been discovered in the maze of the Badlands. Cattle rustlers used the area to hide stolen cattle in the many natural holding pens. (Courtesy of the Kadoka Depot Museum.)

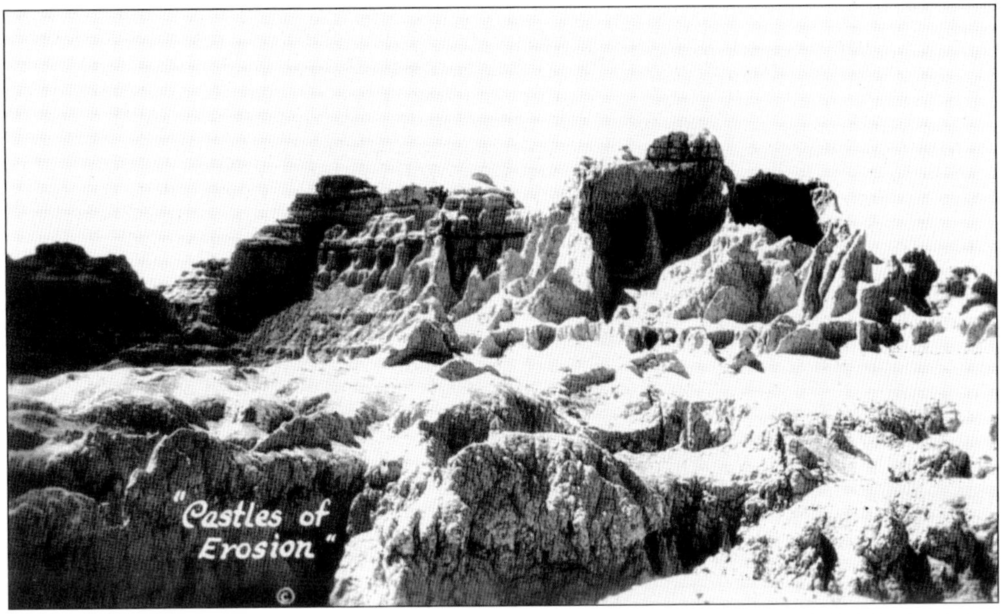

The name "Castles of Erosion" conjures images of a city from a lost era. Early travelers and scientists who came looking for fossils thought formations in the Badlands resembled castles. The Brule formation exhibits colorful banding and is the layer where the magnificent shapes of erosion and fluting are carved by the elements. Fr. Pierre-Jean DeSmet commented that the Badlands appeared as "extensive villages" and "ancient castles from some new world, or ages far remote."

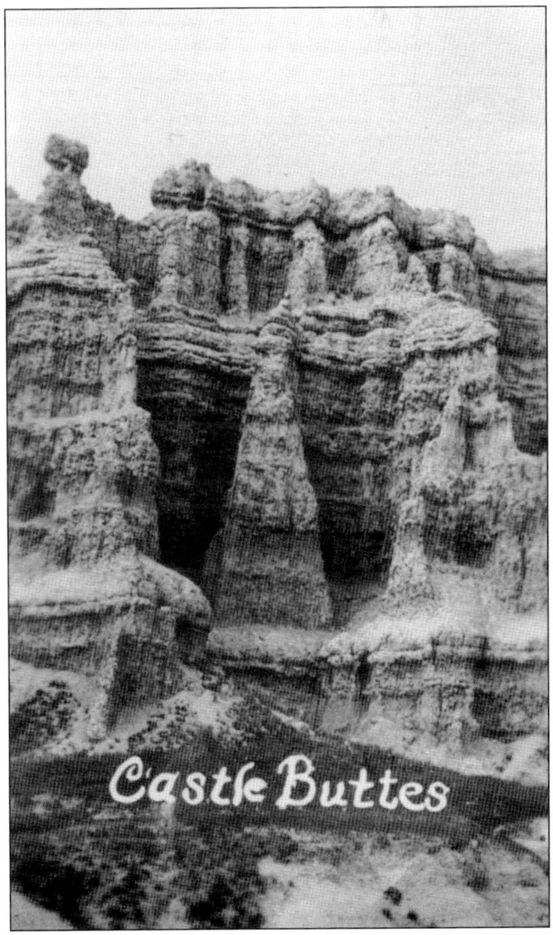

The weathering of layers at different rates creates the sculptured landscape. Castle Buttes displays fluting. Prince Maximilian, of Weid, who accompanied Charles Bodmer on a trip up the Missouri River, expressed regret on not having the opportunity to visit the Badlands and see its "remarkable forms" resembling "fortresses, churches, villages, and ruins."

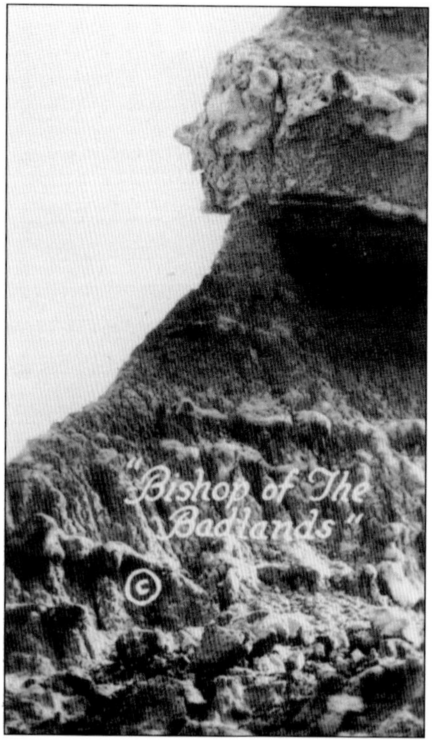

With a little imagination, the discerning eye can visualize a face in profile on the left side of this Badland formation. It was called Bishop of the Badlands. Most often, the early explorers viewed the Badlands as breathtaking architecture such as castles, palaces, lost cities in ruins, and even pyramids. Occasionally, nature also sculpted unusual Badlands denizens such as this.

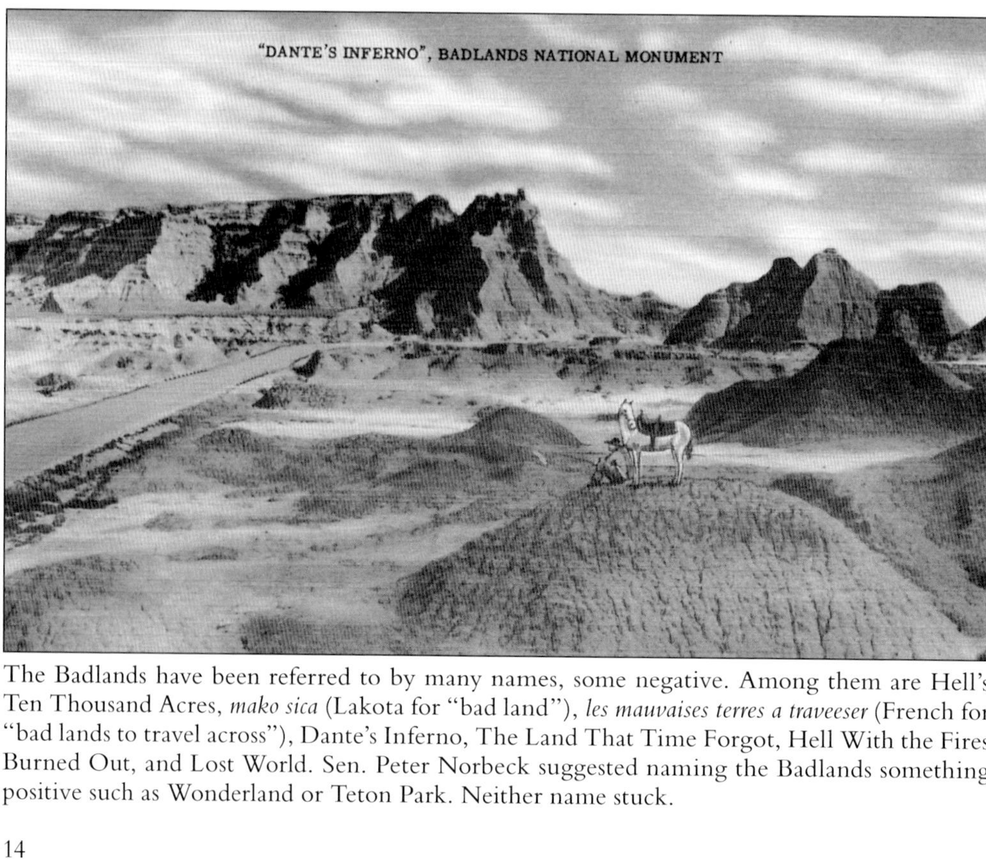

The Badlands have been referred to by many names, some negative. Among them are Hell's Ten Thousand Acres, *mako sica* (Lakota for "bad land"), *les mauvaises terres a traveeser* (French for "bad lands to travel across"), Dante's Inferno, The Land That Time Forgot, Hell With the Fires Burned Out, and Lost World. Sen. Peter Norbeck suggested naming the Badlands something positive such as Wonderland or Teton Park. Neither name stuck.

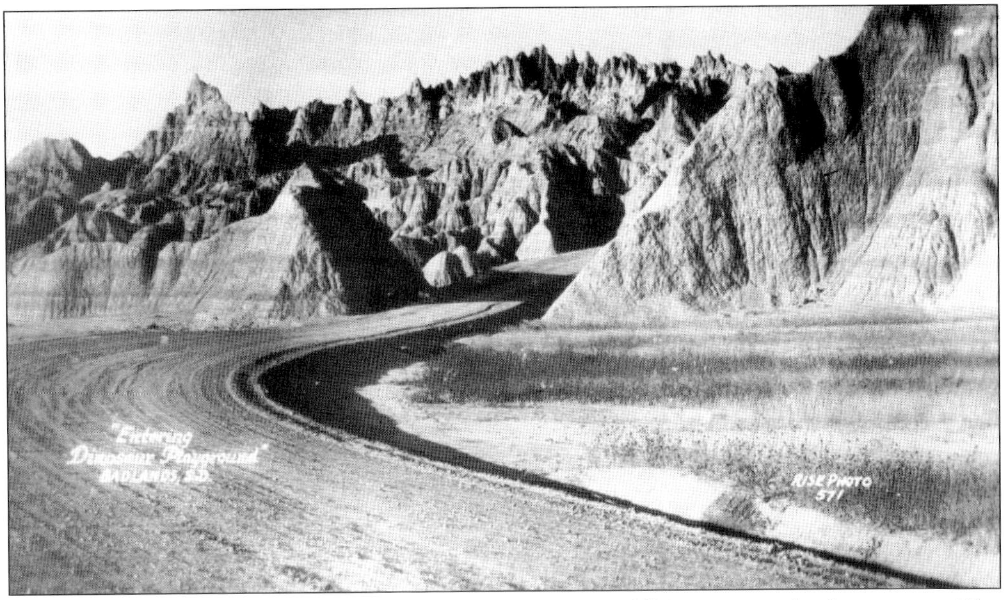

The title on this postcard, "Entering Dinosaur Playground," is not completely accurate. The dinosaurs were all but extinct before the Oligocene animals appeared in the Badlands. The area is known for the fossilized ammonites, oreodonts, titanothere, protoceras, and giant pigs, which spanned the Eocene and Oligocene epochs.

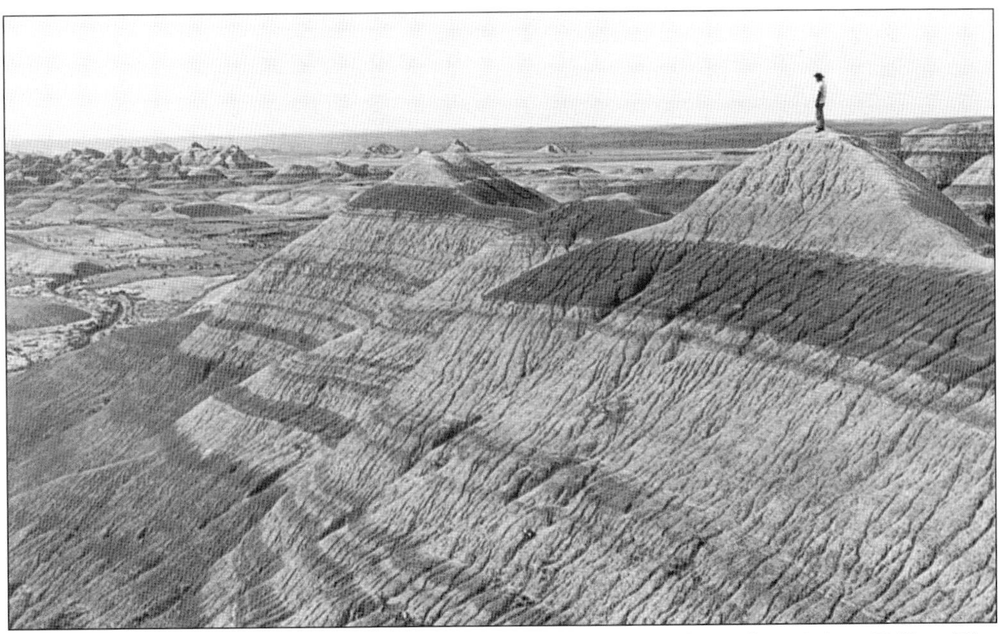

A man stands on the red candy-striped buttes looking over the White River Valley. The banding is characteristic of the Brule formation. Mineral deposits determine the coloring of the Badlands. Oxidized manganese exudes a purple cast. Iron oxide produces the orange and tan layers. The white layers are volcanic ash from the Rockies. Grey layers are a combination of ash, clay, and silt from streams.

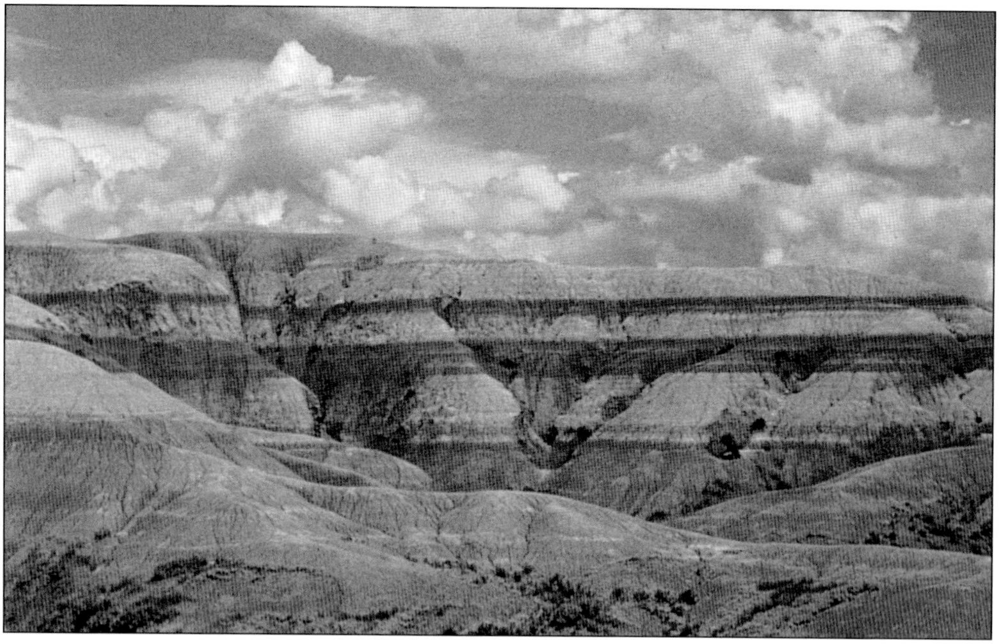

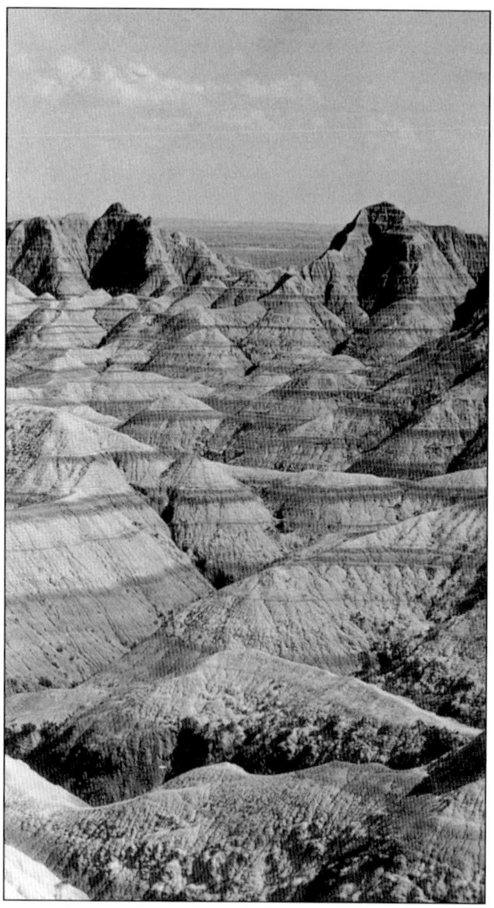

Another view shows the red and beige striping of sedimentary layers that resulted from marine, river, and volcanic deposits. Rivers and streams carved these deposits into fantastic shapes. The upper Brule formations are steep and carved with pillars, steps, fluting, and overhangs. (Courtesy of Wall Drug.)

These striped bands appear to have been drawn with a colored pencil and ruler. The terrain during the Oligocene, 28 to 32 million years ago, was flat, and the silt deposits from rivers were laid down very evenly, giving the illusion of perfection. The fossils found in the red layer have a reddish color.

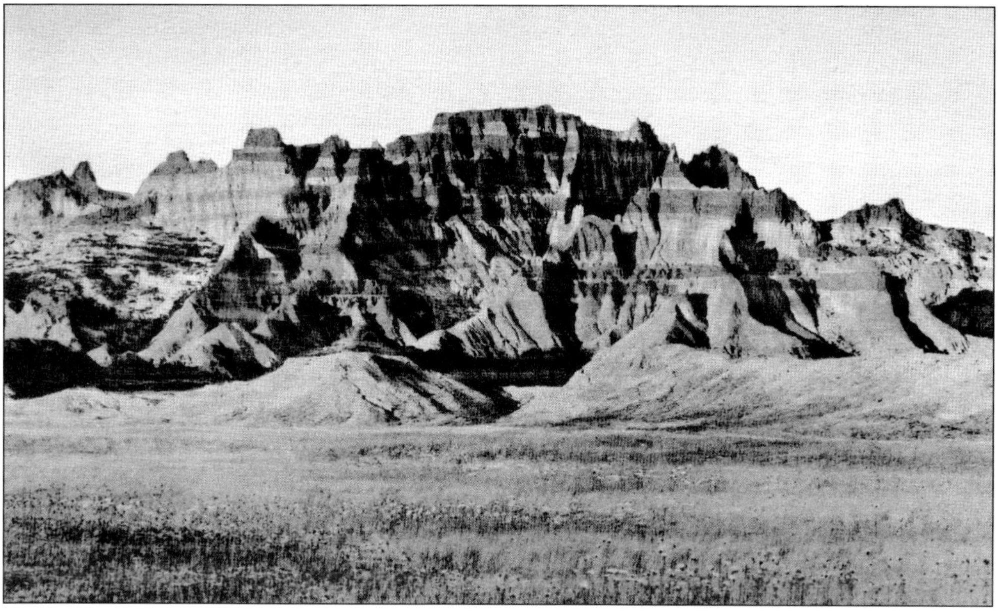

Within the desolate landscape, fossils lie encased in the ancient strata. After hearing reports from early explorers and fur traders, scientists journeyed to the Badlands in the 1840s to gather fossils. Some of those who came were Dr. Joseph Leidy of Philadelphia, who discovered a prehistoric camel fossil now on display at the Academy of Natural Sciences in Philadelphia. Dr. John Evans, Fielding Meek, Ferdinand Hayden, and others hauled away cartloads of specimens. The fragile fossils are now protected under the 1906 Federal Antiquities Act, making removal unlawful on federal lands. Only paleontologists can remove fossils, using special methods. (Both, courtesy of Wall Drug.)

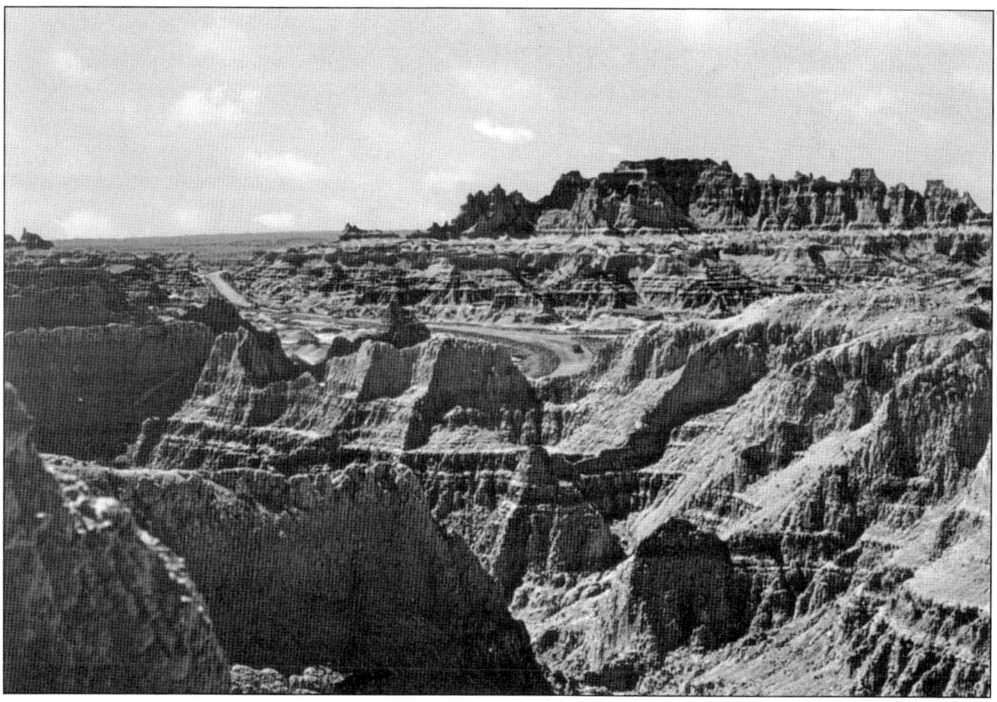

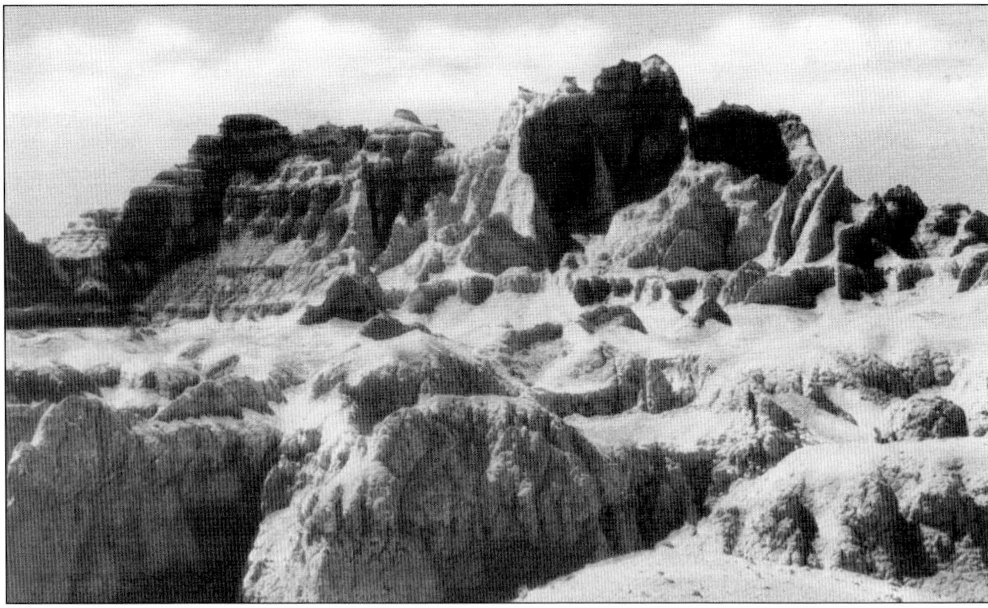

Dr. John Evans, one of the first scientists to visit the Badlands, described the area as "thousands of abrupt, irregular, prismatic, columnar masses, frequently capped with irregular pyramids, and stretching up to a height of from one to two hundred feet, or more."

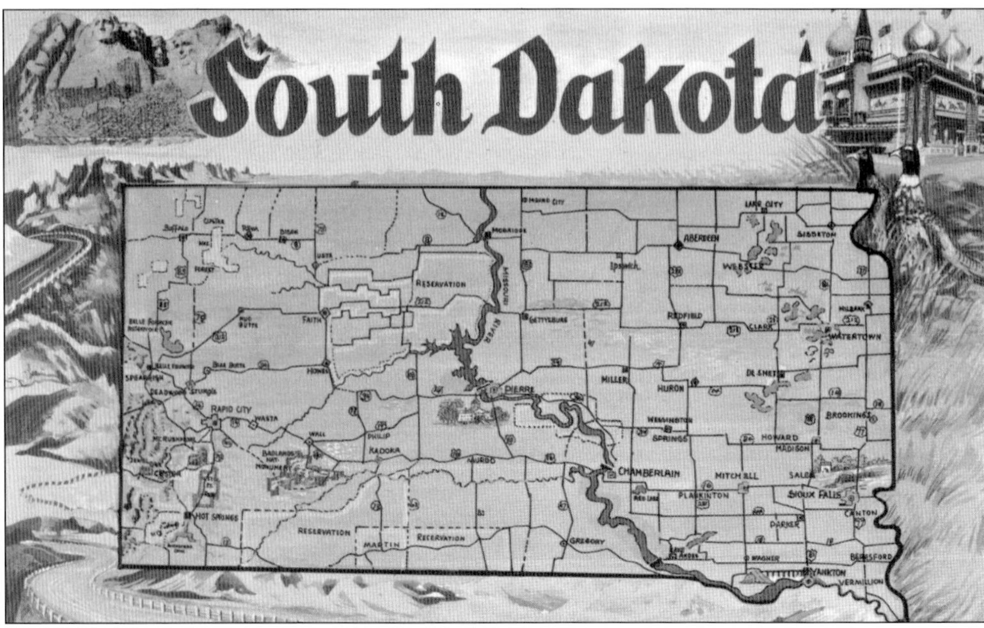

The border of this South Dakota map includes illustrations of the Black Hills, Mount Rushmore, the Badlands, and Mitchell's Corn Palace. Wall, South Dakota, is directly north of the Badlands, and Kadoka is to the east. Interstate 90 has not been built yet. Instead, Highway 16 is the main road to Rapid City. South Dakota is known as the pheasant hunting capital of the nation, even though pheasants are not native to the state.

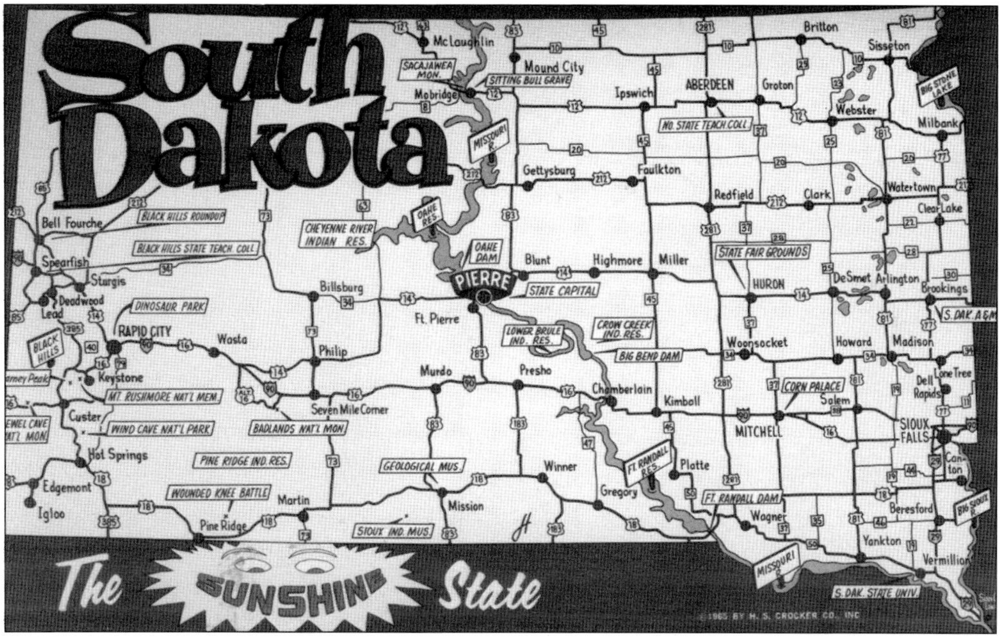

This map shows various points of interest in the state. Rapid City, Badlands, Pine Ridge Indian Reservation, and Wounded Knee are highlighted at lower left. Interstate 90 had been built by the time of this map, following most of the route of Highway 16. Even though Wall and Kadoka are not included, Seven Mile Corner is pinpointed west of Kadoka.

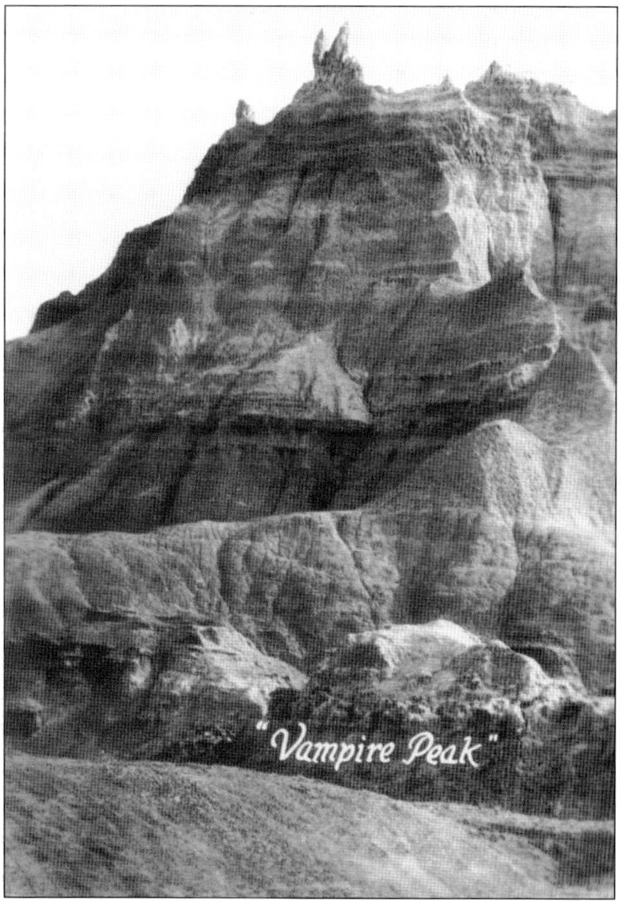

Located at Cedar Pass, Vampire Peak has been photographed extensively. The peak may have been named for its fang-like points. It is also thought to have been named by a traveling artist, J.I. Peterken, who noticed bats around the formations sometime around 1915.

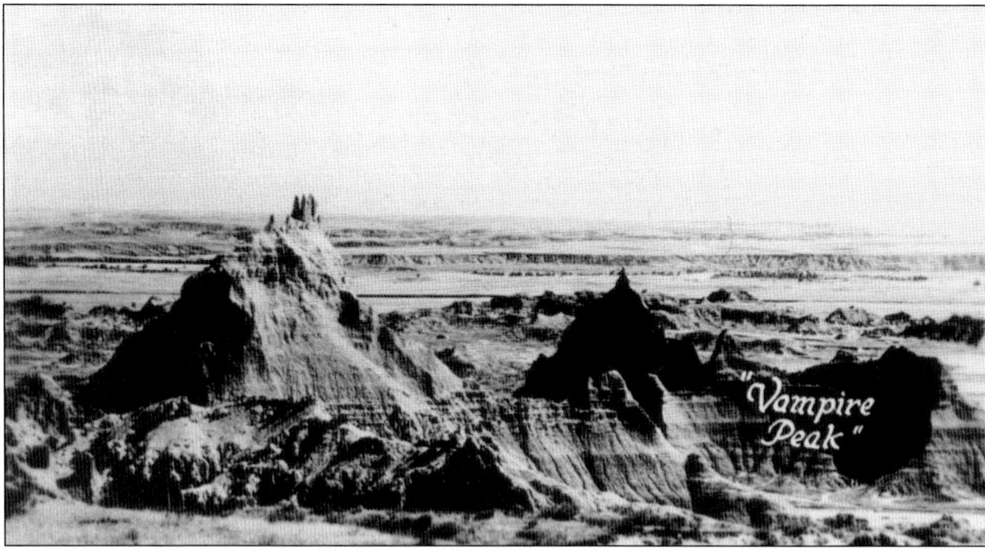

Vampire Peak is seen from a distance in this image. Its surrounding landscape has been referred to as Vampire Valley. The spires are prominent in this early image. The White River, which carries Badlands sediment to the Missouri River, is visible in the background.

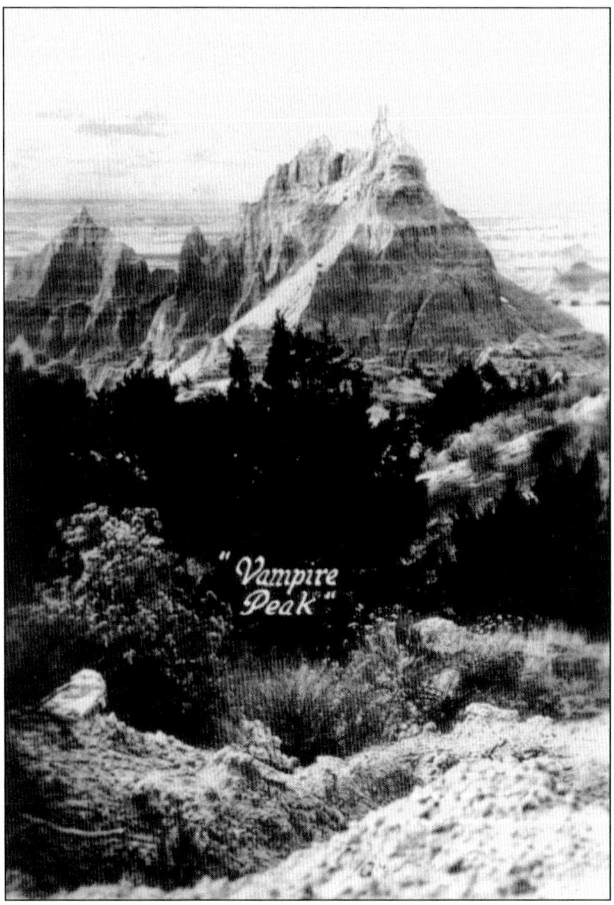

Note that the points in this image of Vampire Peak are not as distinct as in earlier views. Either erosion removed the distinctive fang-like points from the landmark peak, or a thunderstorm in 1950 took down one of the two spires. Because the fangs were composed of ash, they may have eroded at a faster rate, but not all formations erode so quickly. Sandstone, gravels, and nodules wear more slowly.

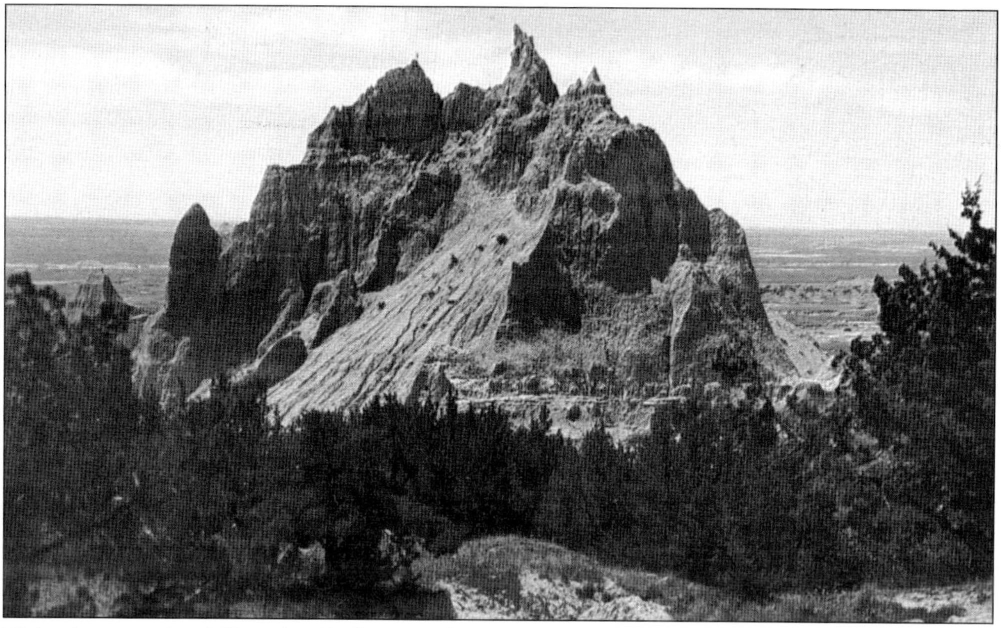

This photograph of Vampire Peak was taken in the 1930s. The sharp points have definitely weathered, and a slide area is visible on the peak. Cedar Pass is on a geological fault, causing rock slides to periodically occur, affecting the Cedar Pass road even today.

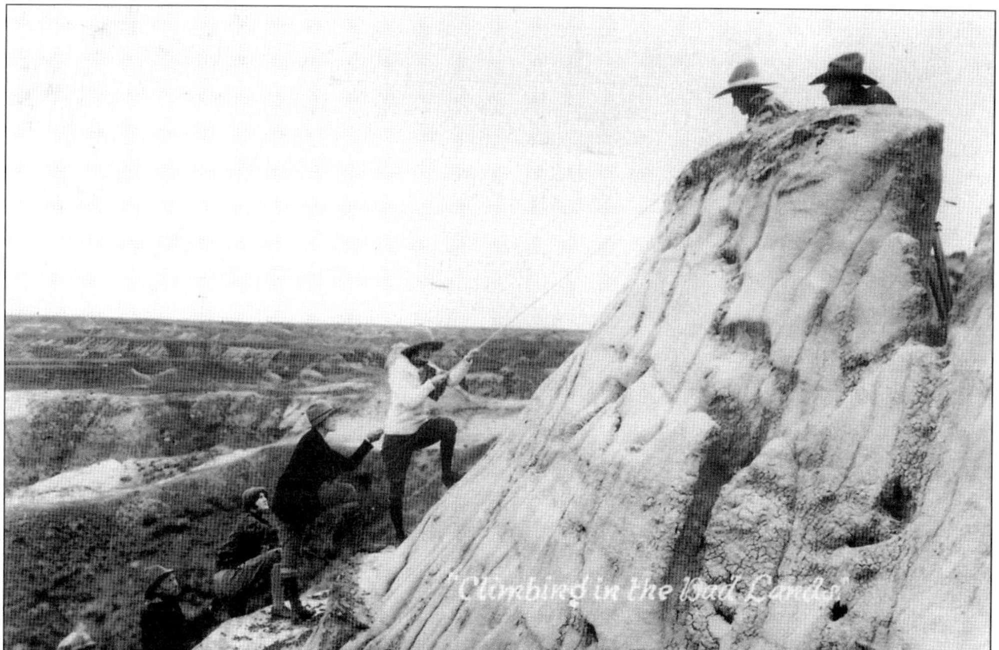

There is more than one way to climb the Badlands. Here, a group of people are using a rope to reach the top. Local people enjoyed visiting the Badlands on Sundays. The loose soil and slick surface often render climbing difficult, especially after a rain. Caution is urged in attempting a climb.

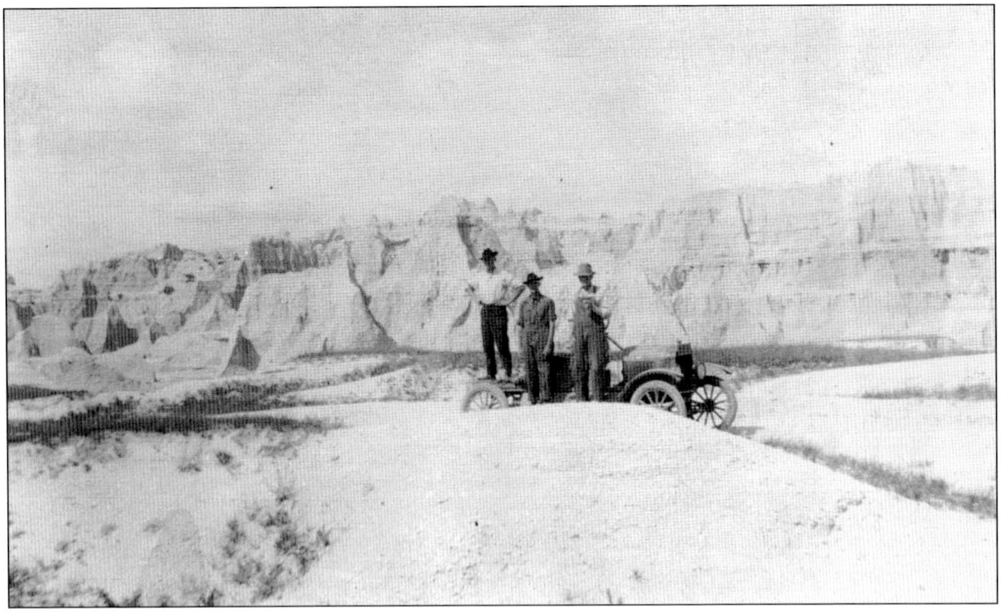

Three men pause for a picture by their automobile, which they probably drove down a crude trail. The advent of more reliable vehicles accelerated the need for better roads and services. However, action was not taken until the late 1920s.

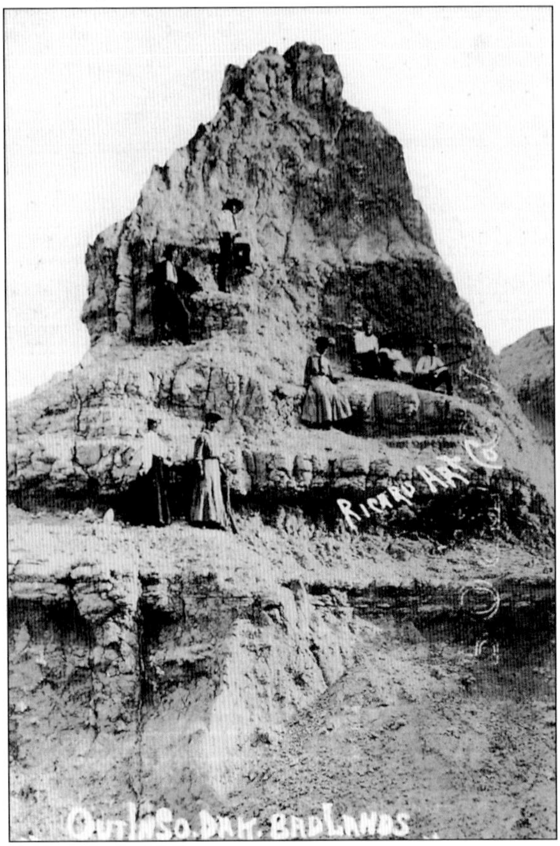

A group of people dressed in their Sunday best pose in the niches of a Badlands formation. A Sunday picnic in the Badlands was a popular event, and exploring the area probably came after lunch. Every formation is different, inviting closer inspection and an opportunity for a memorable photograph.

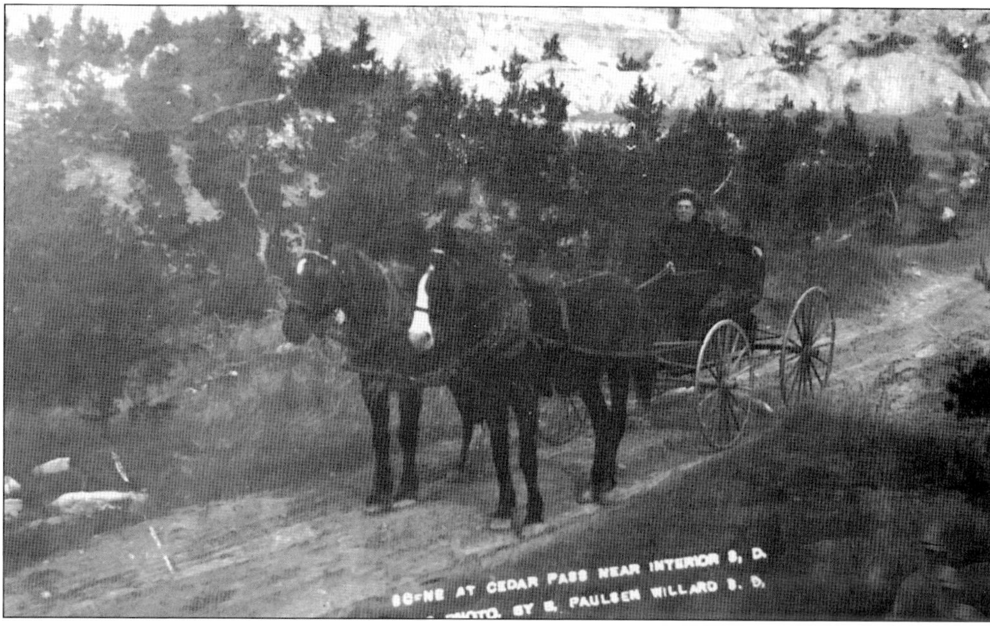

Cedar Pass was one of the main roads into the Badlands. A man in a buggy stops for a photograph in this scenic spot of cedar trees and Badland formations. The Cliff Shelf Nature Trail, a popular tourist stop, is located in this slump area. (Courtesy of the Kadoka Depot Museum.)

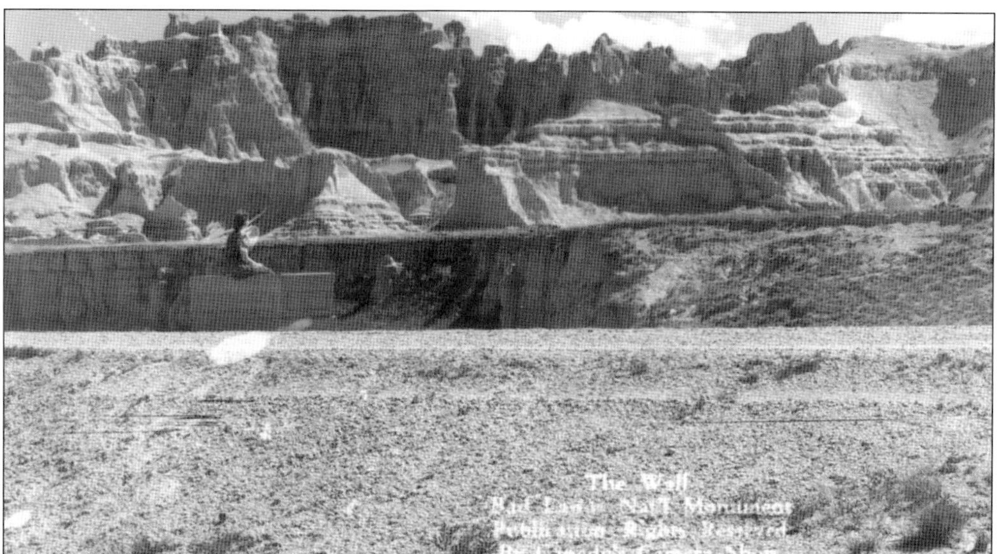

A woman gazes upon the Badlands Wall, which hindered access to the interior from the north until the early 1900s, when crude trails were built. The Badlands Wall is 60 miles long, stretching from Scenic in the west and Kadoka in the east.

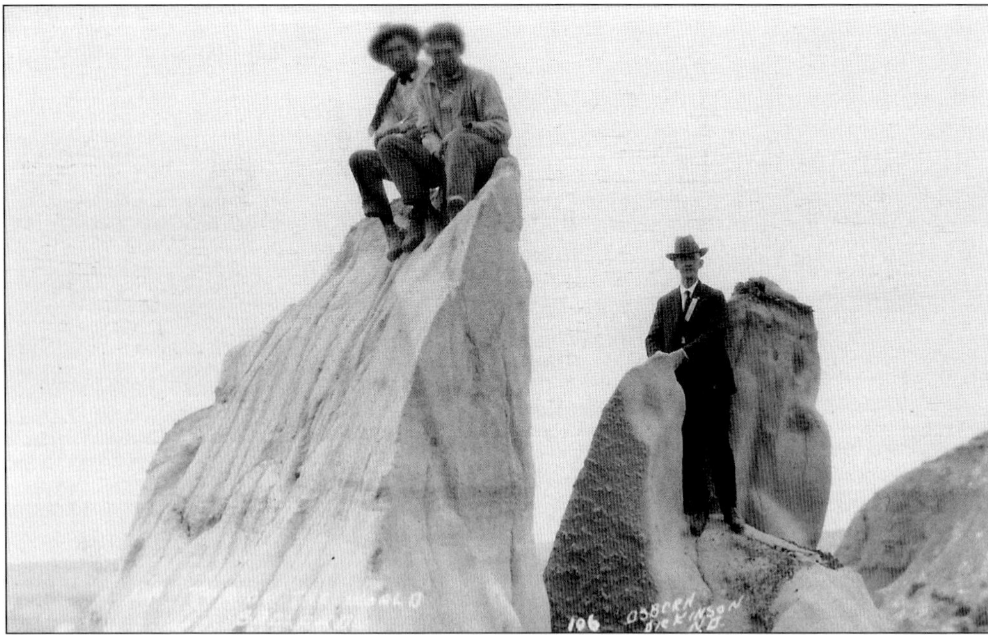

Three men pose in this Badlands scene. Sunday outings to the Badlands were quite common. One man even wears a suit, which does not seem suited to the rough terrain. Summer months in the Badlands can be oppressively hot. Proper clothing, shoes, a map and compass, and water are advised. Hikers have become lost in the twists and turns of formations, which might confuse a novice.

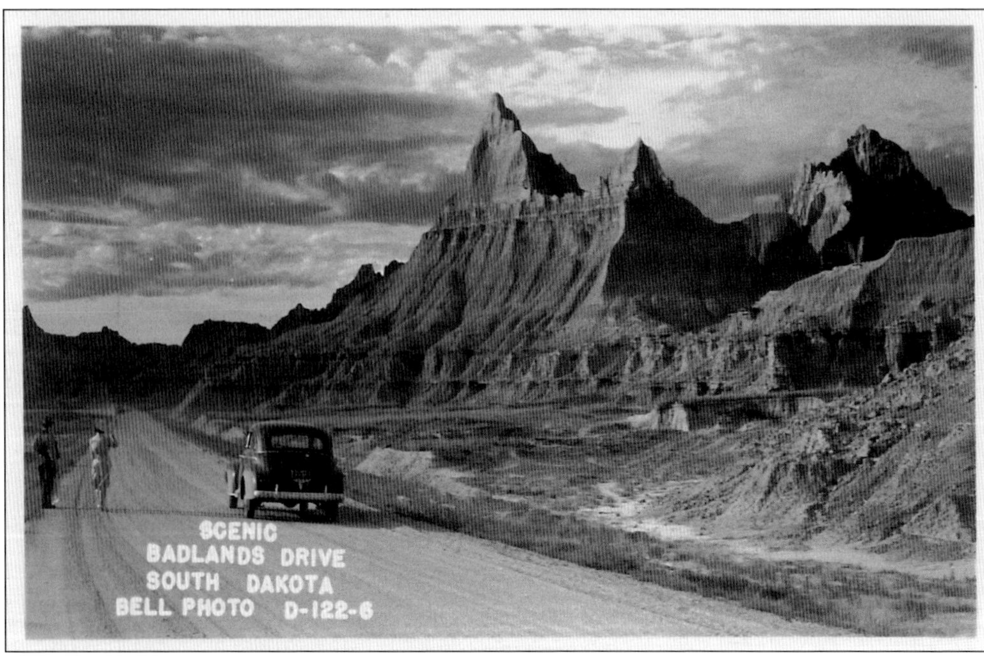

Mailed in 1948, this postcard shows a gravel road through the Badlands. However, blacktopped roads would soon arrive. The skies appear brooding, but a rain shower will bring out the varied colors of the Badlands and perhaps water the semiarid land.

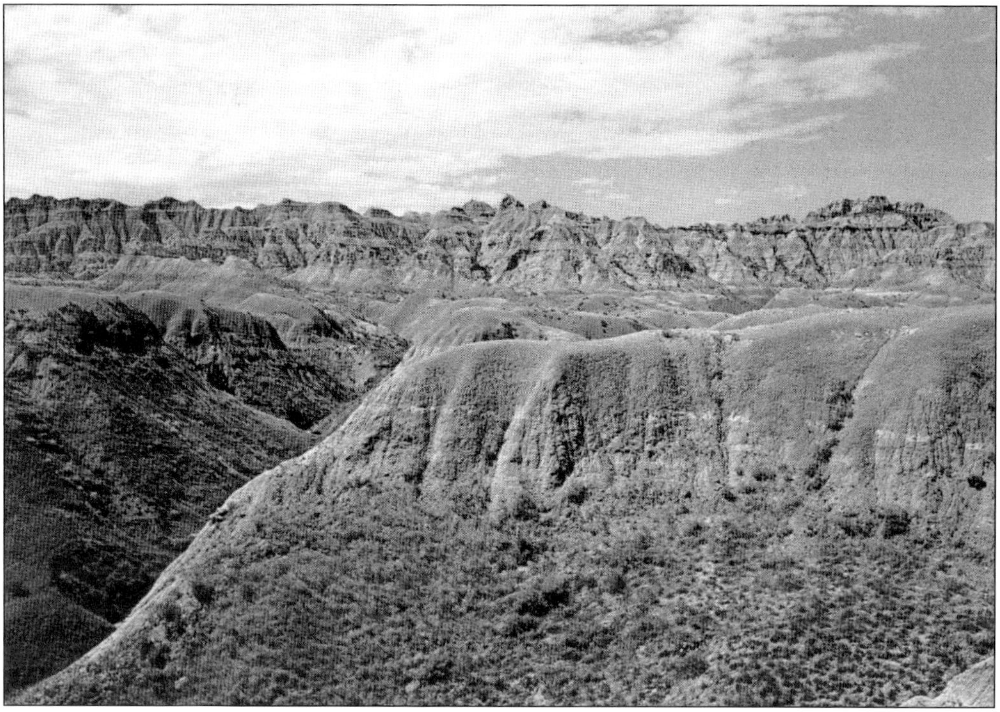

Vegetation struggles to survive in the semiarid Badlands. The annual rainfall is 14–16 inches or less. Drought conditions are not uncommon. Junipers, also referred to as cedars, grow in slump areas where moisture accumulates or along springs and other areas retaining water. There is also a variety of bushes and wildflowers, cactus, and grasses. The ubiquitous cactus blooms on the surrounding prairie in the spring. Pioneers used the cactus pads for fuel and to settle murky water. Jelly could also be made from juicy cactus fruit when the prickly spines were removed. The Native Americans also used parts of the cactus for medicinal purposes. The juice from the stem was used as a fixative to set paint on hides. (Both, courtesy of Wall Drug.)

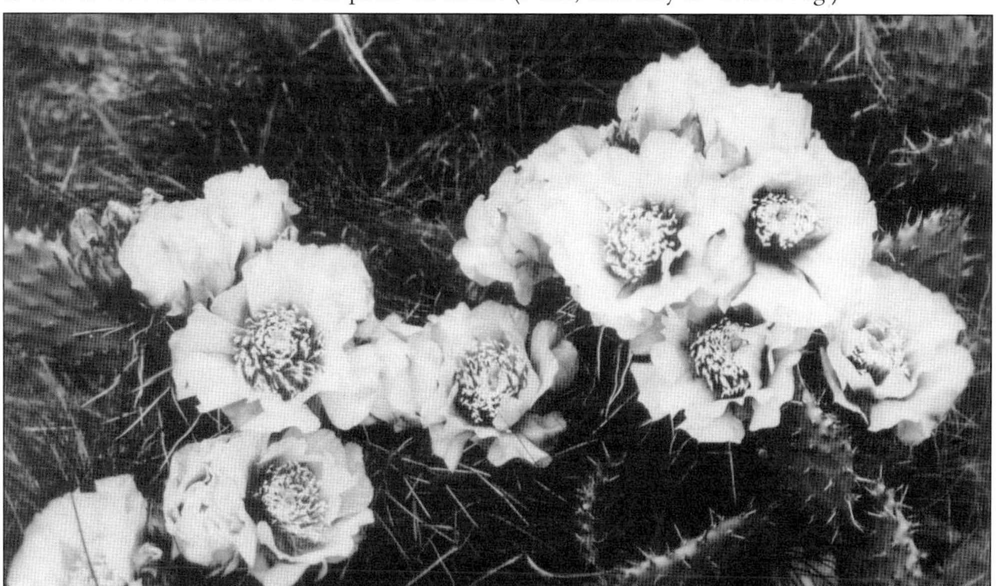

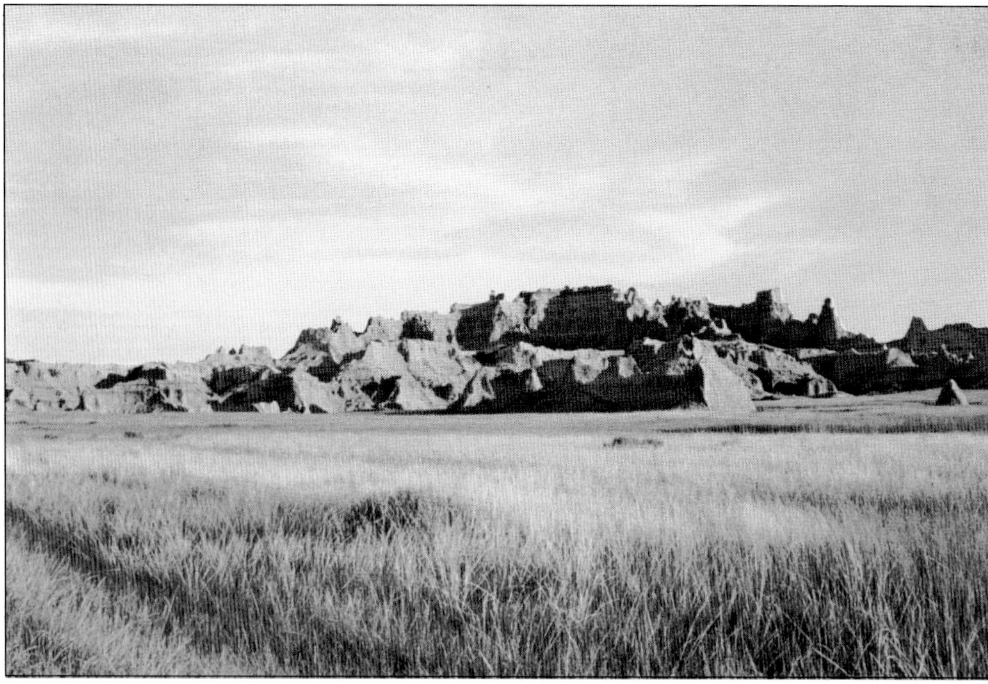

The Badlands is rimmed with prairies and their mixed grasses that once supported herds of buffalo and later great herds of cattle during the open range era. Wildlife such as the antelope, bighorn sheep, and prairie dogs now take advantage of this habitat. Native to the Badlands, the pronghorn antelope roams the prairies in herds. The animal is known for its keen eyesight, curiosity, and speed of 40 miles per hour, rendering it the swiftest of all North American animals. The fur traders and trappers floated animal pelts down the Cheyenne and White Rivers from the American Fur Trading Company at Butte Cache and other posts. By the early 20th century, the antelope and other wild animals in the Badlands had been hunted to near depletion. (Both, courtesy of Wall Drug.)

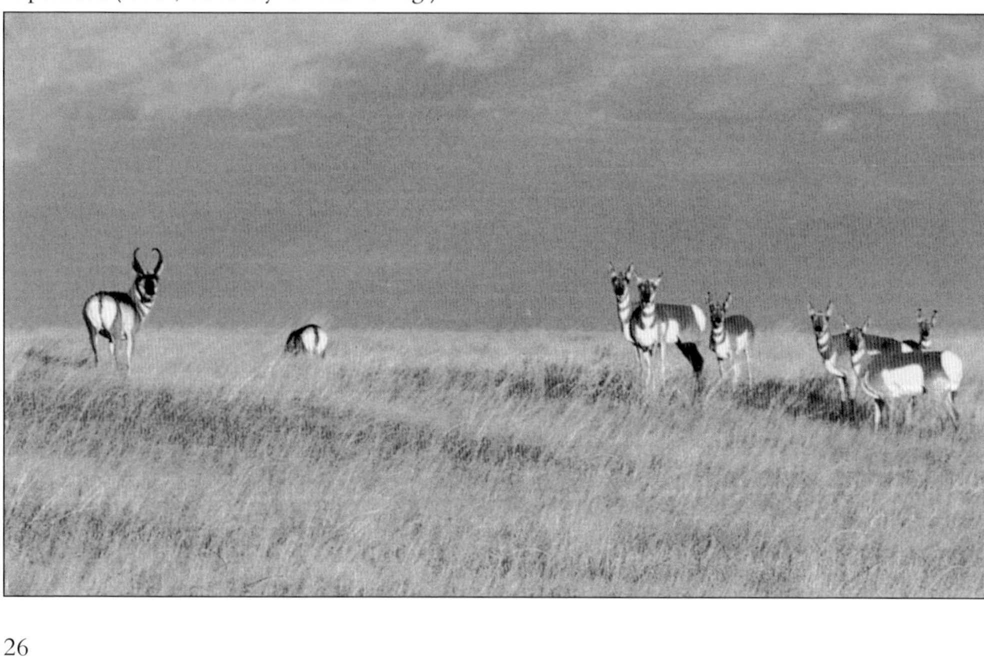

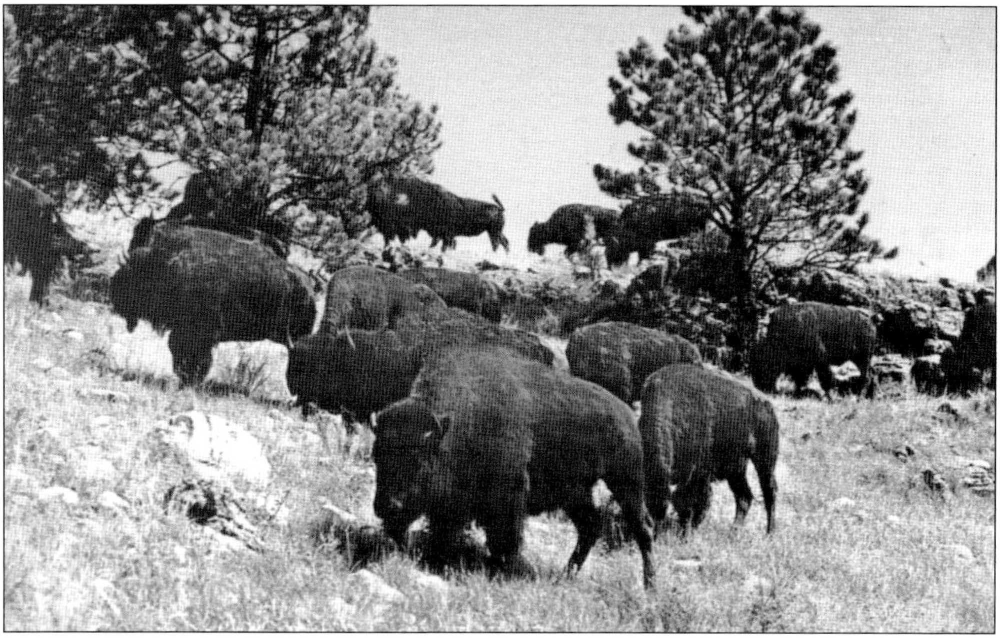

The bison, also known regionally as buffalo, once inhabited the plains by the thousands. The Plains Indians depended on the buffalo for their very existence. Unfortunately, the buffalo were hunted and killed by humans to the point of extinction. A combined drought in 1861 and over-hunting drove the bison out of the Badlands. In 1963, bison were reintroduced from Theodore National Park in North Dakota to replace the herds that once roamed the prairies. By 1970, the herd had increased to 400. The herds are carefully monitored and periodically rounded up for vaccinations. Herds of buffalo can be viewed at Sage Creek Basin in Badlands National Park and state parks in the Black Hills. A few private buffalo ranches also exist.

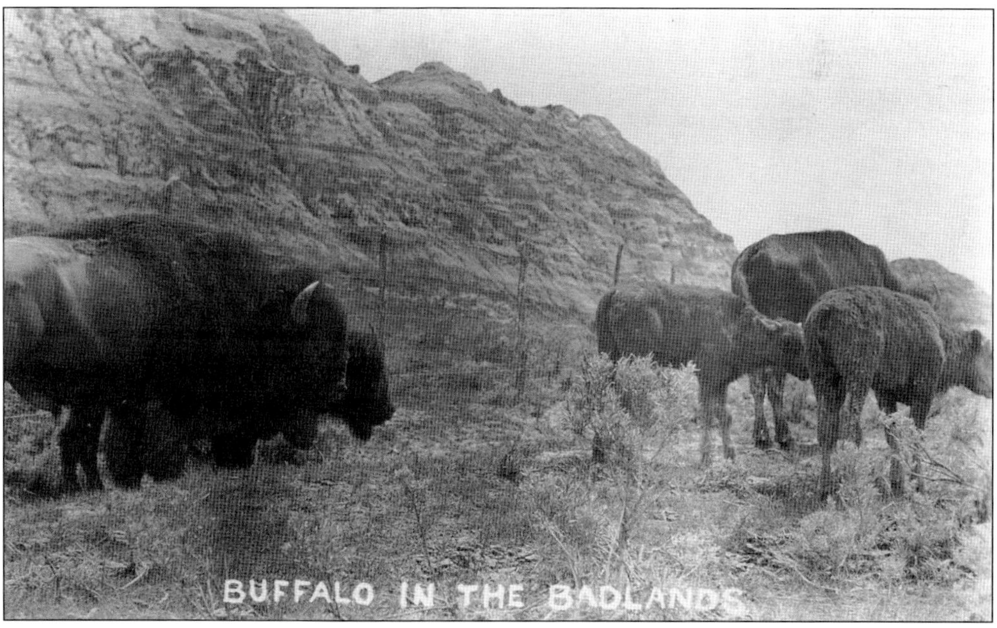

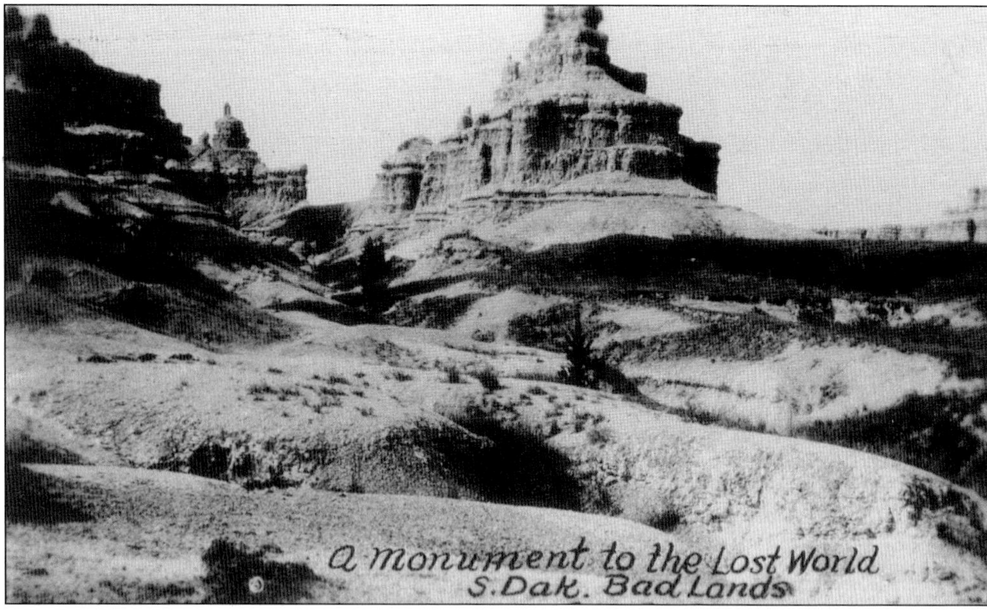

Many formations appear as ancient architecture, like this one dubbed "A Monument to the Lost World." Dr. John Evans described the Badlands as a "city of the dead." The French artist E. De Girardin described them as a "city in ruins." He also thought the formations resembled embattled chateaus and the pillars appeared as gigantic lighthouses.

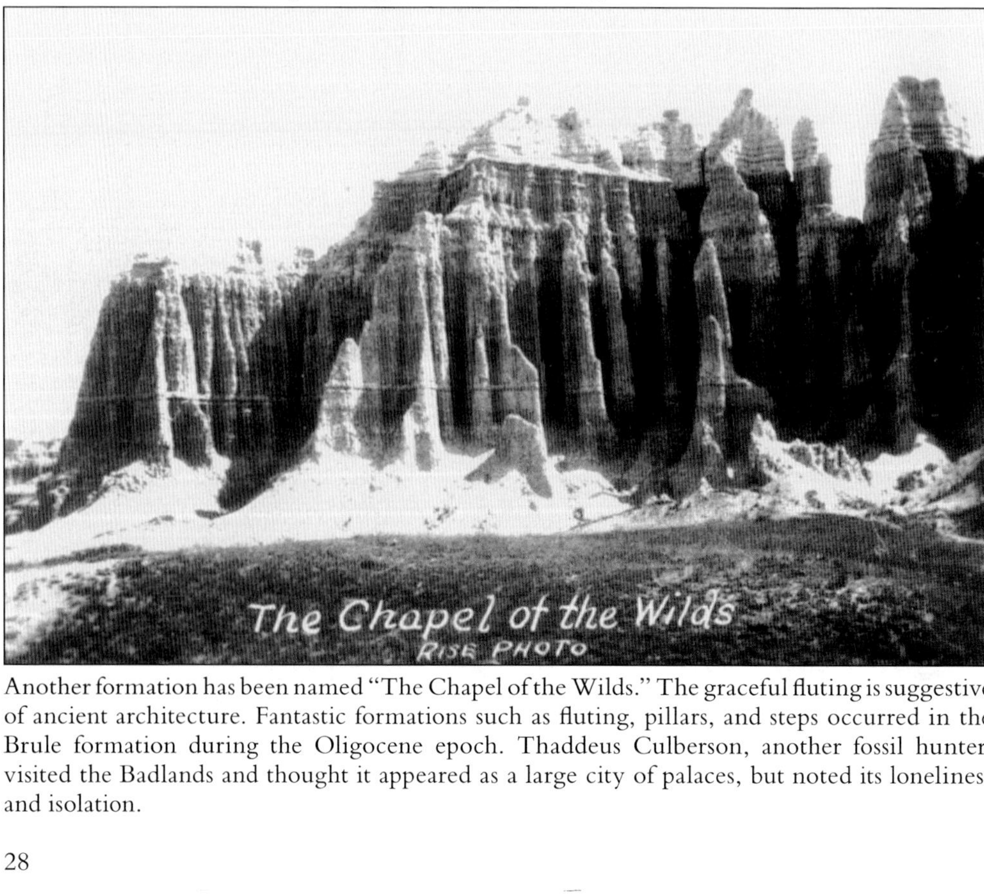

Another formation has been named "The Chapel of the Wilds." The graceful fluting is suggestive of ancient architecture. Fantastic formations such as fluting, pillars, and steps occurred in the Brule formation during the Oligocene epoch. Thaddeus Culberson, another fossil hunter, visited the Badlands and thought it appeared as a large city of palaces, but noted its loneliness and isolation.

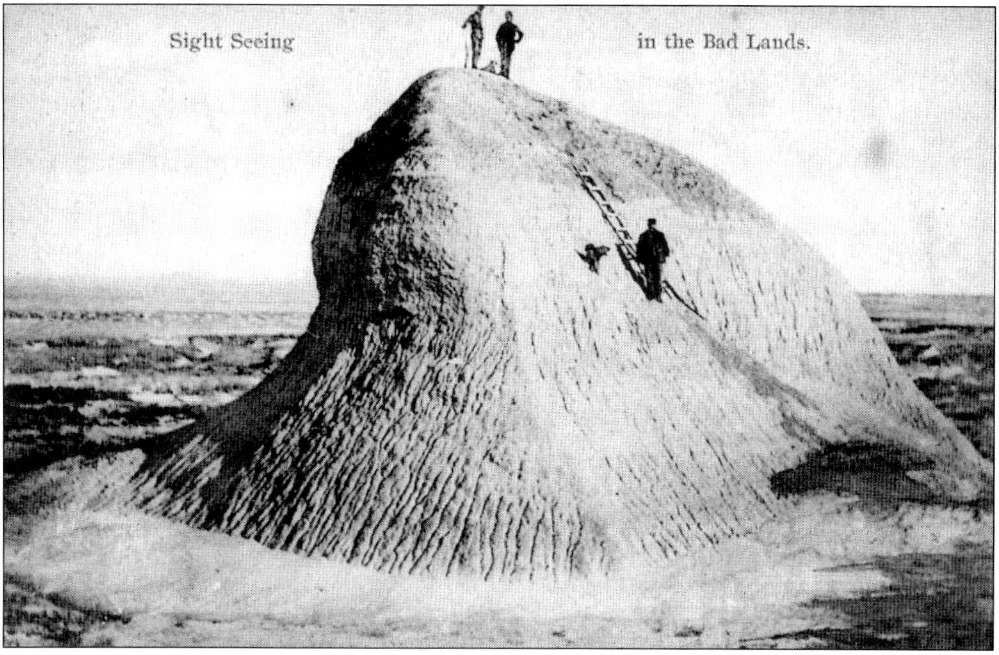

Exploring the Badlands is hard to resist, and good climbing shoes are recommended. This vintage postcard captures the adventurous spirit of three men and a dog climbing a Badlands formation with the help of a ladder. Apparently they had been here before and planned ahead for this visit.

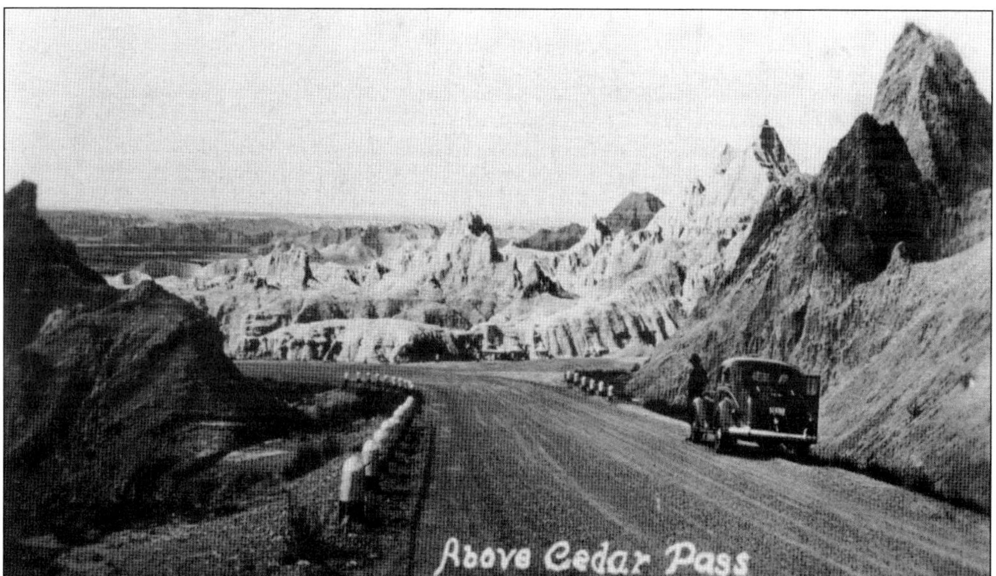

It is not unusual for tourists to stop and inspect Badlands curiosities, as well as its ecosystem. No two formations are alike, and a hiker who veers off a marked hiking trail can become lost easily if not paying attention.

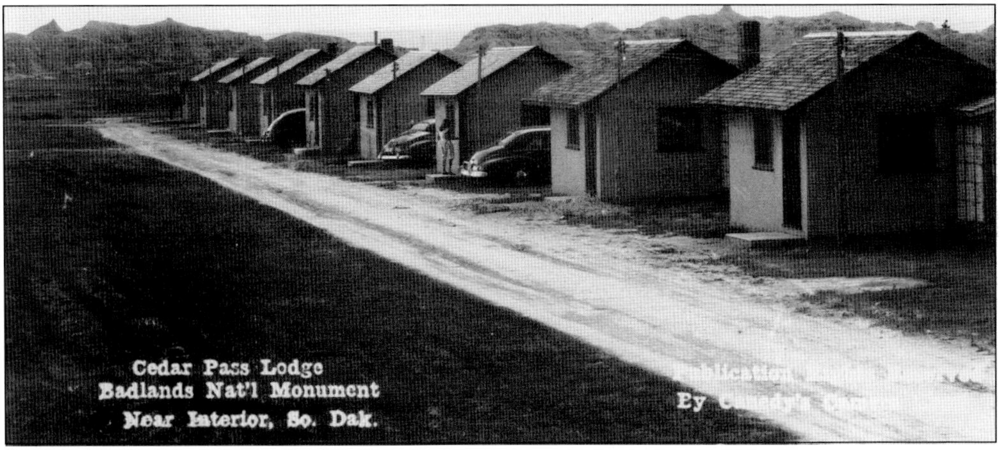

In 1928, Ben Millard assisted his sister Clara Jennings in planning the Cedar Pass Tourist Park. He built a dance hall as well as cabins for the concession personnel and later built cabins to rent to tourists for $1 a day. Most were plain with only a bed, mattress, washstand, and chair. Early tourists traveled with their own bedding and made up their own beds when they stayed in cabins like these.

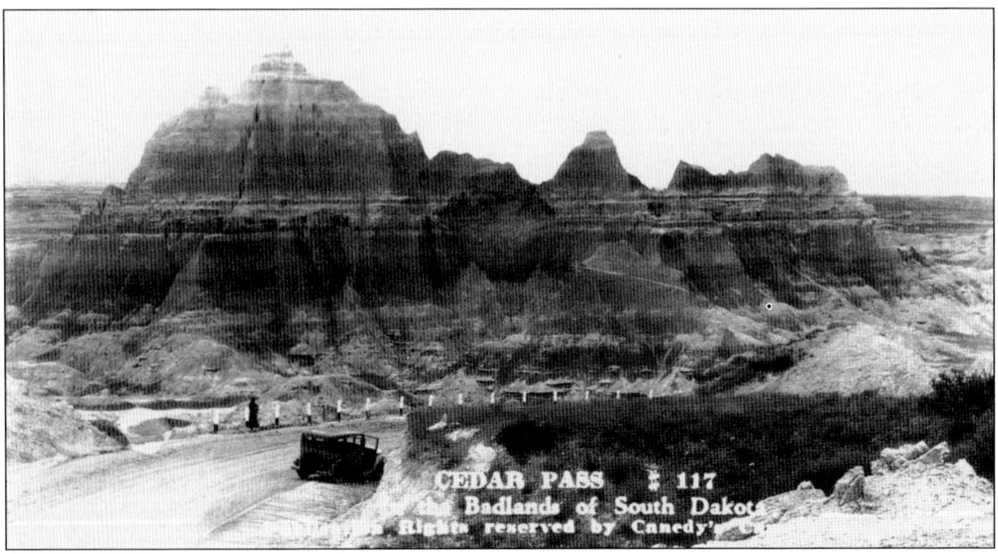

This 1930s postcard reads on the reverse: "Mr. Millard proved grand and sends his regards. The Badlands are gorgeous." Ben Millard operated a lodge at Cedar Pass. He established a tourist business and worked closely with Senator Norbeck to preserve the Badlands for future generations. In 1935, Millard also opened a tourist facility at the Pinnacles, south of Wall, and was a staunch supporter of Norbeck, who worked tirelessly toward gaining national park status for the Badlands.

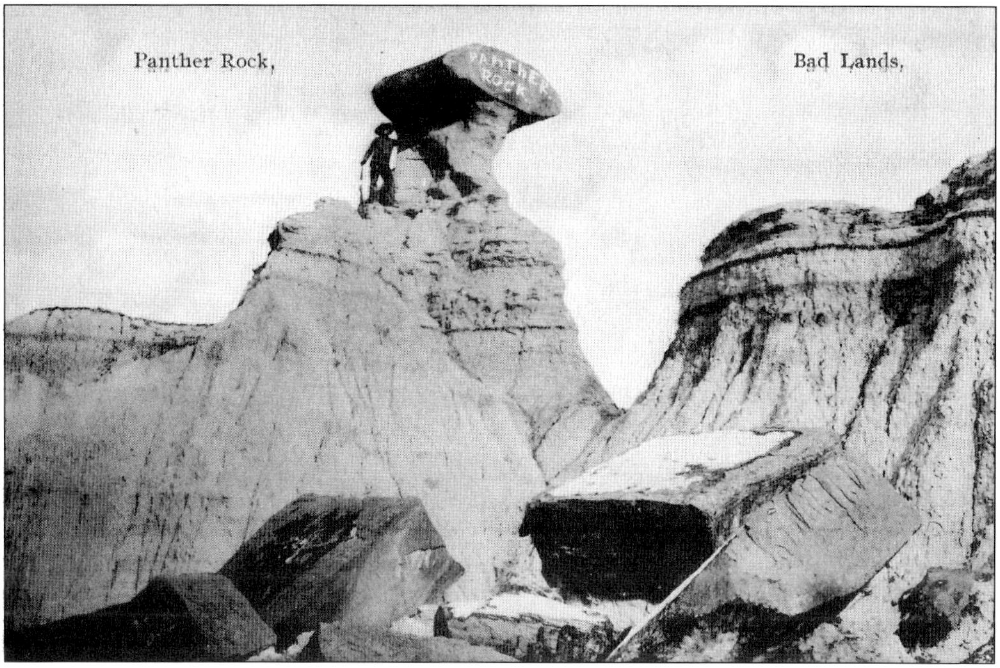

Many unique Badlands formations were given imaginative names, reflecting their shape or location. Above, a man with a gun poses on Panther Rock. The photograph below also contains a man with a gun. The Badlands was a hunting paradise before it was settled. Over a period of years, many of the native wildlife were hunted to near extinction. The wolf, elk, and bighorn sheep in the area were totally wiped out. The National Park Service reintroduced bison in 1963 and bighorn sheep in 1964. Deer and antelope have made their own returns.

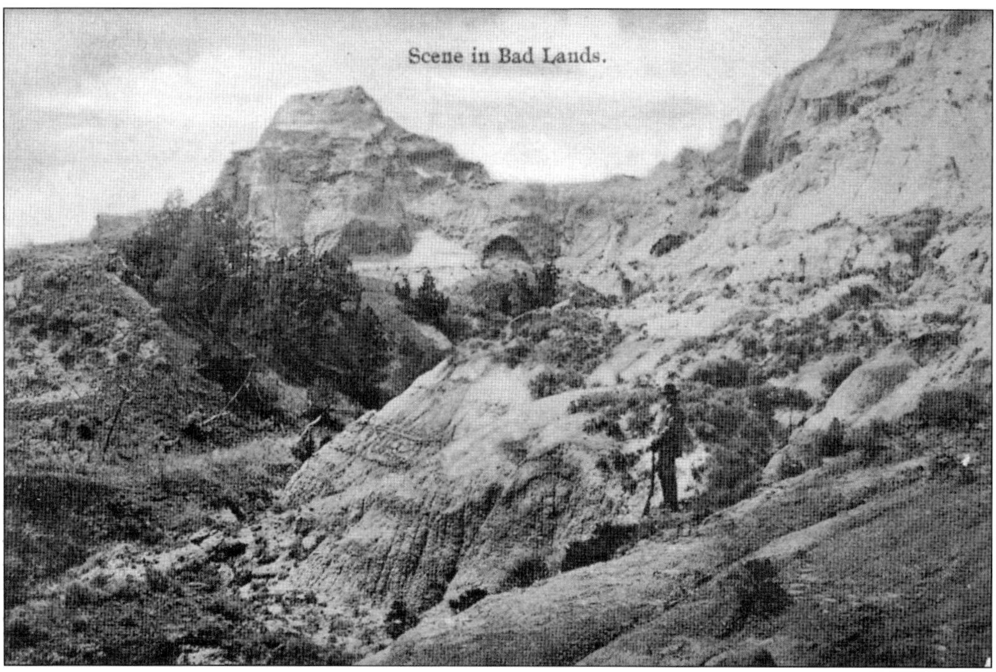

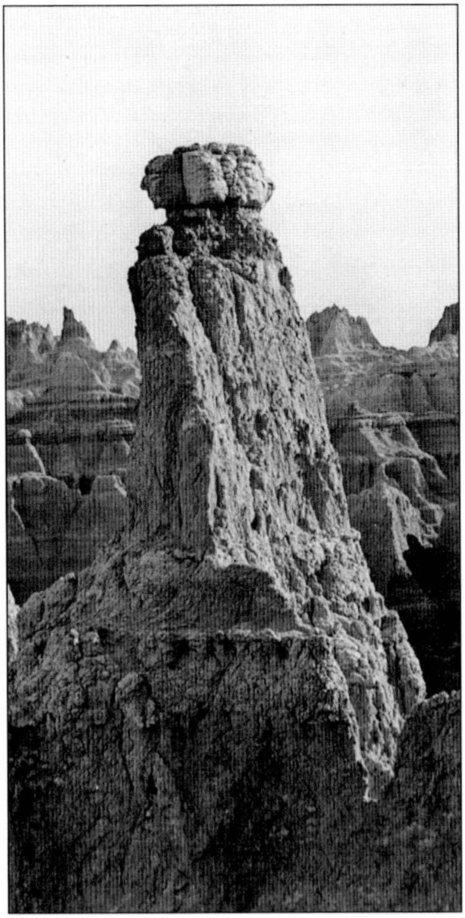

This pillar with its cap is an example of artistic erosion in the Badlands. The Badlands clays can vary from loose to very firm, determining their rate of weathering. This washing away at different rates creates the rough and alluring landscape, which will continue to change over time.

This formation is called Battle Ship Butte. Father DeSmet visited the Badlands in 1848 and described them: "Viewed at a distance, these lands exhibit the appearance of extensive villages and ancient castles, but under forms so extraordinary, and so capricious a style of architecture, that we might consider them as appertaining to some new world, or ages far remote."

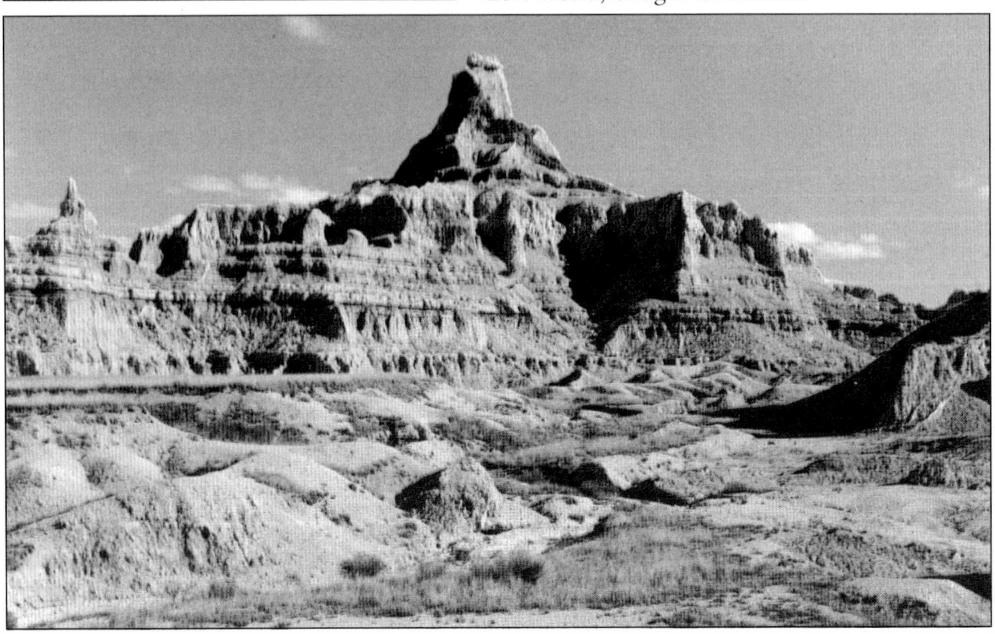

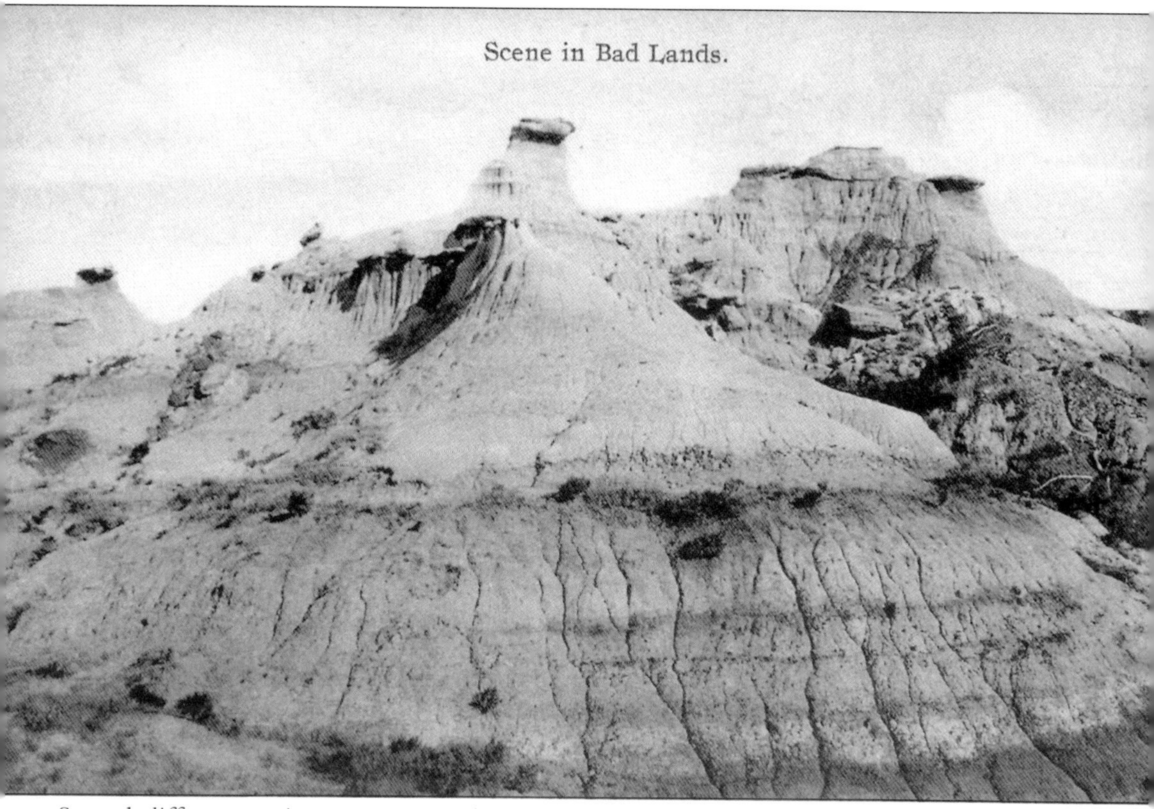

Several different environments existed in the Badlands region, which began as a sea and progressed to a tropical forest and then a savannah while supporting an array of animals. Each environment also produced varying sediments, which were deposited layer by layer. Sand, silt, and clay form the sediments that have been compacted together into sedimentary rock. The knobs on this formation show where erosion was the most successful, wearing away the softer sediment and leaving the curved protrusions. Erosion occurs every time it rains, freezes, or the wind blows, changing the Badlands landscape on an ongoing basis. It has been estimated that one inch of erosion occurs annually, depending on the soil composition. Storms can topple a pillar or remove a spire. Formations photographed 50 years ago may not look the same today. Geologists have estimated that the Badlands will completely erode in another 500,000 years.

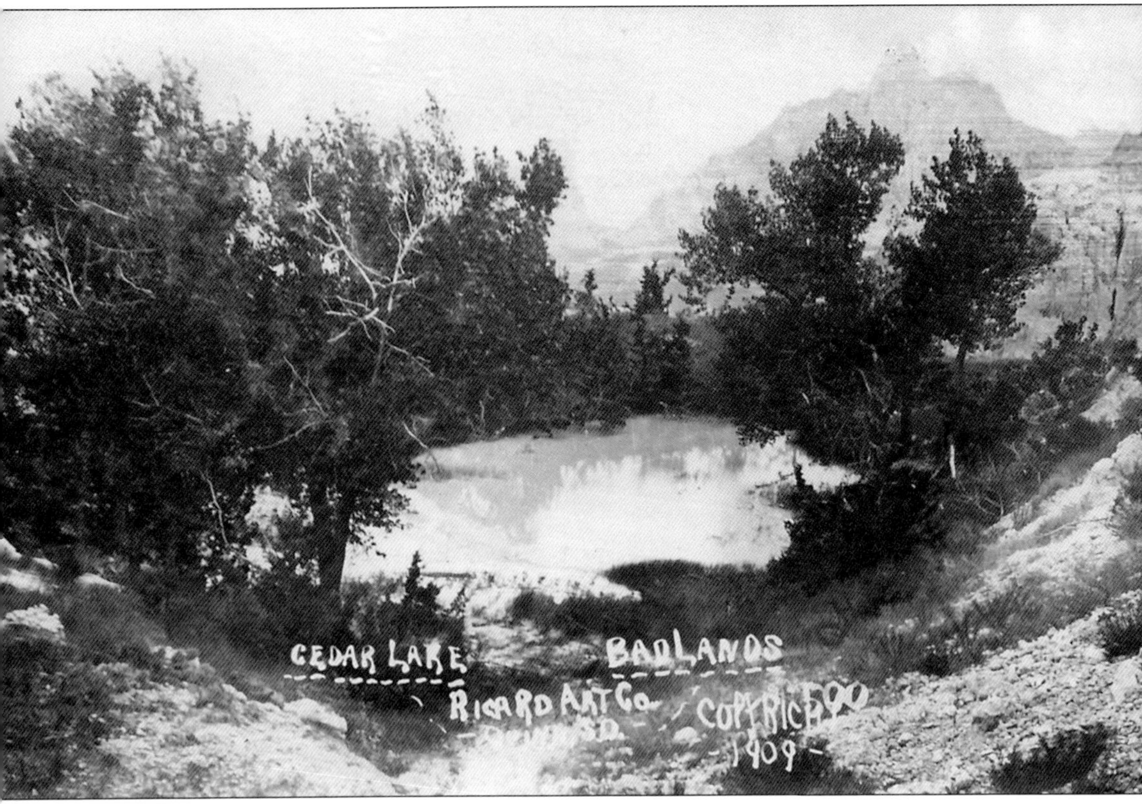

This scene was captured in 1909 at the area known as Cliff Shelf, a slump where a cliff at the Cedar Pass area broke loose, disrupting the normal drainage pattern. As a result, holes, pits, and ponds were created, enabling the area to hold water from rain and melting snow. In 1909, Cedar Lake stood here. Cedars and other vegetation still flourish, even though the lake is gone. Cliff Shelf has been developed into a half-mile paved loop walking trail. A pamphlet explaining the plants and other features of this unique place is available at the trailhead. There are other slumps in the Badlands, recognizable by their lush vegetation. This postcard was manufactured by the Ricard Art Company of Quinn, South Dakota. Arthur and Joseph Ricard filed on homesteads in the area in 1908. Herman Ricard established a photography business in Quinn and took many photographs in the early 1900s, including this one.

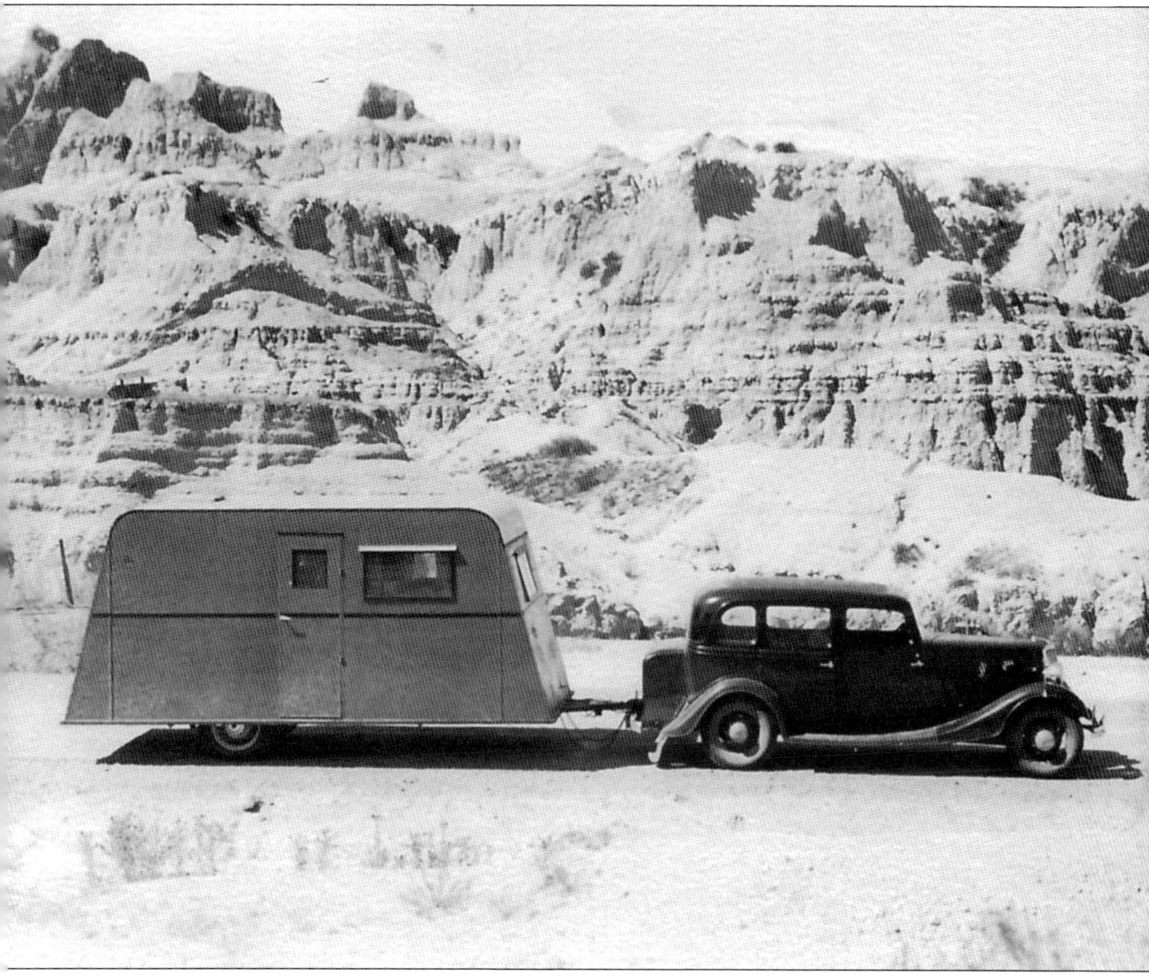

Some of the early visitors brought their own accommodations with them. The sender of this 1935 postcard wrote on the reverse: "This has taken the place of the old Dodge—Very comfortable if you don't get too far off the beaten trails." None of the roads were blacktopped at this time. Camping is permitted in designated areas at Badlands National Park. The Cedar Pass Campground is only a few miles from the town of Interior and close to the Cedar Pass gift shop and restaurant. During the summer, an evening program is presented at the Sholly Memorial Amphitheater. Camping is also available at the Sage Creek Basin. Cabins can be rented at the lodge in the park. Motel accommodations and other camping facilities in Interior, outside the park, are another choice. A night in the Badlands is a memorable experience.

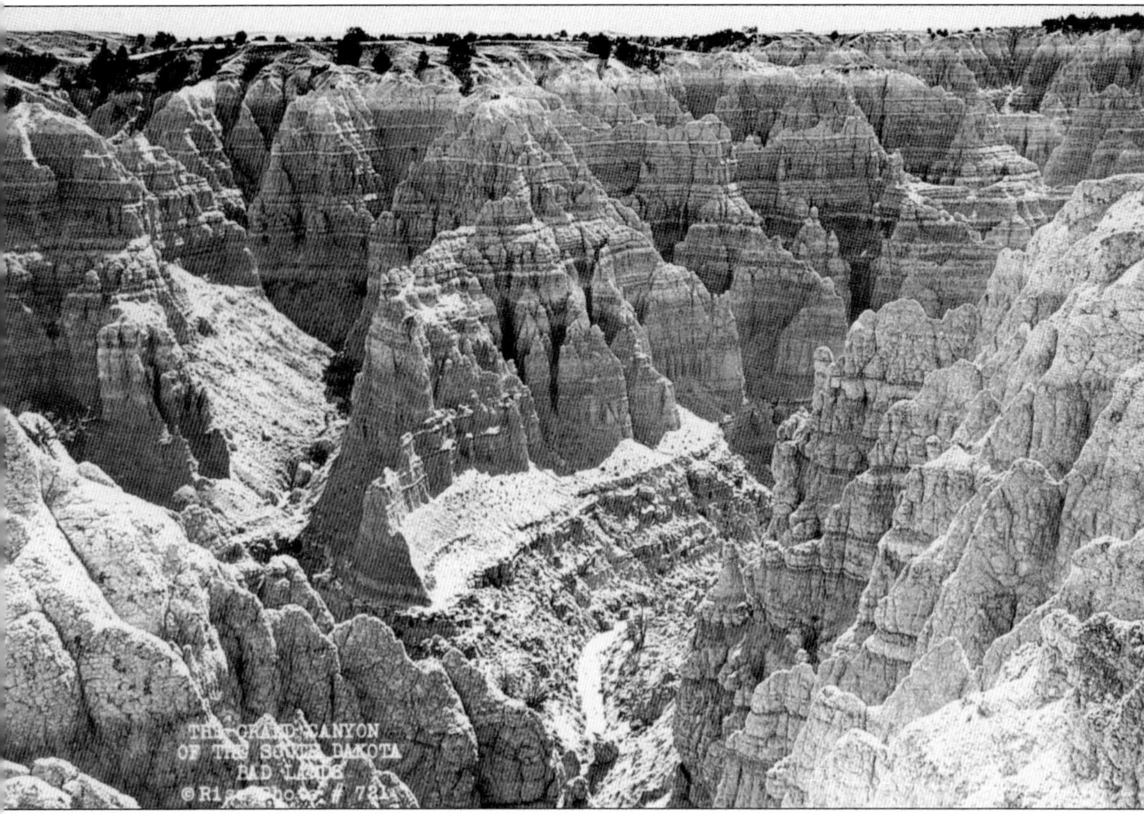

This view, entitled "The Grand Canyon of the South Dakota Bad Lands," thought to rival the Grand Canyon in splendor, is a part of Sheep Mountain in the South Unit, which contains some of the most spectacular Badlands scenery. Even though it appears impressive, the Badlands did not qualify for national park status until 1978. Senator Norbeck became interested in a 1909 Congress resolution to set aside a South Dakota Badlands National Park. He visited the Badlands in 1911, when homesteaders had fenced most of the land in sections. He realized the spectacular scenery of the Badlands should be set aside as a national park, and predicted the futility of homesteaders attempting to farm the land, especially during drought years.

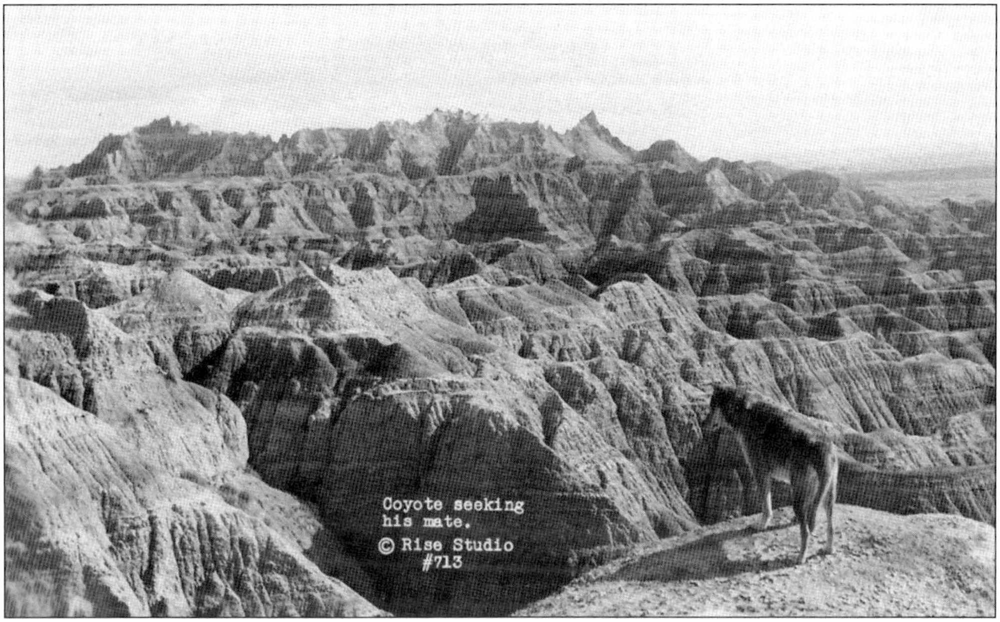

Badlands National Park is a sanctuary for wildlife. The prairie is composed of 56 species of grass in which plants and animals live. Even predators such as coyotes, foxes, and bobcats are protected within its boundaries. Wolves harassed early ranchers by killing livestock. Wolfers, men who hunted them, exterminated them in the Badlands. Prairie dogs, ferrets, deer, pronghorn, bison, bighorn sheep, deer, chipmunks, squirrels, jack rabbits, 206 bird species, 69 butterfly species, reptiles, and amphibians also roam safely within the park's borders. More information on the grasslands is available at the Buffalo Gap National Grasslands visitor center in Wall.

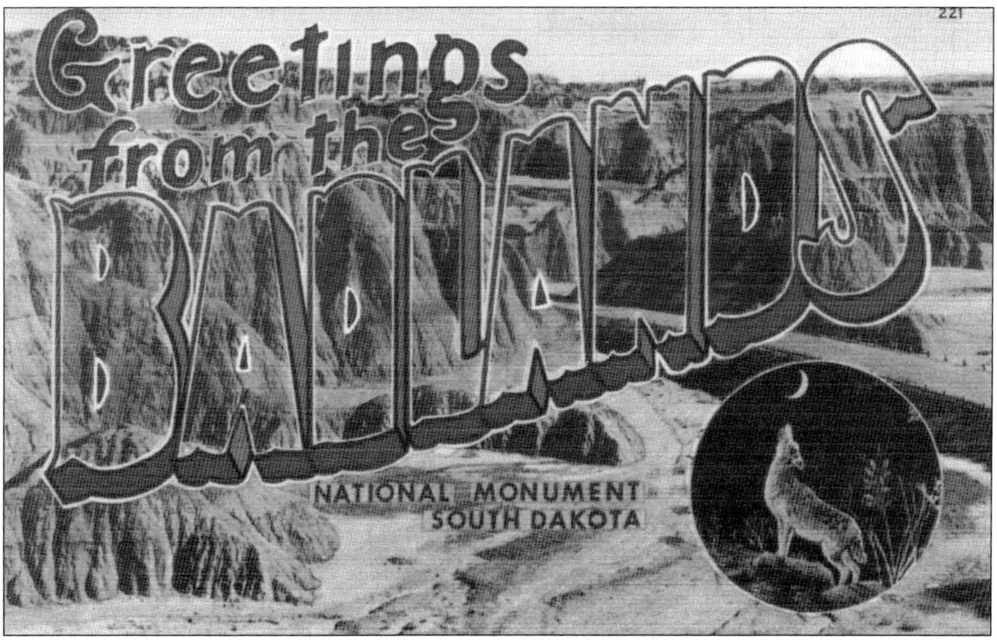

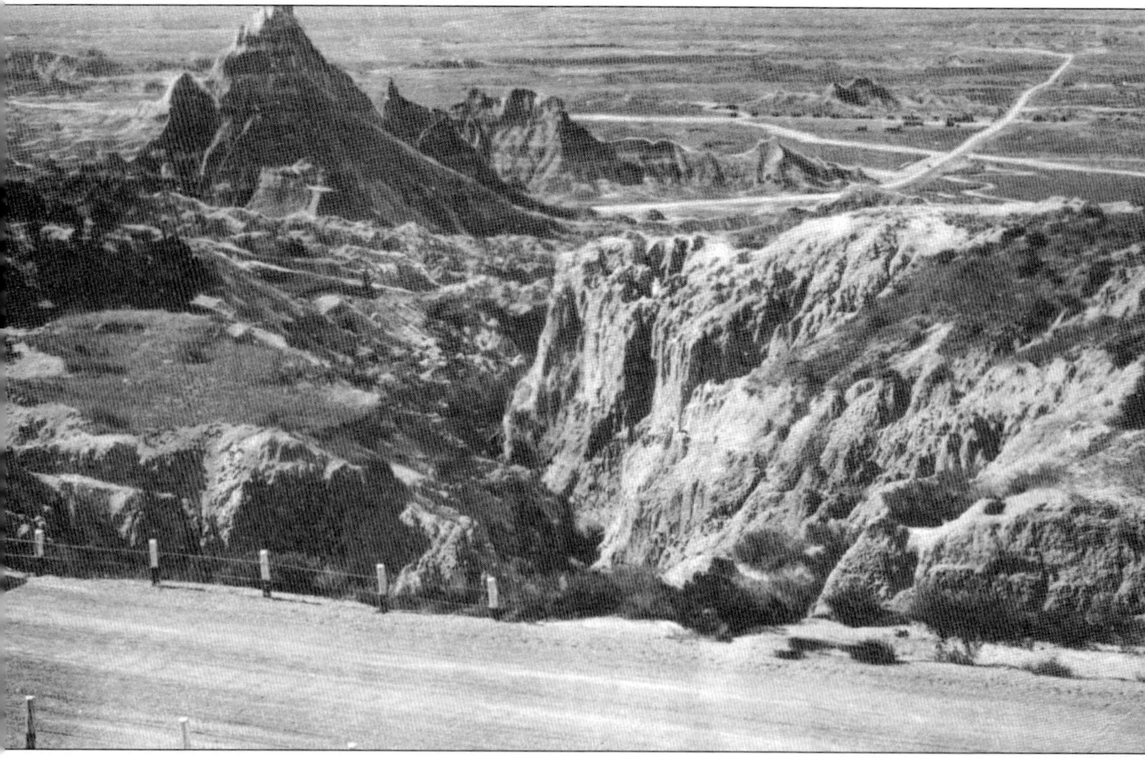

This view of Vampire Peak, postmarked July 4, 1941, overlooks Cedar Pass Lodge and the monument headquarters. In 1940, the National Park Service intended to have its office in Wall with additional facilities at the Pinnacles, south of Wall. However, Ben Millard donated 28 acres at the foot of Cedar Pass to the park service. Several years earlier, Millard had purchased the land from his sister and begun to establish a tourist business. Later, he donated an additional 160 acres to the park service, where a custodian's house was built. In 1991, the visitor center was renamed Ben Reifel Visitor Center for a congressman of Lakota Sioux and German American descent who served five terms from January 3, 1961, to January 3, 1971. Reifel was affiliated with the Bureau of Indian Affairs, served as a consultant for Indian programming, and was a member of the National Park Service Advisory Board. The road pictured here continues to the town of Interior.

Two

Inroads to a Lost World

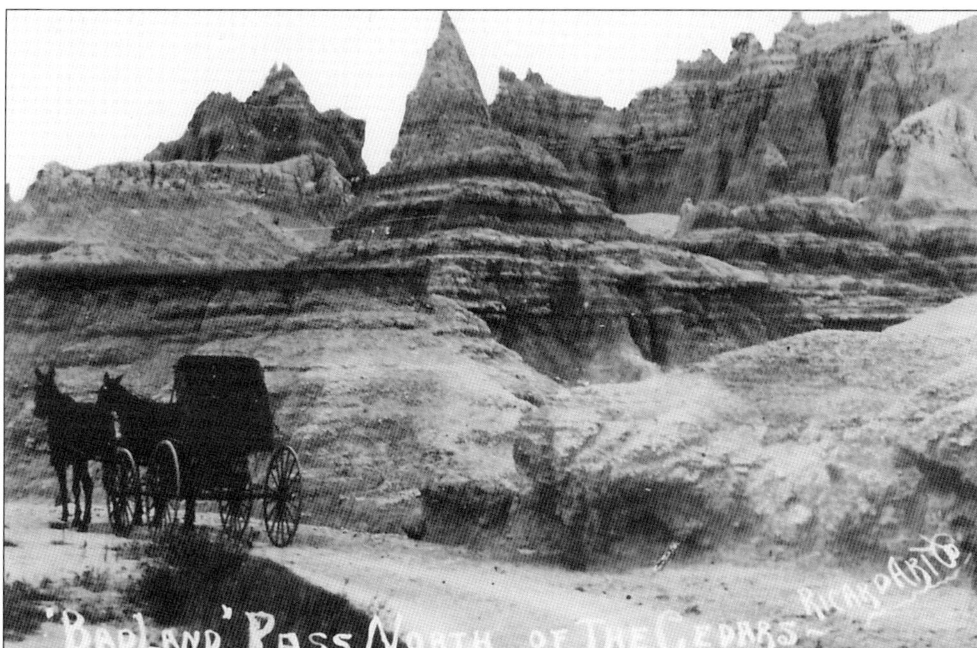

A two-horse buggy pauses at the pass north of "the Cedars." The Cedar Pass road was one of the first roads constructed, enabling the residents to penetrate the Badlands Wall. The rough terrain of the Badlands forms a wall that divides the upper and lower prairies. The four major passes are Cedar, Norbeck, Dillon, and Bigfoot. The passes render travel across the north rim possible.

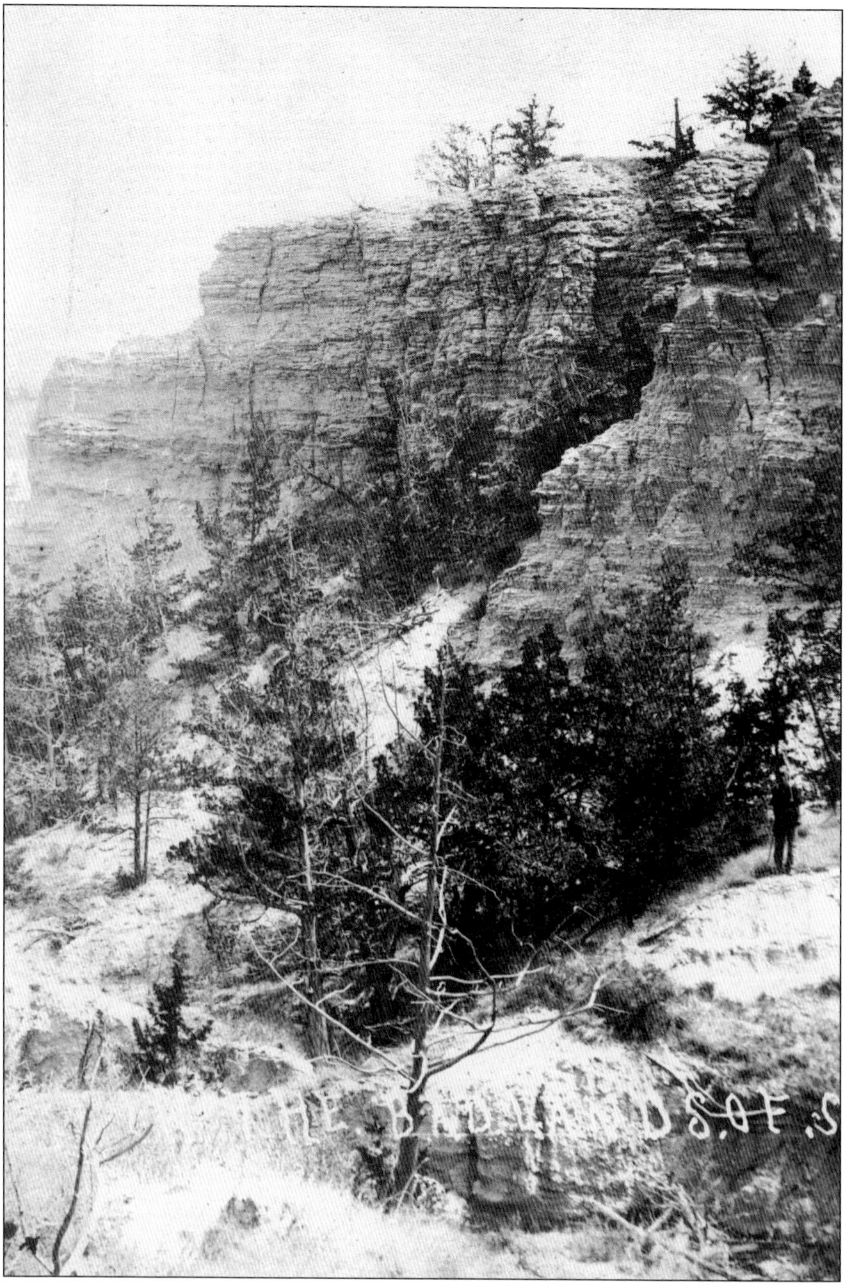

This postcard sent from Midland, South Dakota, on June 21, 1907, reads, "Small sample of the Bad Lands. We are 30 miles from there. Can only go on horseback." A road through the Badlands had not been built yet when this postcard was sent. Only a few trails existed for horse and wagon traffic. One was Saddle Pass, a steep, narrow horseback trail connecting the interior of the Badlands and the prairie below with the prairie above. For a time, Saddle Pass was a mail route from Interior to the north. If a homesteader lived above the Badlands Wall and needed to get to Old Interior (known earlier as Black) for supplies, he would leave his wagon at the top and ride a horse down Saddle Pass, bring up the supplies from the trading post, load the wagon, and return to his homestead.

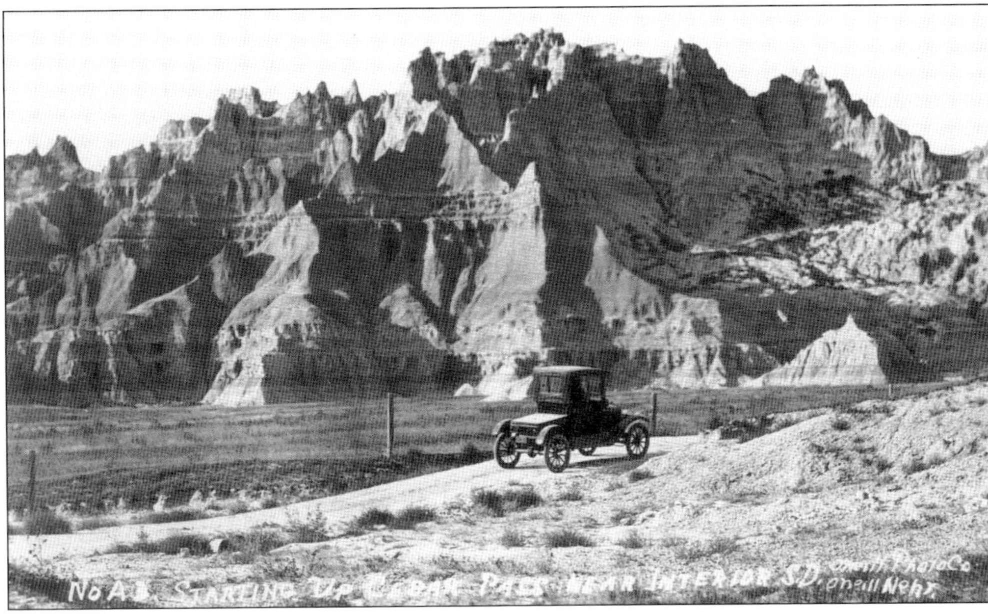

This car at Cedar Pass was one of the many Model Ts, Chevrolets, Maxwells, and Star motorcars that began to appear in the Badlands around 1914 and 1915. The roads were mere trails, often worn with deep ruts by wagon wheels. These early cars, which required a crank to start the engine, would often get stuck in the ruts or in the mud during wet weather.

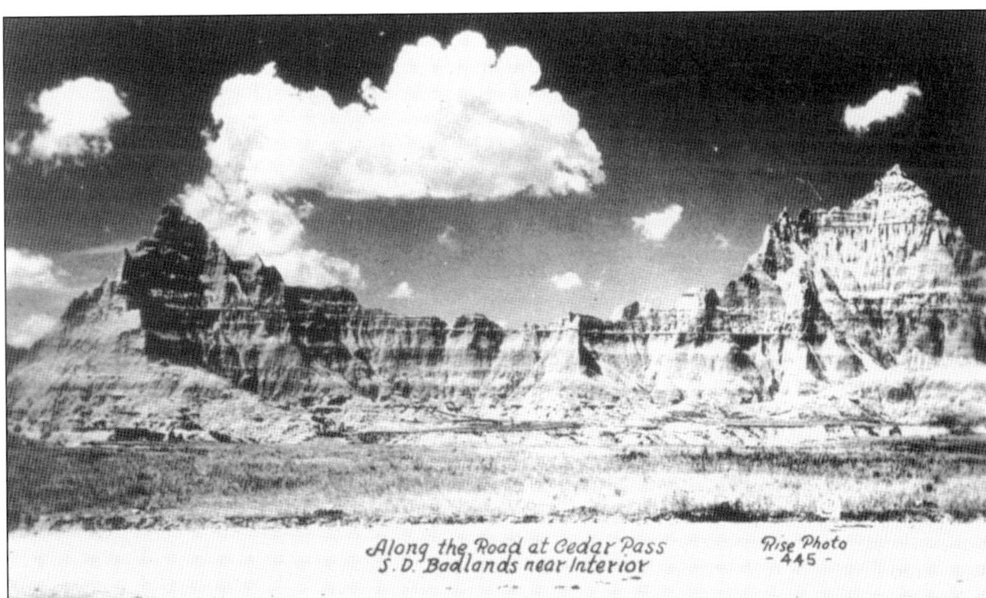

The road through Cedar Pass began as a trail and then improved as a dirt road when the residents requested a better road. The road progressed to gravel in 1936 and finally to a paved road in the 1940s. The pass shown in this c. 1935 postcard is called Cedar Pass because of the profusion of cedars growing near a well-watered area.

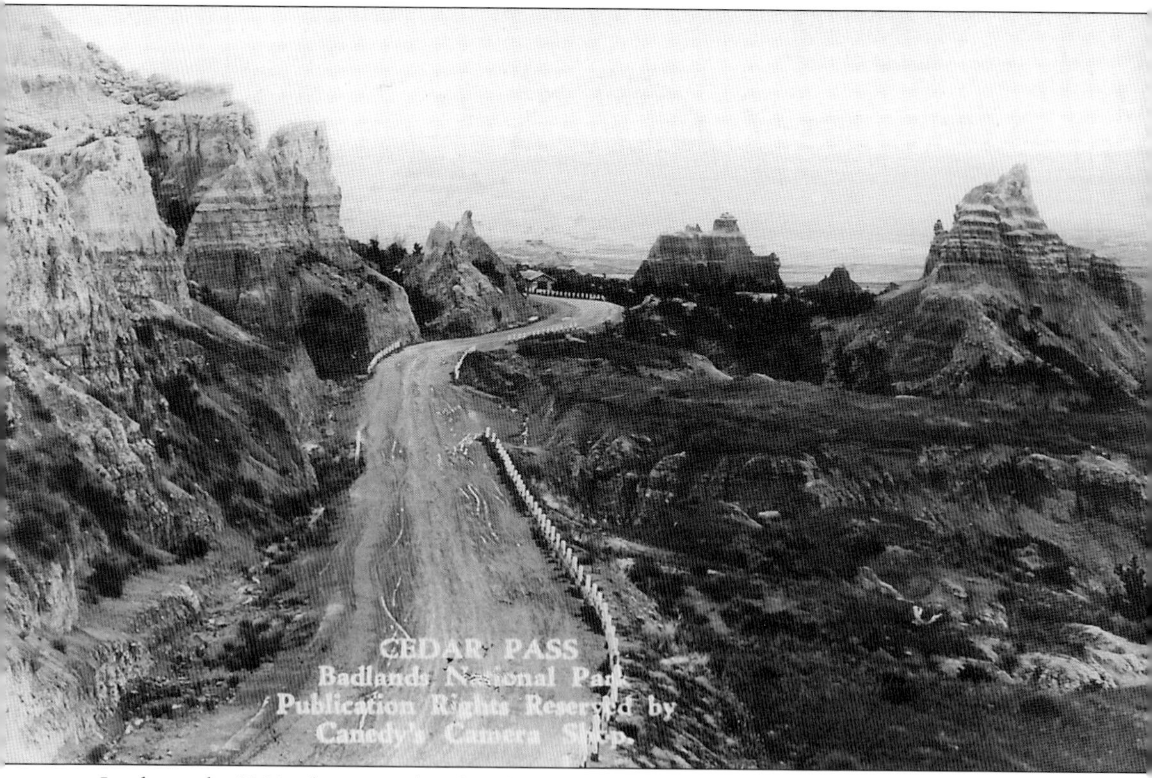

In the early 1900s, homesteaders banded together to build a makeshift road through Cedar Pass in order to reach the town of Interior to buy supplies. Interior was isolated in the interior of the Badlands without a safe road to travel from the north. In spite of organized efforts to bring improved roads through the Badlands, no action was taken until the 1920s, when Interior businessmen earnestly promoted travel through the Badlands. The state highway commission took notice and estimated the cost to build a road would be $10,000. In 1929, a dirt road through Cedar Pass to Interior was completed. Designation of the Badlands as a national monument was in the works, adding impetus to constructing highways throughout the Badlands in the 1930s. The dirt roads were eventually graveled, and then blacktopped in the 1940s. Mailed in 1937, this postcard offers an early view of the Cedar Pass dirt road with guardrails.

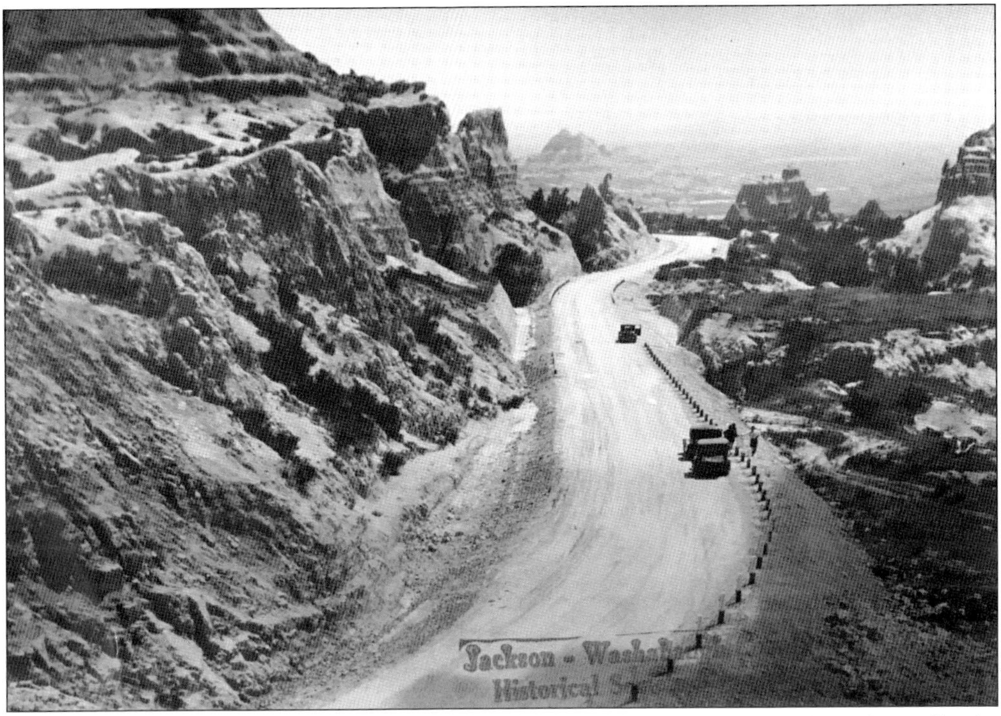

Cars pause along the road at Cedar Pass. By 1941, there were 70 miles of roads in the Badlands. Almost 30 miles were graveled, and 40 miles were dirt. Toward the end of the 1940s, blacktopping began. (Courtesy of the Kadoka Depot Museum.)

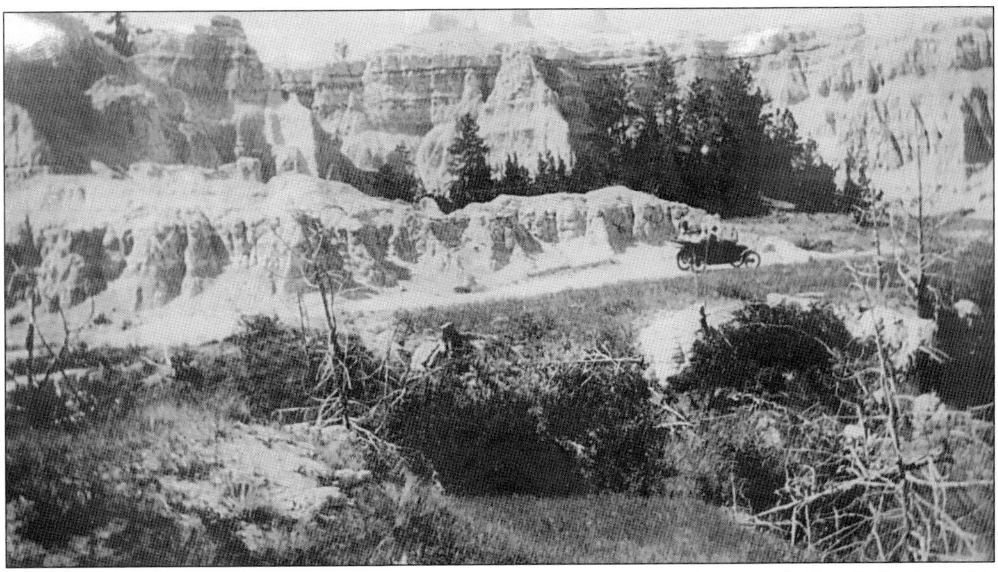

Highway 73, south of Kadoka, leads to Kodak Point, overlooking a Badlands basin with formations dotted with cedars. The highway continues out of the basin and ascends Quiver hill, where this photograph was taken. (Courtesy of the Kadoka Depot Museum.)

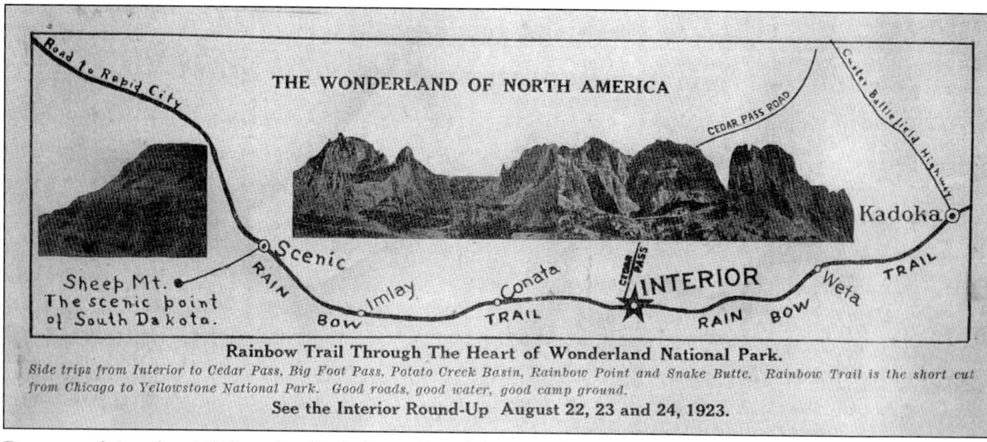

Promoted in the 1920s, the Rainbow Trail began from Kadoka to Weta, Interior, Conata, Imlay, and Scenic. From the trail, routes branched off to Cedar Pass, Bigfoot Pass, Potato Creek, Rainbow Point, Snake Butte, and Sheep Mountain. The improved road through Cedar Pass had not yet been completed. The Rainbow Trail was also known as Highway 40 or the White River Road.

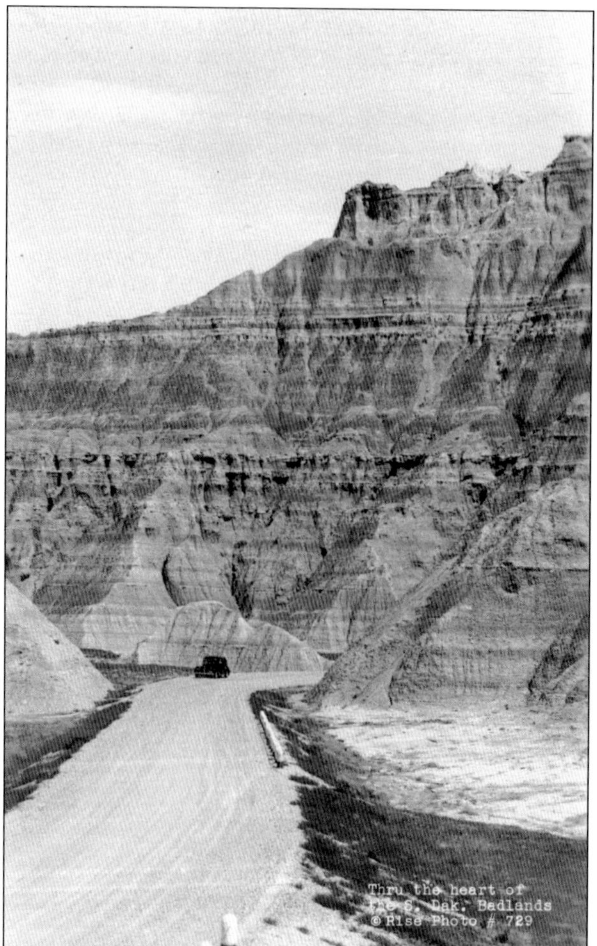

In 1928, a bill was drafted to give monument status to the Badlands, stipulating that South Dakota acquire 90 percent of the private lands within the proposed boundaries at its own expense. Furthermore, South Dakota was to donate the acquired land to the federal government as well as build a 26-mile road along the Badlands Wall. Here, a car wends its way through the heart of the awe-inspiring scenery. Note that the road is graveled.

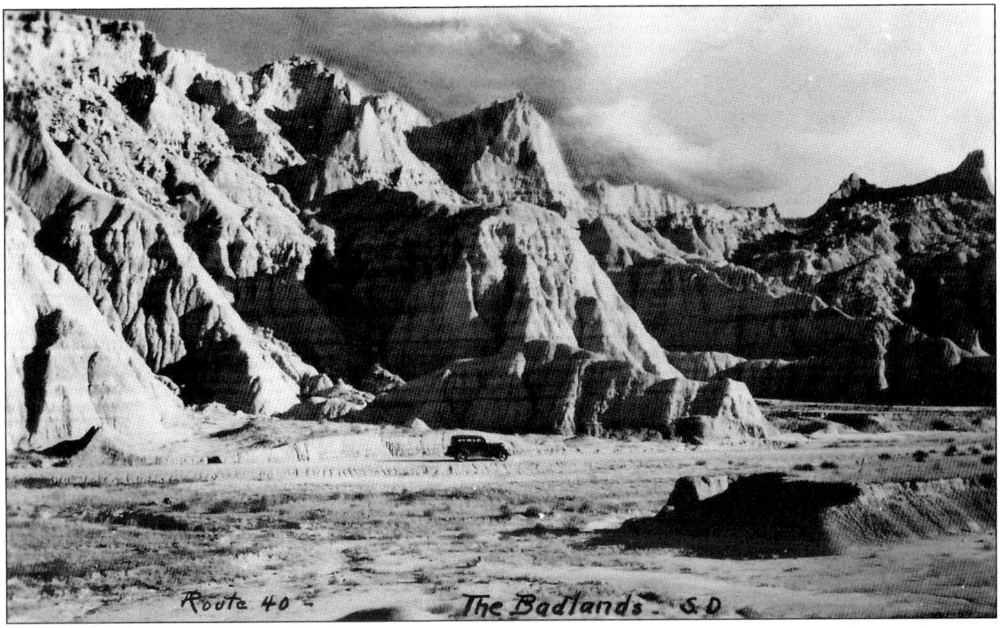

A car travels Route 40 through the Badlands. Perhaps influenced by a suggestion of Ranger Louis Knowles, Senator Norbeck mapped out the most scenic route in the Badlands, while engineers proposed an easier route, which would bypass the best scenery. In 1922, Norbeck introduced the first bill in Congress to make a portion of the Badlands a national park.

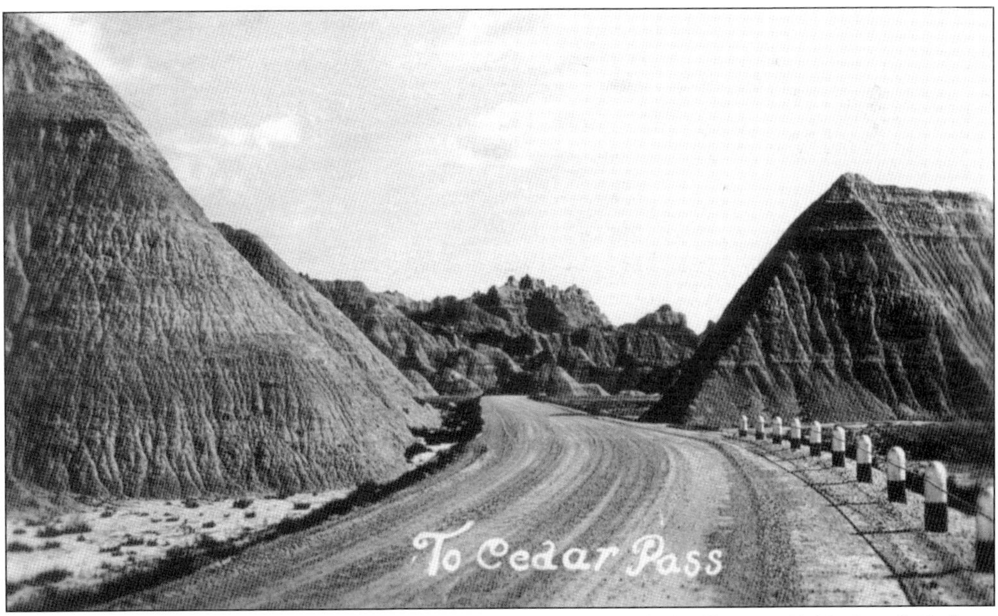

Gravel roads were completed in the park in 1936 after a unified effort. In 1920, South Dakota addressed the issue of building roads across the state. Two proposals were mapped out. One was known as the Black and Yellow Trail, from Brookings to Pierre and Philip. The other, from Sioux Fall to Kadoka, was known as the Custer Battlefield Highway, later Highway 16.

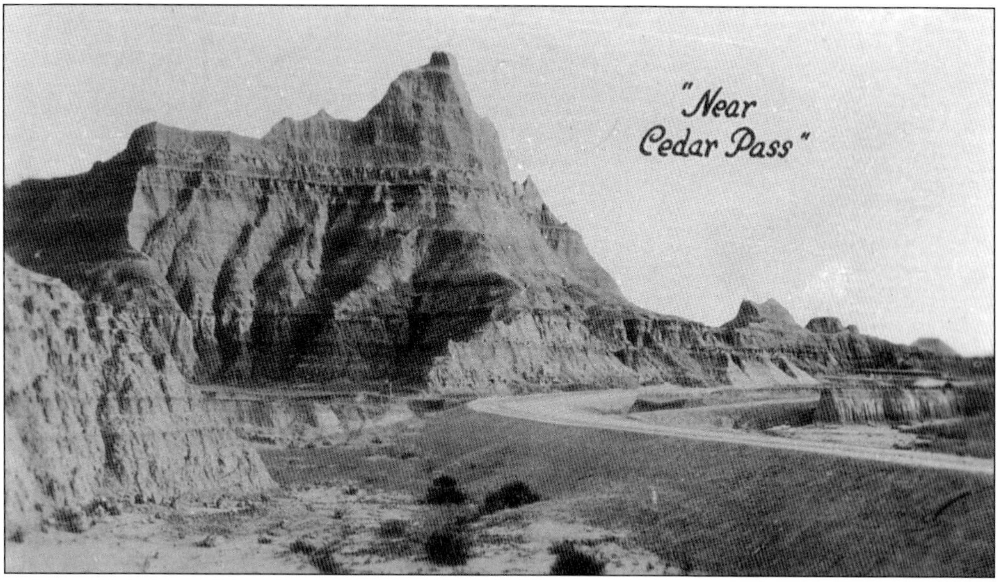

Interior and the Badlands were not included in the push for roads crossing the state, but the Interior businessmen would not give up their desire to bring tourists to the Badlands. At first they promoted the road below the wall called the Rainbow Trail, from Weta to Interior and on to Rapid City. In 1921, the Interior Commercial Club proposed a scenic loop west of Kadoka, through Cedar Pass to Interior, Scenic, and Rapid City. By 1929, the state-graded dirt road through Cedar Pass was completed. President Coolidge signed a bill in 1929 proposing monument status for the Badlands, adding further impetus for road building. In June 1936, the roads were graveled.

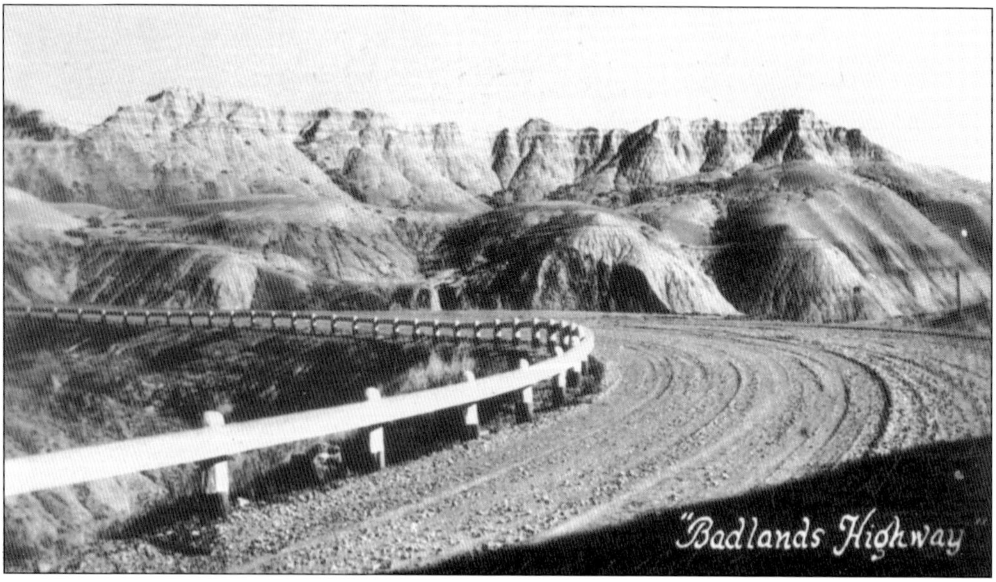

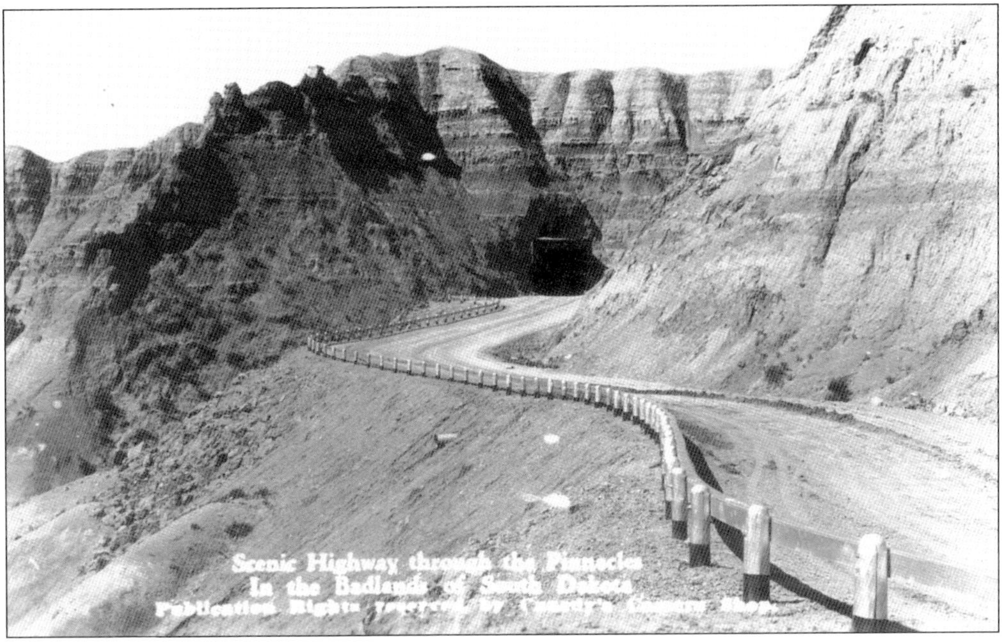

In 1940, Emergency Relief Administration (ERA) labor under the Public Roads Administration removed two tunnels constructed during the first half of the 1930s. One was the Pinnacles, a 175-foot tunnel. The engineers noted that the timbers supporting the tunnel were in poor condition. Because of rockslides and the soil's instability, the tunnels were in danger of collapsing. Under the leadership of the National Parks Conservation Association and relief organizations such as the ERA, the Resettlement Administration, Works Progress Administration, and the Civilian Conservation Corps, many projects were completed in the Badlands.

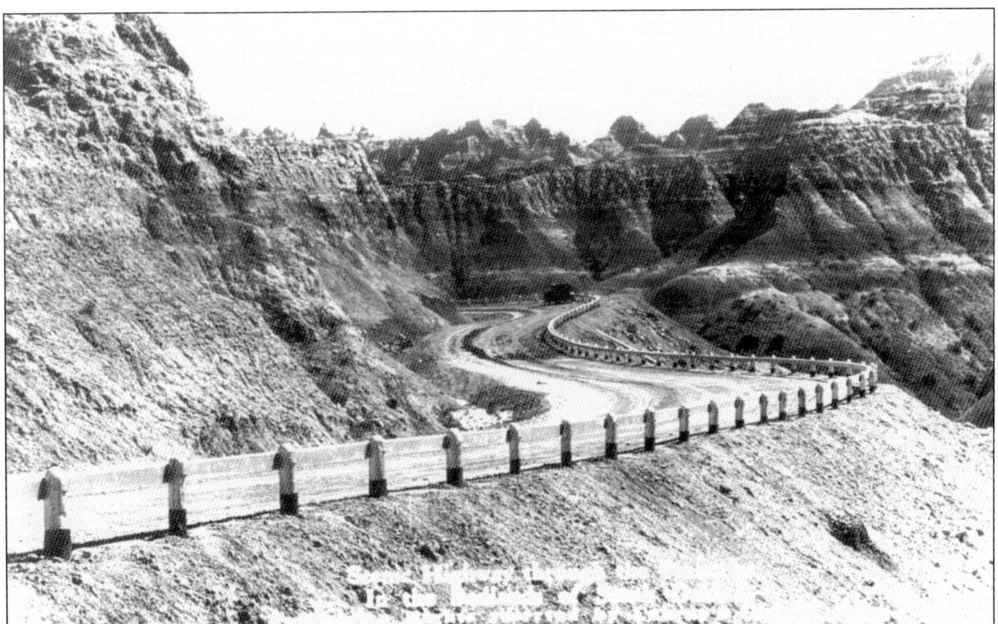

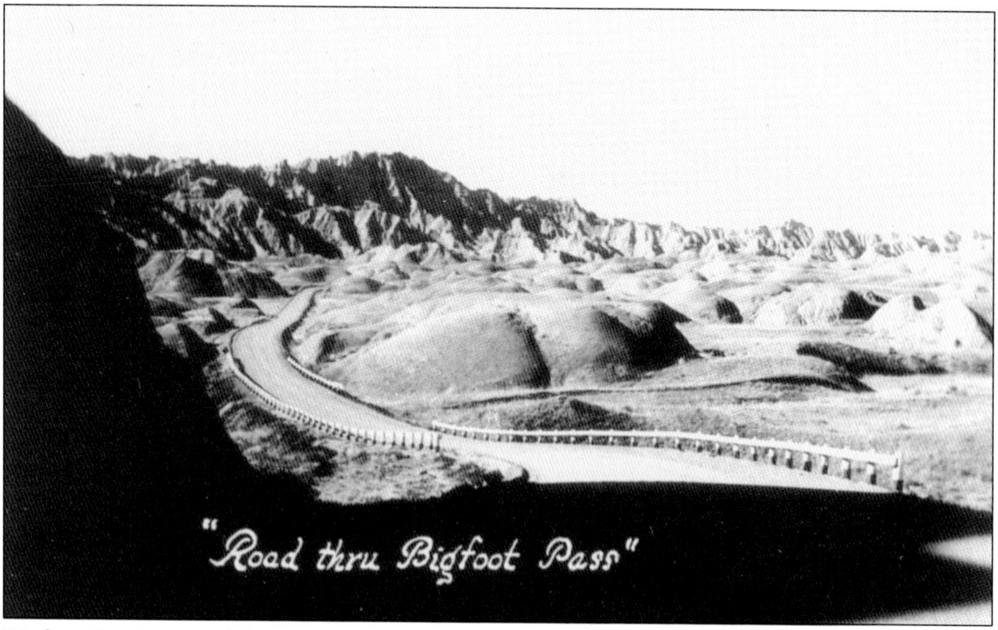

Bigfoot Pass is named for Chief Bigfoot (Spotted Elk), a Minneconjou Lakota Sioux who led his people from the Cheyenne Indian Reservation through the Badlands. Soldiers intercepted his band en route to Pine Ridge and someone fired a shot, leading to a massacre near Wounded Knee in December 1890.

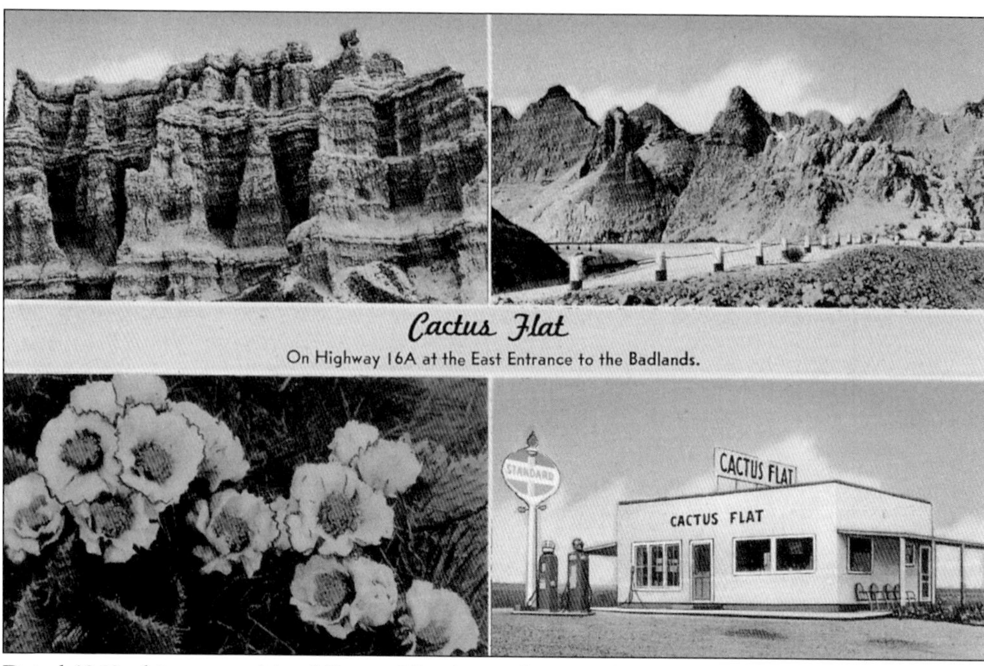

Dated 1962, this postcard is of Cactus Flat, located on Highway 16A at the east entrance to the Badlands. Leonard and Fern Emry built the original gas station to the west of the one pictured and named it Cactus Flat. The card reads, "The last stop before entering the Badlands to buy gas, oil, souvenirs, photograph supplies, ice cream, pop and beer. Leonard Emry, Cottonwood, South Dakota." The gas station is no longer in operation.

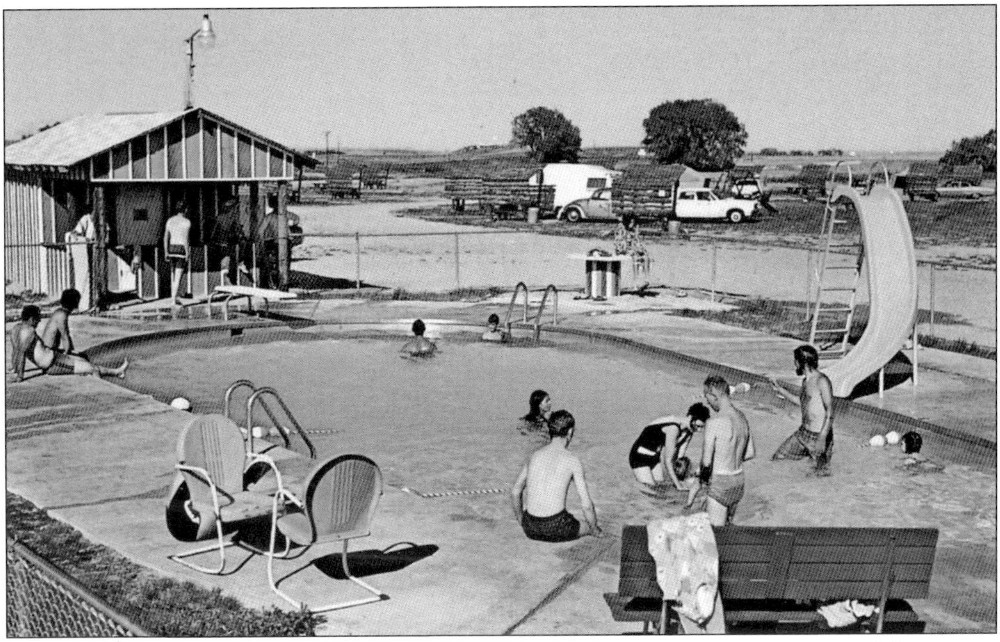

Across from Cactus Flat is the Circle Ten Campground, originally built and named the Cactus Flat Campground by Leslie and Jessie Crew. The name was changed as a tribute to the open range when cattle were rounded up at this location and sorted off to their respective ranges. In the 1970s, a pool was added to the campground. The Crews eventually sold the campground. Ownership has changed several times since then.

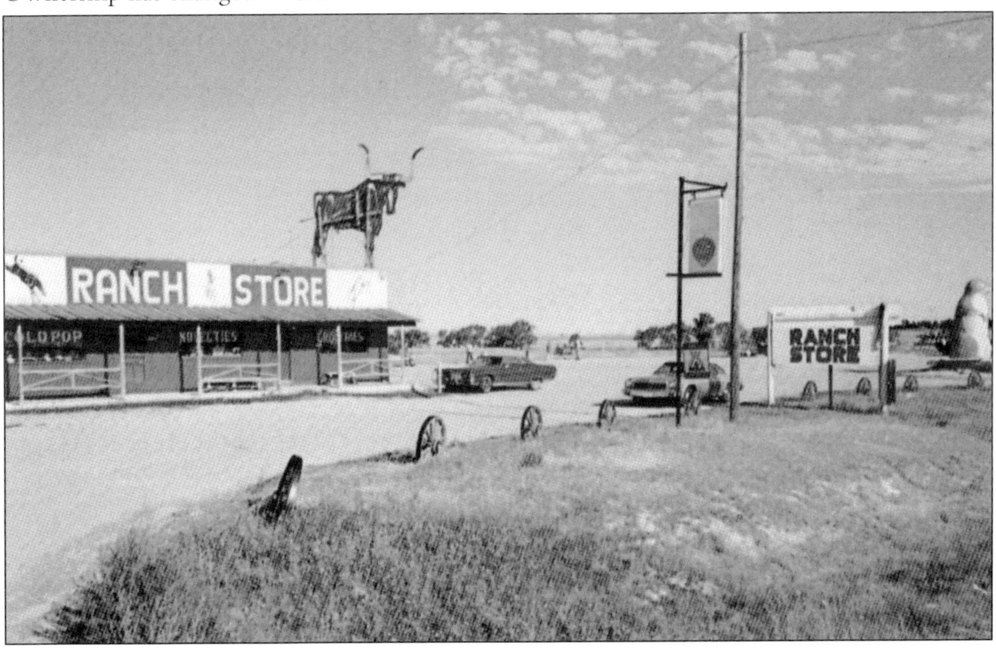

The Ranch Store was originally located in Kadoka before it was moved a few miles south of Cactus Flat at the east entrance to the Badlands. The Ranch Store has changed hands several times and sells the usual tourist items, at one time even exhibiting rattlesnakes. Situated near a prairie dog town, the Ranch Store is a favorite spot to stop and view the animals.

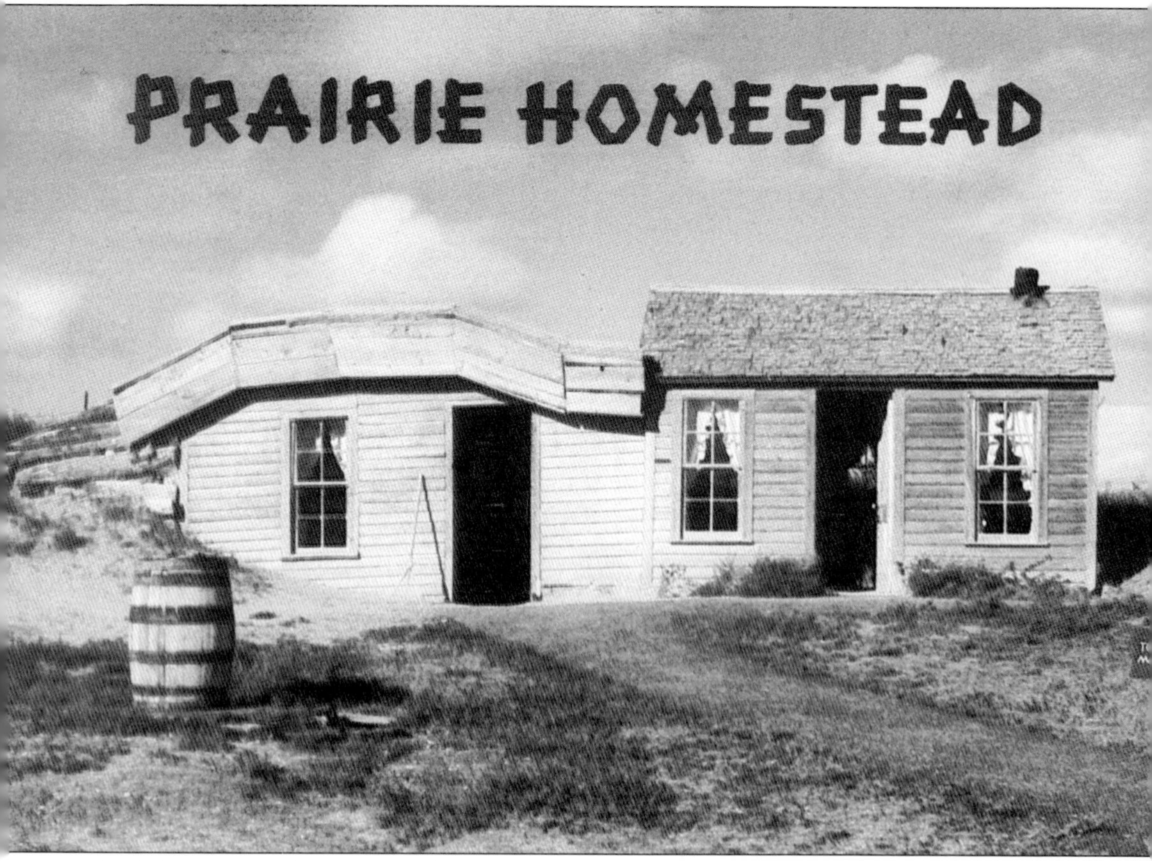

Prairie Homestead, the original sod dugout home of Ed and Alice Brown, is located past the Ranch Store and before the east entrance to the Badlands. Ed Brown filed a 160-acre claim in 1909, farming the land and raising livestock. He paid 50¢ per acre, a total of $80 for right of patent on April 24, 1911. In 1912, Brown moved an abandoned claim shack and attached it to the sod dugout. When Ed died in 1920, their son Charles took over the operation. Alice moved to California in 1934. A year later, George and Charles Carr moved in until Charles too moved to California. George remained in the sod dugout home until 1949. The Brown home is listed in the National Register of Historic Places and is open to tourists.

Three

Native Americans

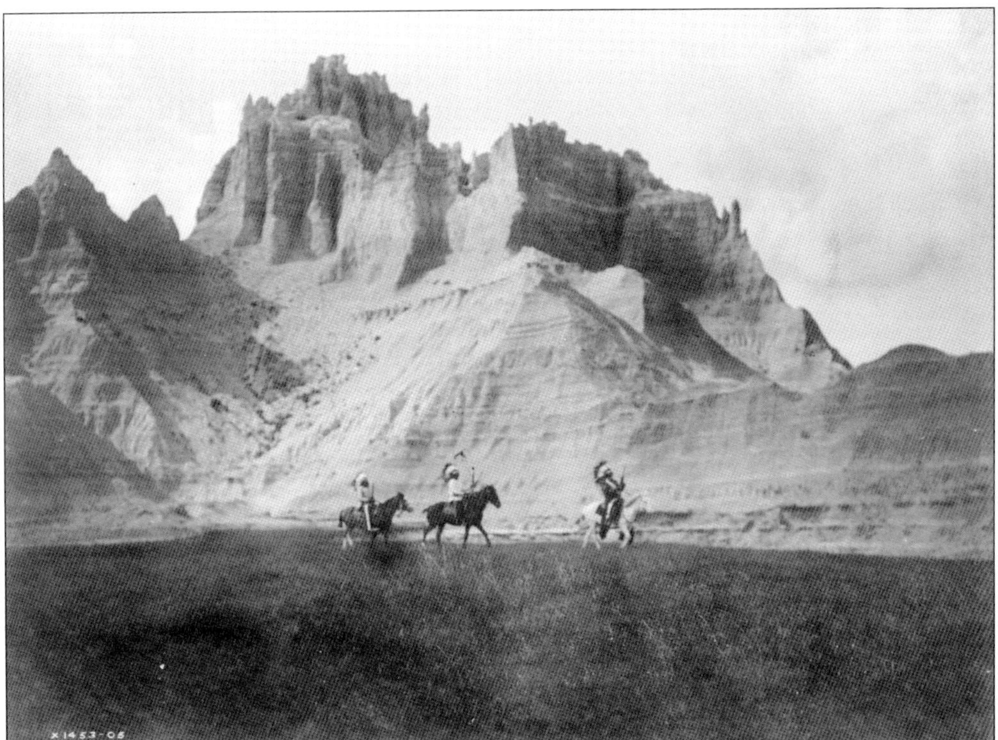

The discovery of fire pits in the Badlands dating to 900 AD confirm that early inhabitants used the area for hunting. The Sioux did not arrive in western South Dakota until around 1775. Referring to themselves as Dakota, their legend records that they originated from Wind Cave. (Photograph by Edward Curtis; courtesy of the Library of Congress, LC-USZ62-107913.)

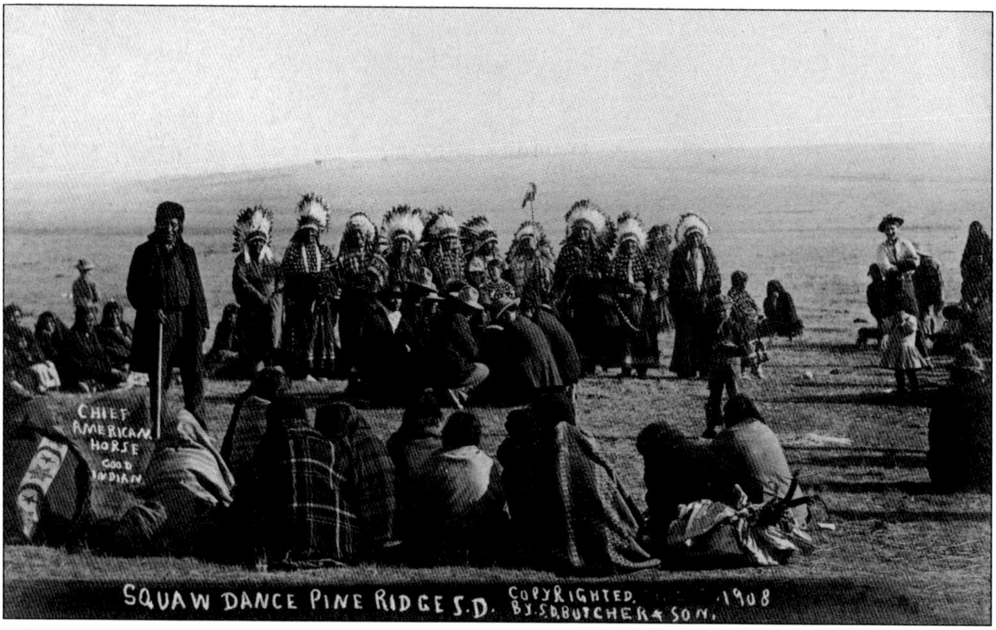

After a series of wars and shifting US government policies, the roving bands of Dakota were confined to reservations. Pictured is a 1908 dance on the Pine Ridge Indian reservation south of Badlands National Park. By that year, the open range was dwindling, and homesteaders took up homesteads on the prairies around the Badlands. (Photograph by Solomon Devore Butcher; courtesy of the Library of Congress, LC-DIG-ppmsca-08386.)

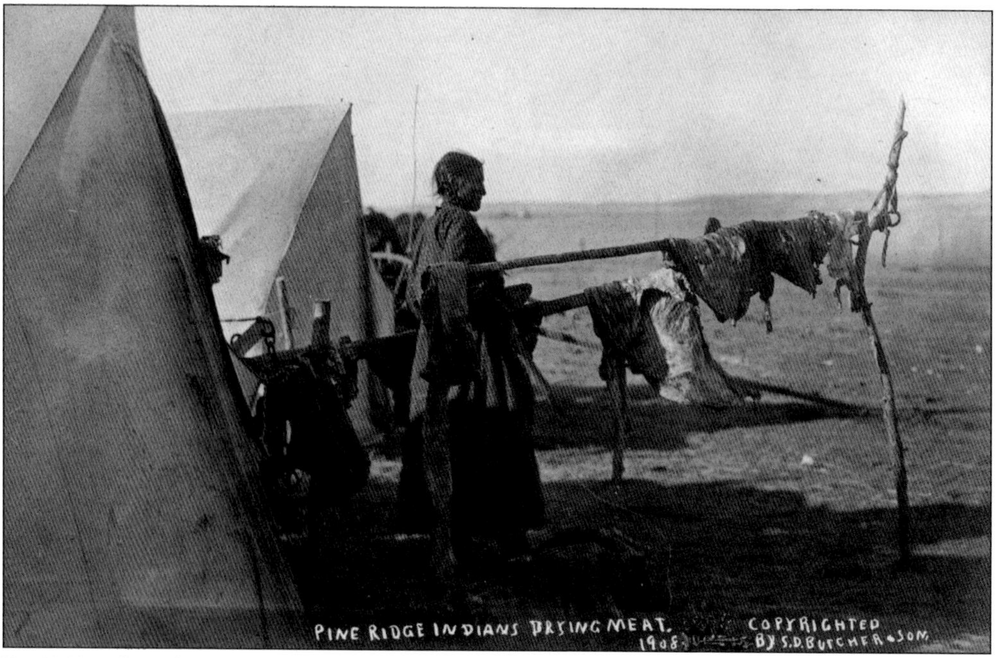

By 1908, when this photograph was taken, the buffalo that had been the chief sustenance of the American Indian were gone. The government issued rations and beef on the hoof, which was killed and butchered. The meat was preserved the old way, by drying it on racks. (Courtesy of the Library of Congress, LC-DIG-ppmsca-08384.)

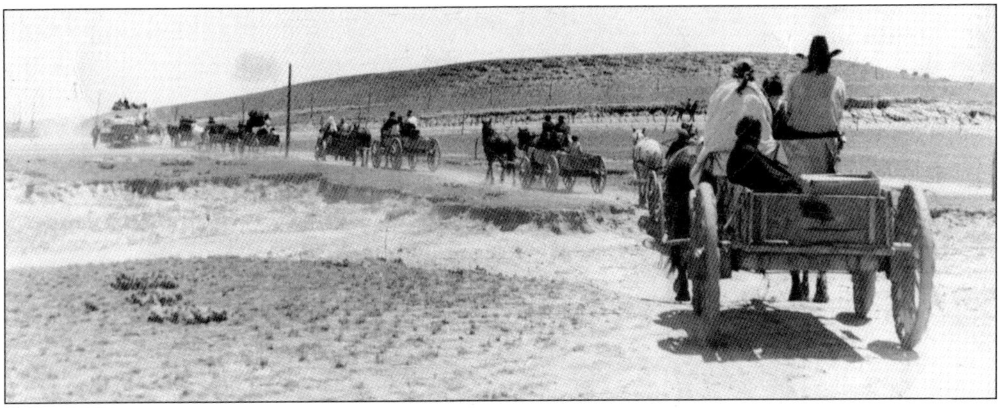

The government encouraged the reservation Indians to give up their nomadic lifestyle, distributing teams and wagons and plows so they could farm; however, this plan did not always succeed. This convoy of wagons may be going for rations or for a day's outing. The Lakota (a sub-tribe of the Dakota) participated in the frontier towns' celebrations and events. (Courtesy of Badlands National Park.)

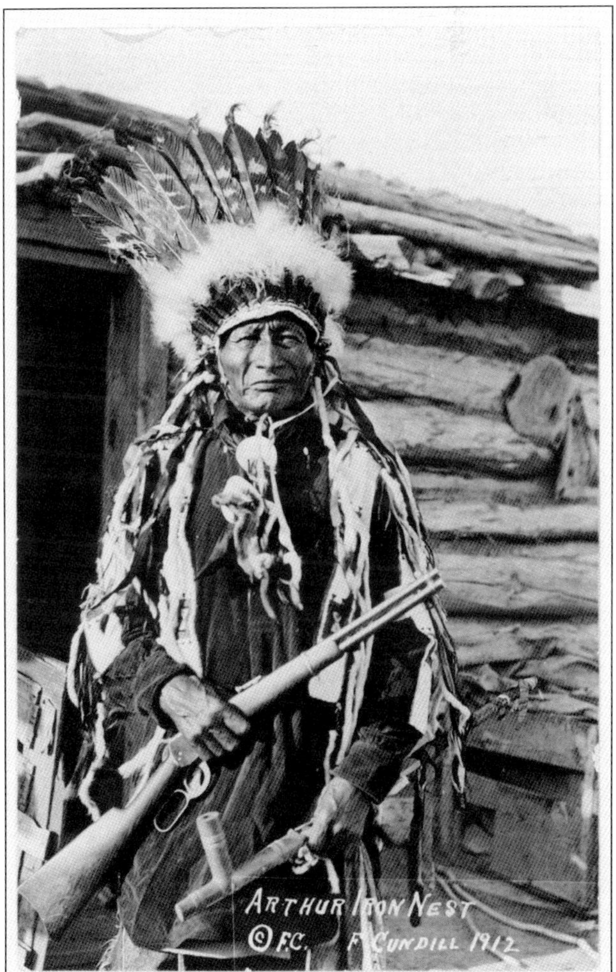

Arthur Iron Nest stands beside his cabin in 1912 while photographer Frank F. Cundill takes his picture. The Lakota were living in log cabins after being relegated to reservations, but some preferred living in tepees and canvas tents, especially during the summer. (Courtesy of the Library of Congress, LC-USZ62-107139.)

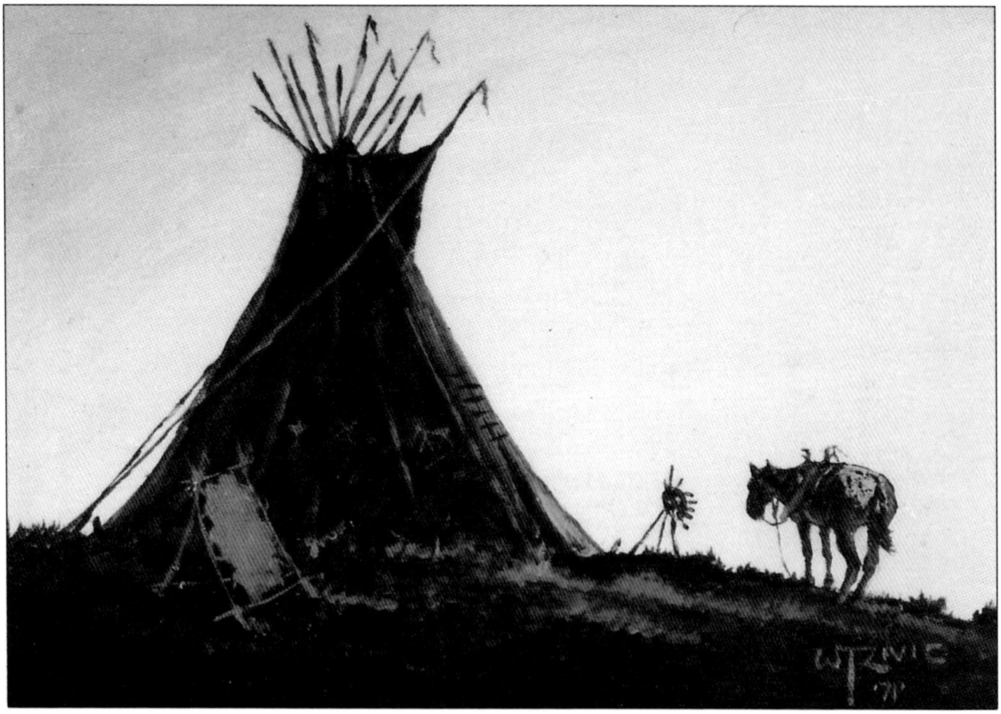

Artist William Zivic painted this scene of a Plains Indian's home. Tepees were made of buffalo hides, rendering them convenient for the nomadic peoples, who could pack up and leave their camp at a moment's notice. (Courtesy of Wall Drug.)

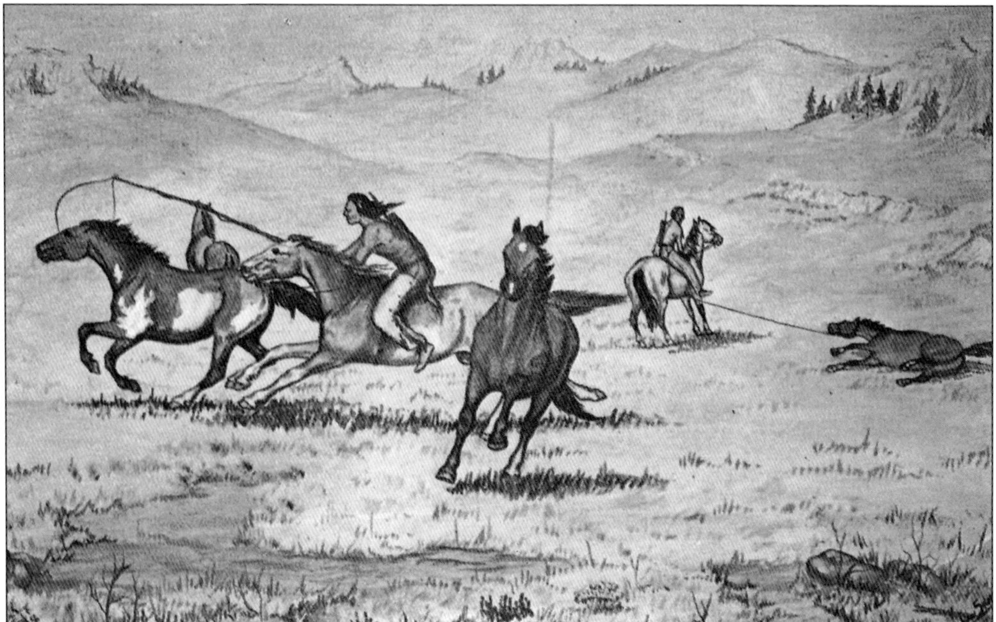

Artist Andrew Standing Soldier, a Native American from Pine Ridge, painted many pictures depicting the Pine Ridge area where he grew up. In this painting, Standing Soldier illustrates the Indian way of catching wild horses. Pine Ridge Indian Reservation is south of the Badlands.

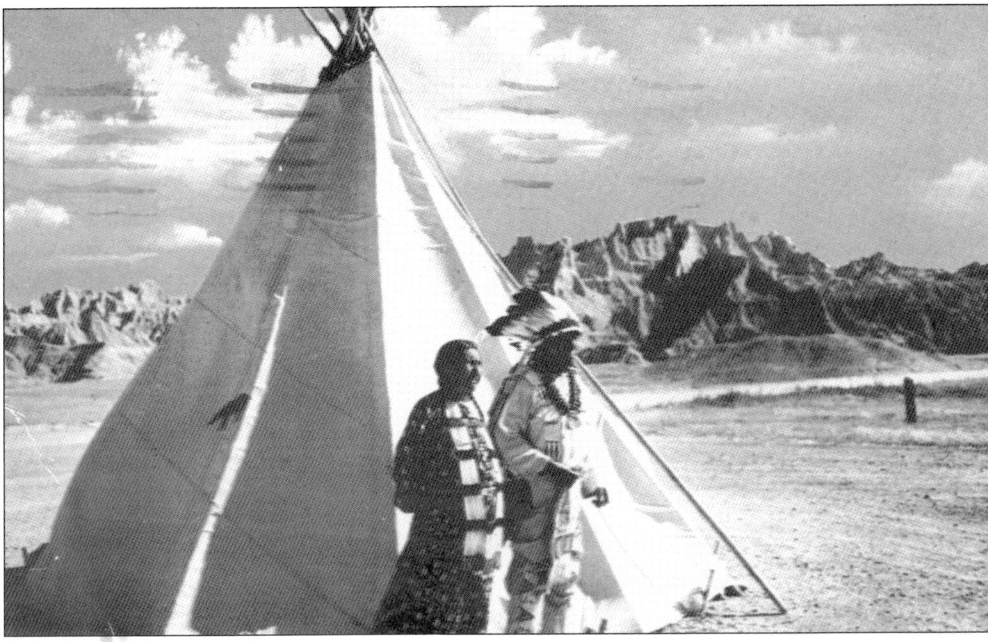

Dewey Beard, a Minneconjou Lakota, was first known by the name of Masu Maza (translated as "Iron Hail"), later calling himself Dewey Beard. He lived a lifetime filled with struggle and sorrow. He witnessed many historical events, outliving his children and dying on November 2, 1955, as the last of the Little Big Horn survivors. Dewey Beard was present when Custer and his men were annihilated. He survived the massacre at Wounded Knee in 1890 where his mother, father, two brothers, his first wife, and their infant died. The last event affected him greatly. He became an advocate for the Wounded Knee survivors as well as a supporter of compensation or the return of allotted acres that had been used as a bombing training range.

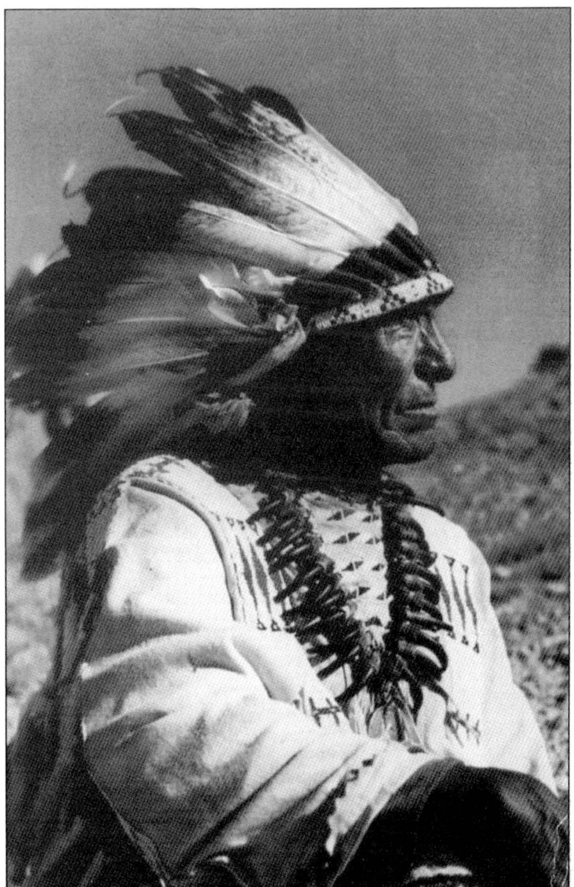

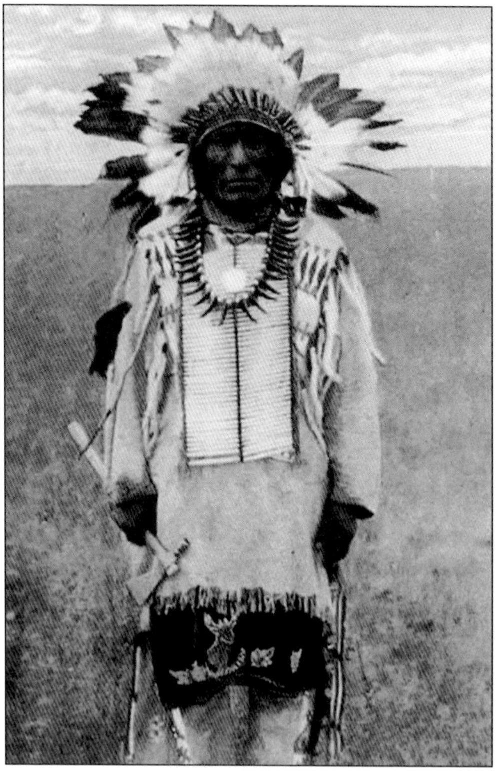

Chief Iron Hail is possibly pictured here in 1920 in ceremonial dress; the bear claw necklace that he wears around his neck appears in most of his photographs. Prior to 1920, Iron Hail celebrated the first annual roundup or three-day rodeo in Interior. The Chicago, Milwaukee & St. Paul Railroad brought spectators and tourists from all parts of the country to watch rodeo contestants and Native Americans dancing traditional dances.

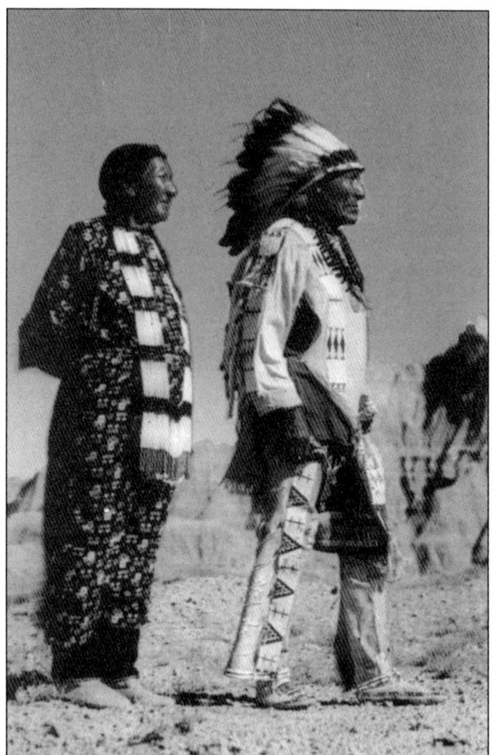

Dewey and Alice Beard lived on an allotment until the government forced them off, giving them their $60 payment each month for their lost land. The government intended to use the allotments for bombing ranges. The allotments were intended to encourage farming, but Dewey Beard turned his into a horse ranch with a house, potato patch, and chickens. Without their allotment, the couple were hard-pressed to make a living.

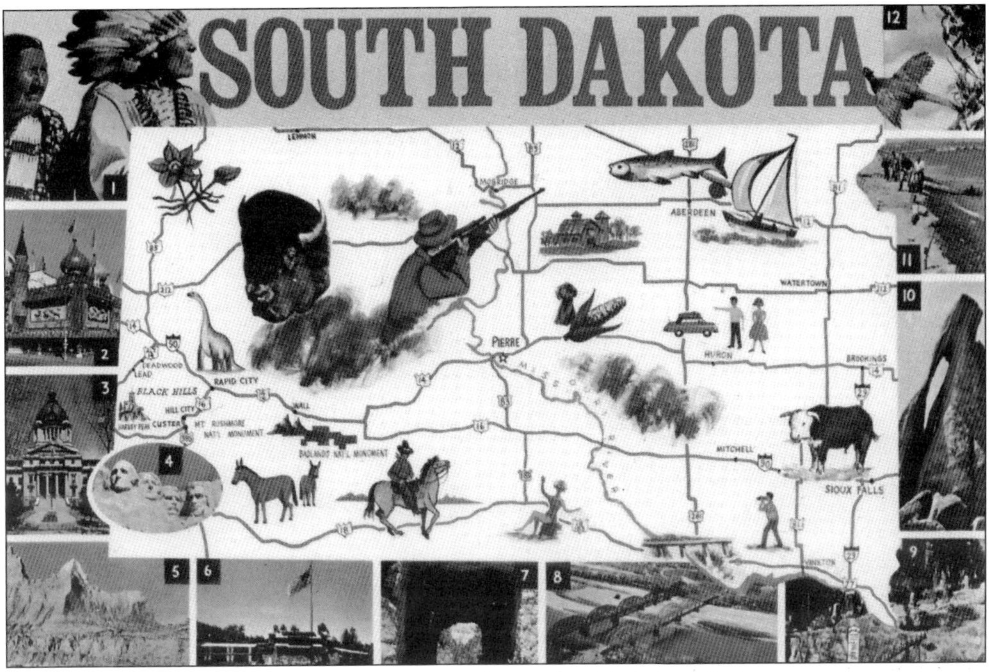

Alice and Dewey Beard appear in the upper left corner of the South Dakota map above. Dewey toured with Buffalo Bill Cody's Wild West show in 1895 and was hired to participate in a Wounded Knee movie, *The Indian Wars*. Dewey garnered attention because of the movie, but he criticized the film on various points, especially the absence of women and children who had been killed during the horrific event. During the 1950s, he played small parts in several movies with pro-Indian themes. Dewey Beard continued to appear with his wife on tours and postcards; however, he was rarely identified. The c. 1913 image below is of Buffalo Bill and Dakota Sioux children during the filming of *The Indian Wars*.

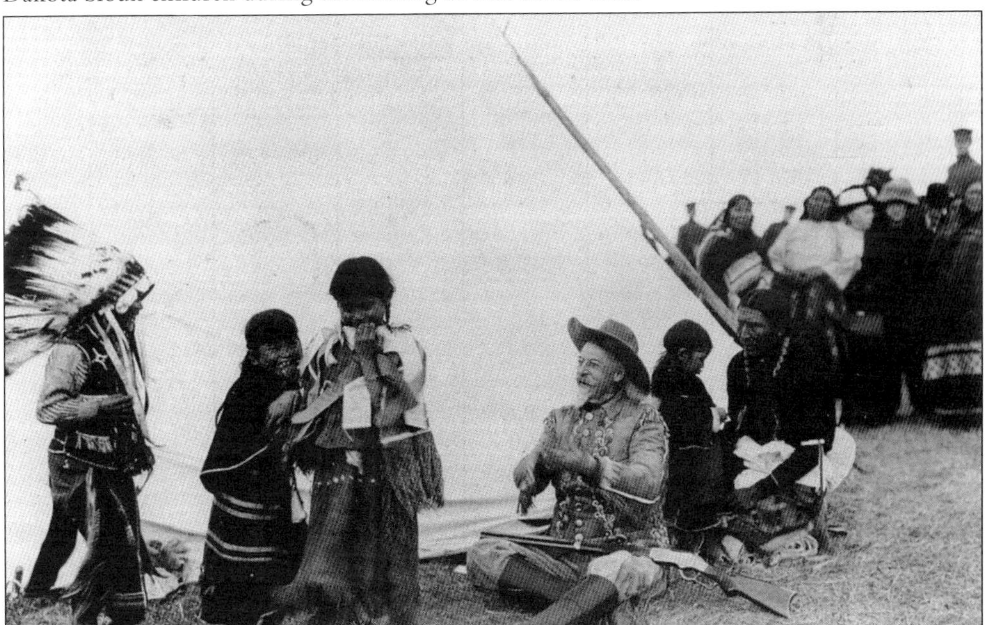

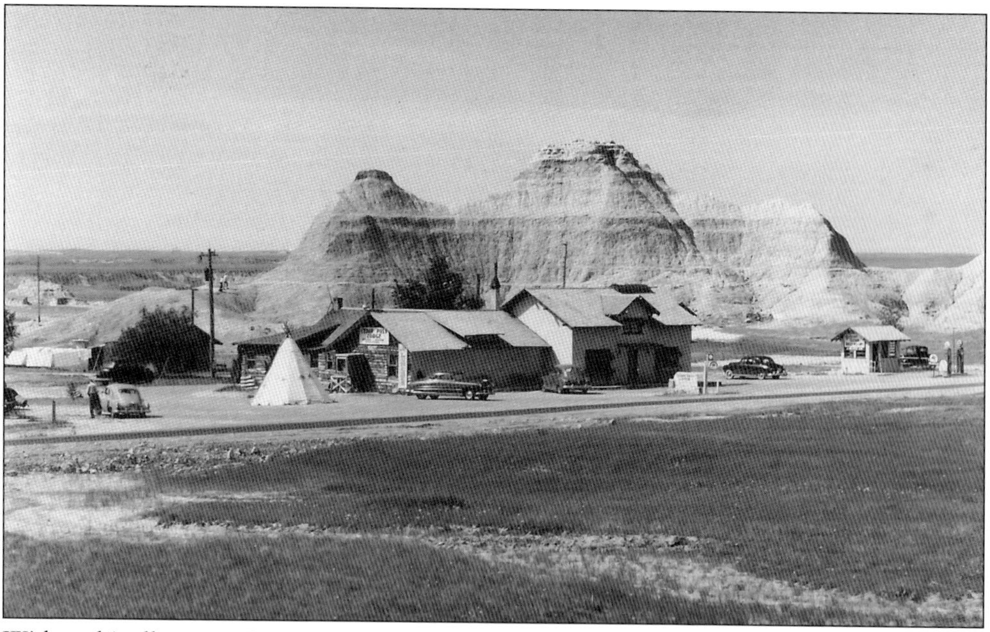

Without his allotment, Dewey Beard pitched his own tepee painted with various animal shapes at Cedar Pass Lodge, where he and Alice spent the summers during the Depression. During their last 20 years, they summered in the Badlands. Dewey, dressed in his ceremonial regalia, and Alice posed for pictures for a small payment of 25¢ or 50¢. Alice took care of the money. A lodge employee remembered that she would hold out her hand and say "more" when the payment was not enough. In 1948, Dewey attended the reunion of Big Horn survivors at Custer State Park in the Black Hills. Later, the Badlands and Lakes Association sponsored Dewey and Alice to travel as unofficial ambassadors to several different states. They enjoyed these excursions and came home with suitcases full of presents for their relatives.

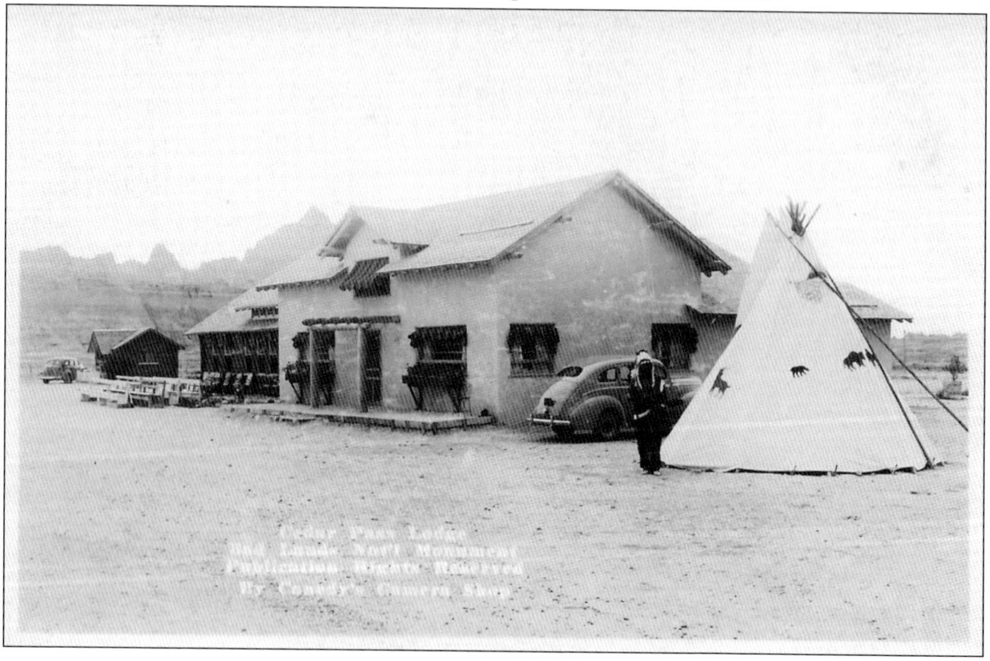

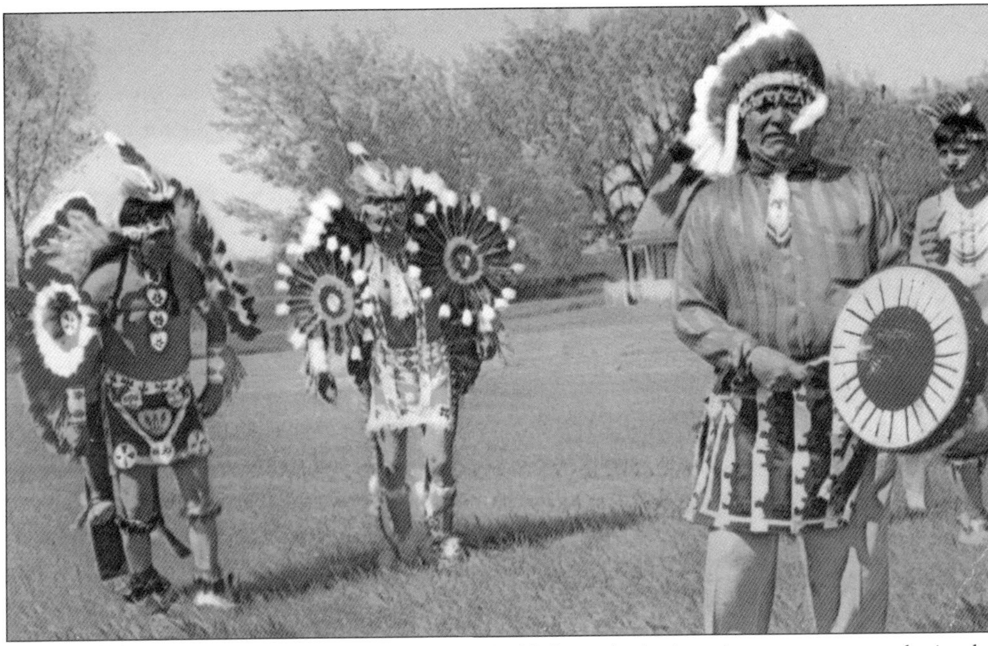

The different sub-tribes of the Dakota Sioux hold festivals during the summer months in the form of powwows, fairs, and special events. Some events are private, and others are planned especially for tourists and are held in the Black Hills and Badlands. Powwows provide an opportunity to socialize, preserve traditions, and dance in colorful regalia.

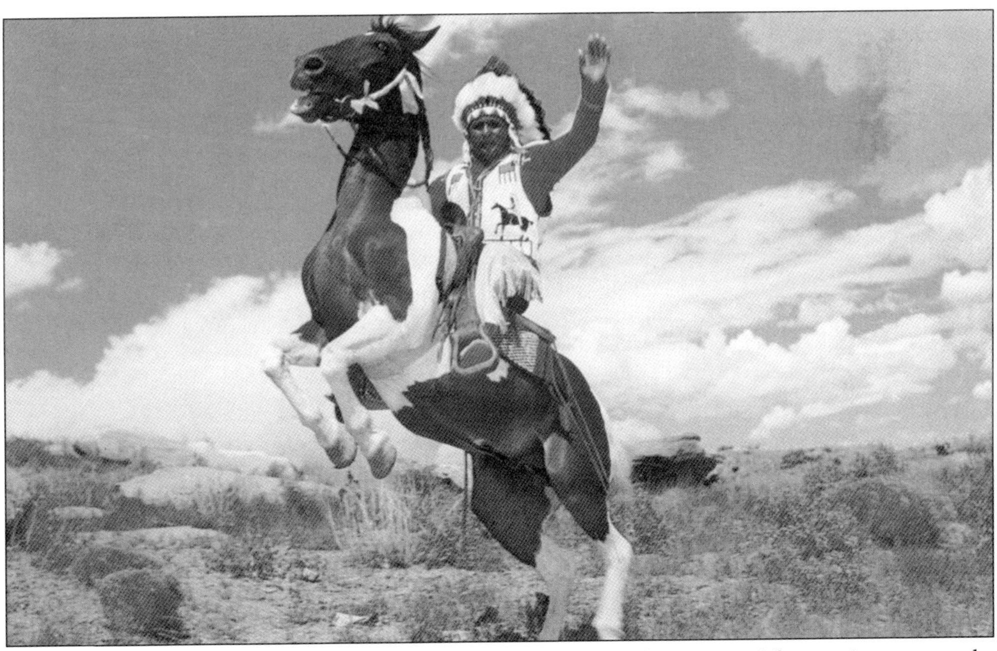

This view of a Native American on a paint stallion may have been staged for tourism postcards. Many beautiful paint horses graze the reservations today. The horse holds a very special place in the hearts of the people and is a symbol signifying mobility, stamina, strength, and power. The horse is often used in pictograms and ledger paintings.

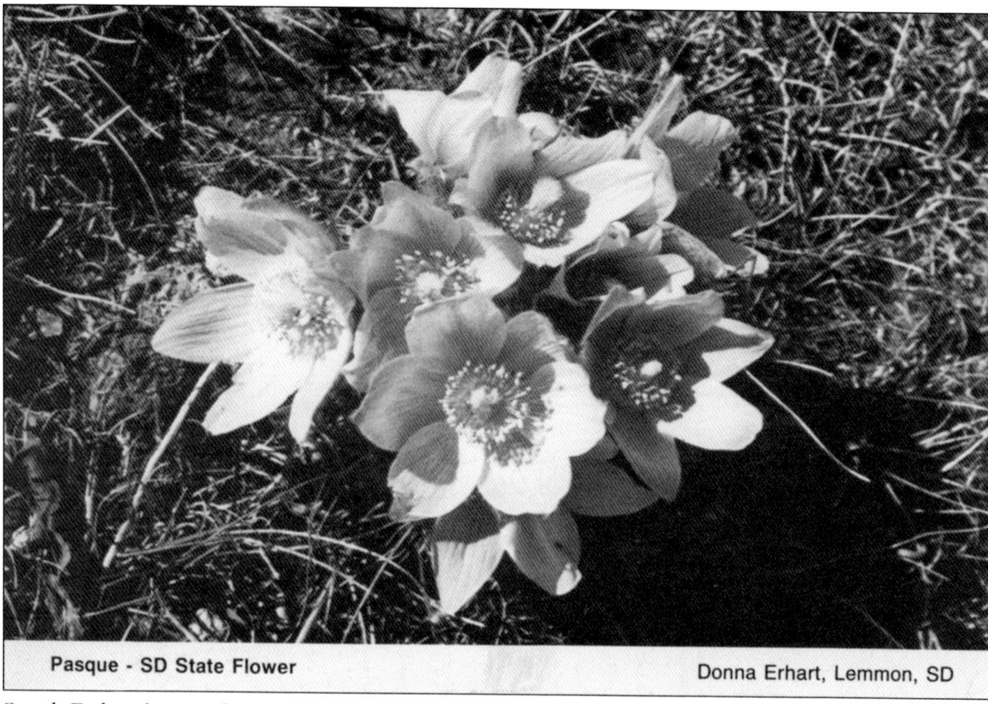

South Dakota's state flower, the pasque, is one of the first wildflowers to bloom on the prairie in the spring even before the grass greens. Its bluish, lavender-colored flowers are also referred to as "prairie smoke." The Dakota people wove several stories around the pasque flower. In one, the flower shows its friendliness to humans by nodding in the chilly spring wind.

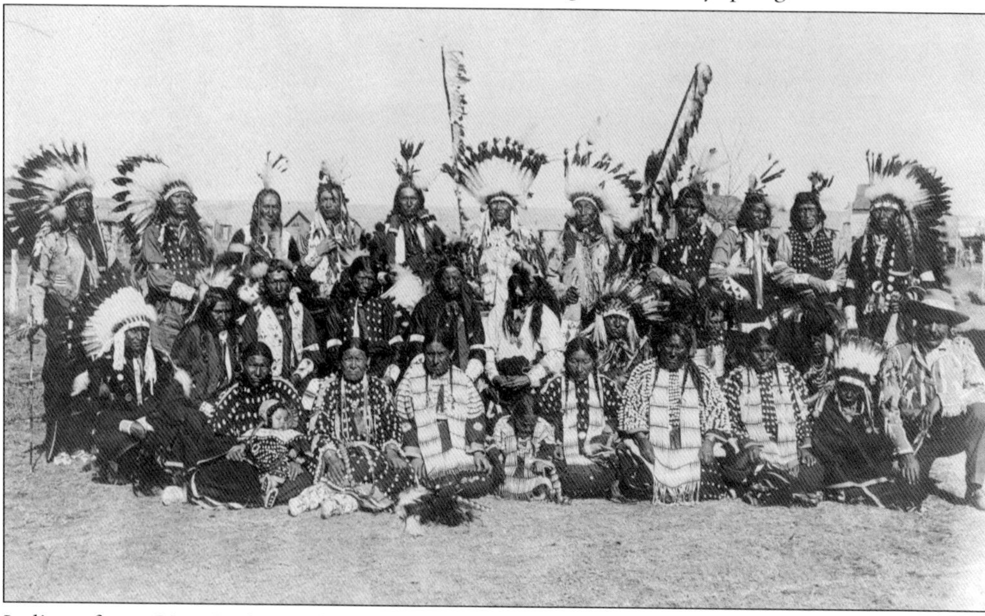

Indians from Pine Ridge and other reservations took part in the region's activities. They participated in parades and in the rodeo action. They performed native dances at powwows and continue to do so today. This photograph was taken around 1910. (Courtesy of the Library of Congress, LC-USZ62-115459.)

Four

Cattlemen and Homesteaders

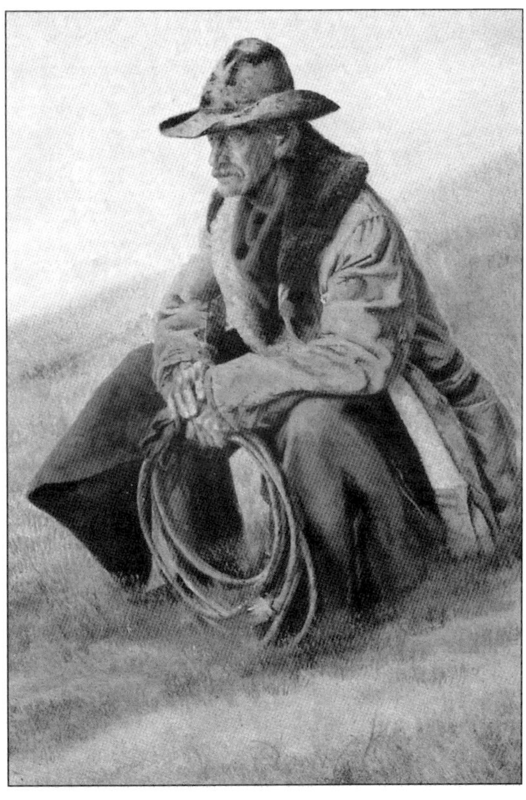

Artist Gerald Farm captured the sentiment and apparel of the working cowboy. A cowboy's life was demanding and subject to the ever-changing weather on the plains. Cattle herds were driven into South Dakota in the late 1880s and 1890s when the land was considered open to the public. Cattle were allowed to graze the unfenced land. The cattle companies conducted roundups to bring their cattle back to the home range. (Courtesy of Wall Drug.)

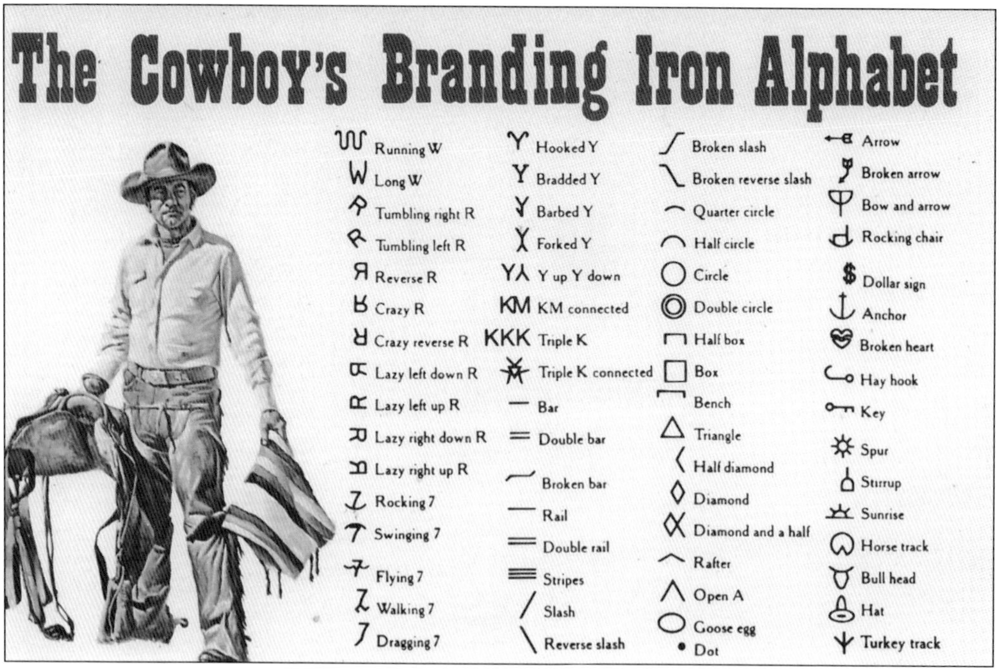

A rancher's brand signified ownership of his cattle. The branding symbols pictured are still used today, with the addition of other symbols. Often ranches were named after their brands. The *Kadoka Press* newspaper published area brands to help determine ownership of stray cattle. (Courtesy of Wall Drug.)

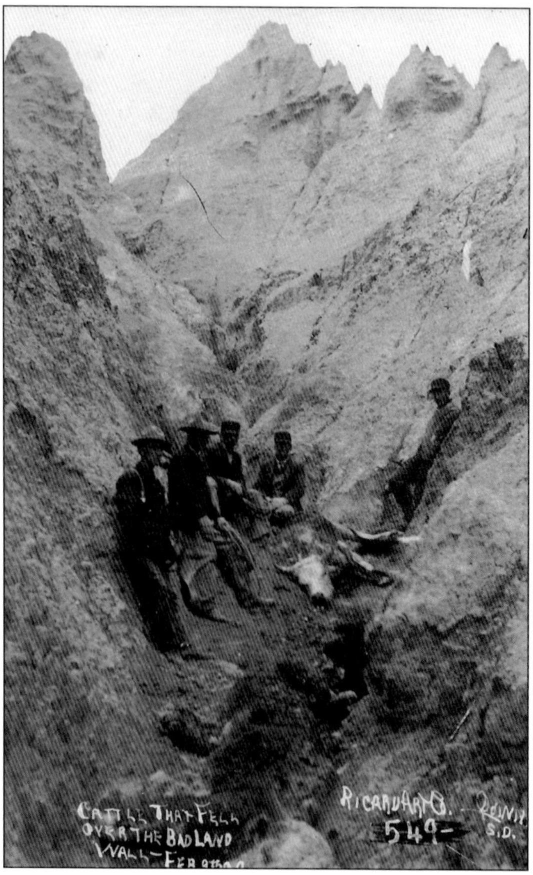

Ranches lost a number of cattle when blizzards and storms hit, either killing the cattle or driving them over the Badlands Wall where they fell to their death. Blizzards and the encroaching homesteader contributed to ending the free range. A few of the names associated with range days are John Massengale, George Porch, Corb Morse, Gus Craven, and Dude Rounds. Today, the Badlands Wall is still a threat to local cattle herds.

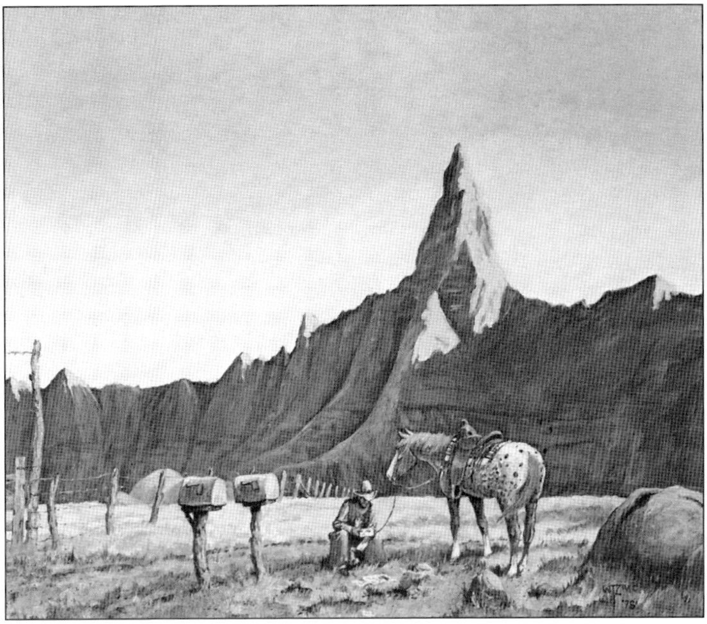

William Zivic painted this scene. Mail service came early to the Badlands region. A trading post called Lodge, on the north side of the White River at the mouth of Bear-in-the-Lodge Creek, provided mail service from December 8, 1890, to July 20, 1893. In 1891, Whitfield, near Pass Creek, provided mail service for one year. Black, also known as Old Interior, began postal service in June 1894 and continued when the town moved. (Courtesy of Wall Drug.)

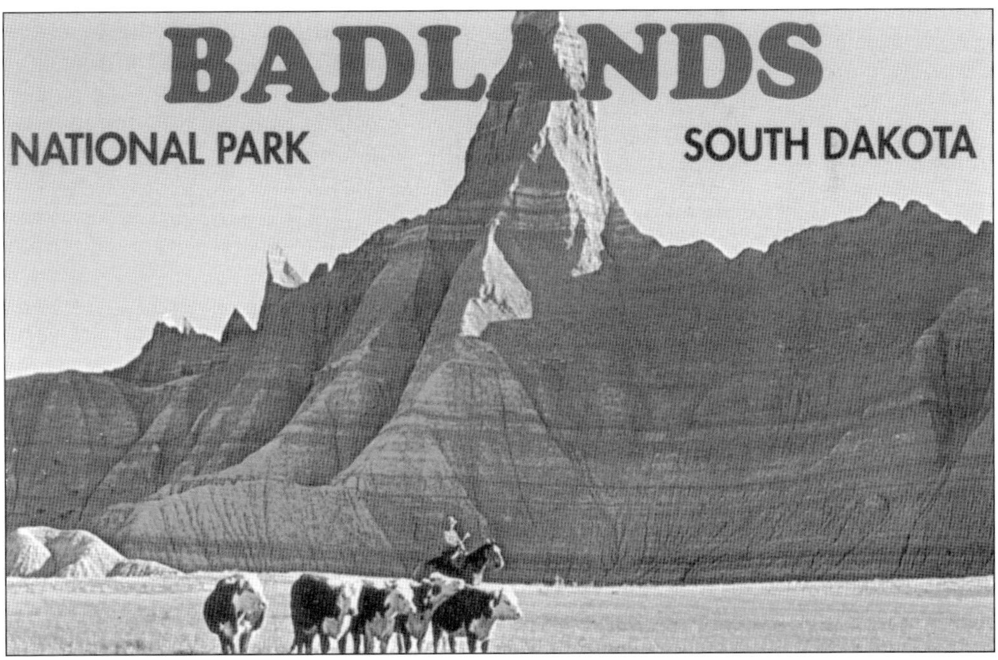

These are Badlands Herefords on the Ed Huether ranch. Herefords replaced the Texas cattle from the open range era. Some of the famous ranches in the early days were the 6L, 15 Irons, Open Buckle, Circle Bar, and the Rake ranch. Today, additional cattle breeds dot private ranch land. (Photograph by Ted Hustead; courtesy of Wall Drug.)

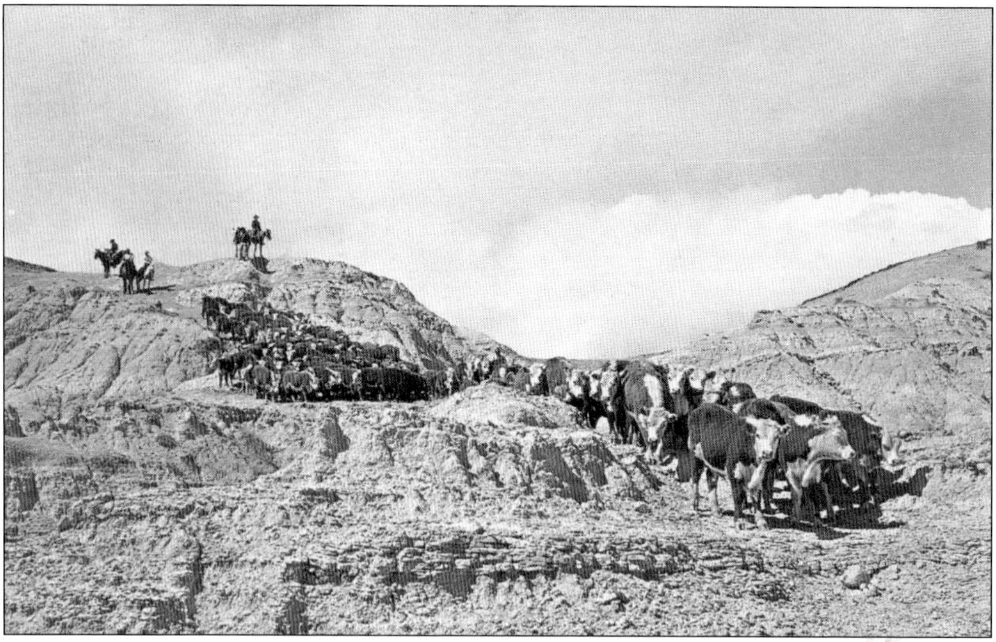

Badlands Hereford cattle are being driven either to pasture or to market. Cattle and sheep thrive on the rich grasses but require extra care during the winter months. Many ranches exist on the mixed grass prairie in and around the Badlands.

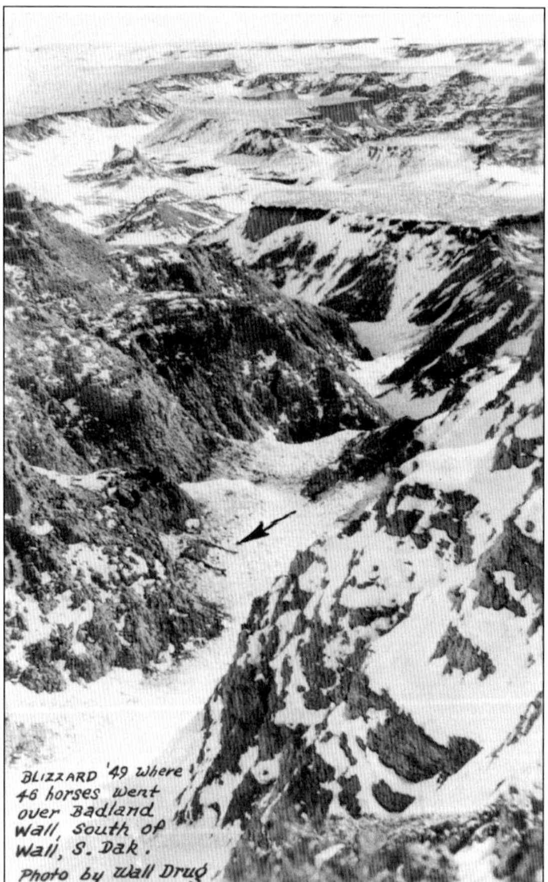

The blizzard of 1949 sent 46 horses to their death over the Badlands Wall, south of the town of Wall. Blizzards in the area are also known to drive cattle over the wall. Such a loss in 1905 devastated ranching and sped up the end of the open range.

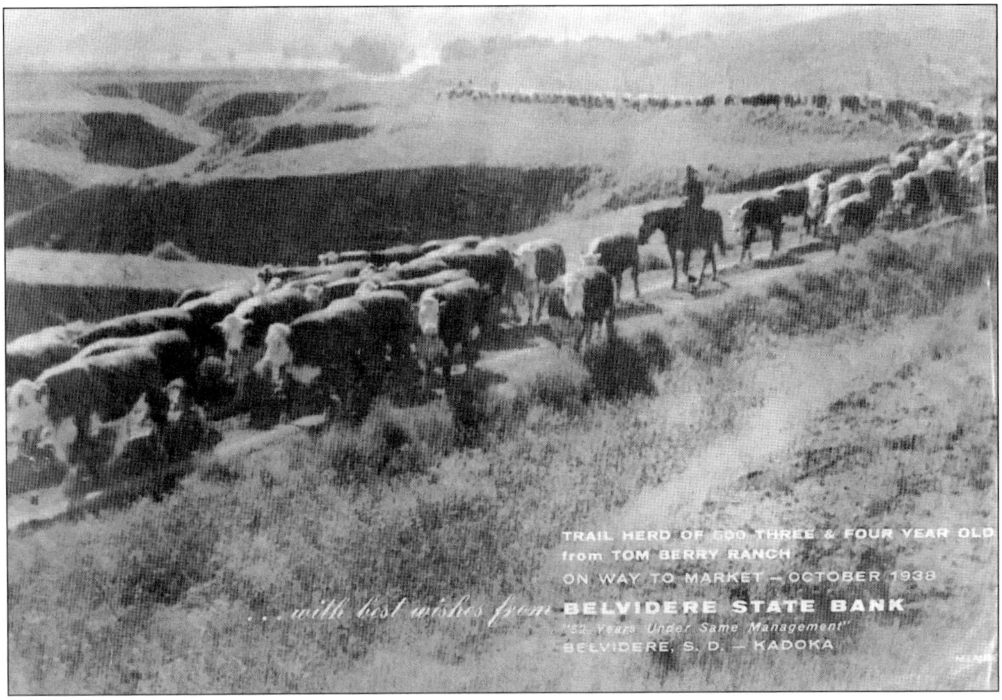

Tom Berry's cattle are being trailed to the railroad to be loaded and shipped in this 1938 photograph. Known as the "Cowboy Governor," Tom Berry was a legislator before he became the 14th governor of South Dakota. He served two terms, from 1933 to 1937, during the years of drought and blowing dirt. He spent his administration working to alleviate the suffering of his constituents during the Dirty Thirties. (Courtesy of the Kadoka Depot Museum.)

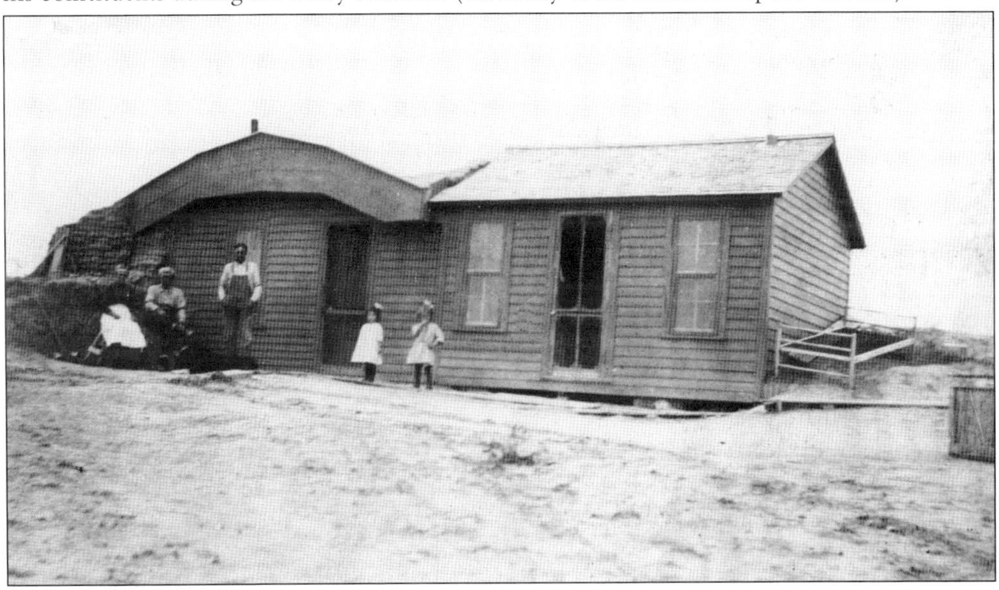

This is a 1913 view of the 1909 Prairie Homestead. Restored by Dorothy and Keith Crew in 1962, this sod dugout home was the original home of Ed and Alice Brown. Pictured are Ed and Alice with their granddaughter and a neighbor's daughter. This prairie home, with no additional improvements, was occupied by a bachelor neighbor until 1949.

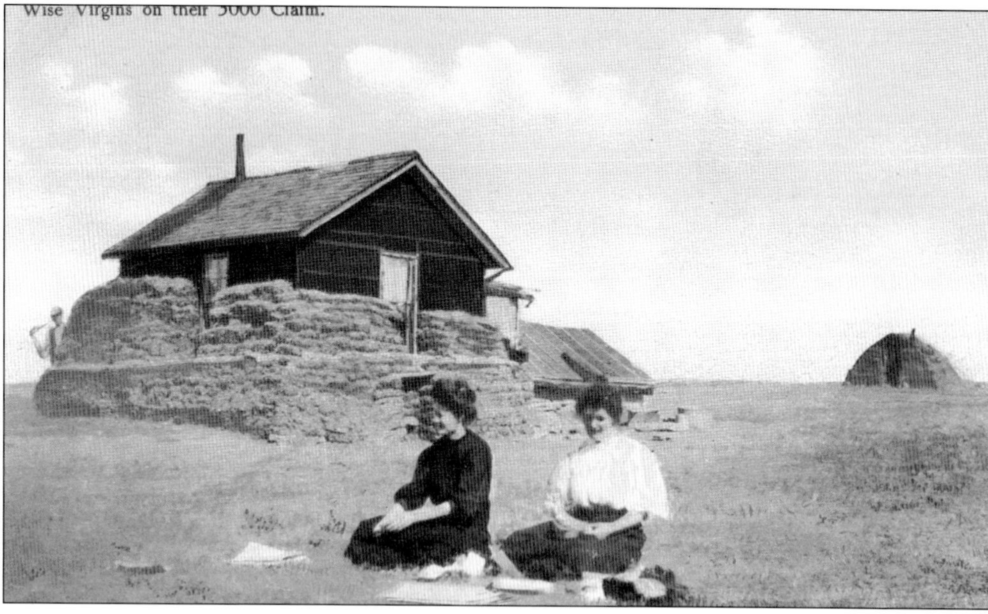

These two women pictured on their homestead in 1910 took advantage of the Homestead Act of 1862, which had been amended several times before the 20th century. Single, divorced, deserted, and widowed women were allowed to file on 160-acre homestead claims in their own name. The length of residency varied over the years, and other provisions were added to prove up and attain title to the land much sooner than the original Homestead Act provided for.

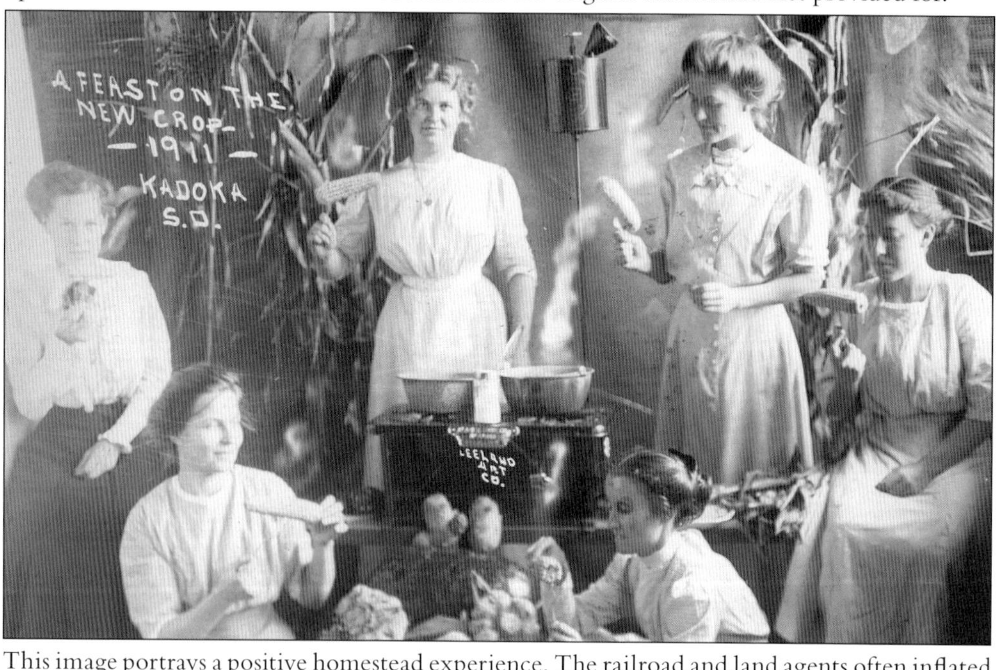

This image portrays a positive homestead experience. The railroad and land agents often inflated the potential of homesteads in semiarid country, touting the area as an agricultural mecca. Much of the land open for settlement in the West was not always conducive to agriculture, although the first few years were mostly productive. Many hopeful homesteaders left defeated, especially during the drought years of 1910, 1911, and the 1930s. (Courtesy of Bonnie Riggins.)

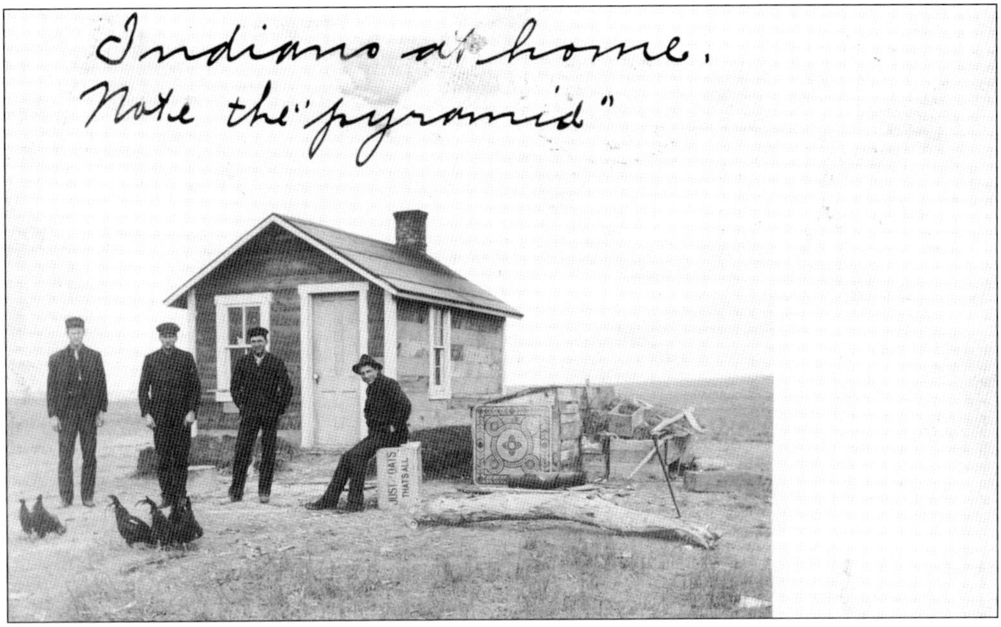

The Kopac brothers settled near Okaton, South Dakota. This 1908 postcard image, taken by Ed Kopac, included a message that read, "Will go to Interior tonight or in the morning." No doubt the brothers rode the train from Okaton to Interior. The Chicago, Milwaukee & St. Paul Railroad made two trips daily, one west to Rapid City and one east from Rapid City.

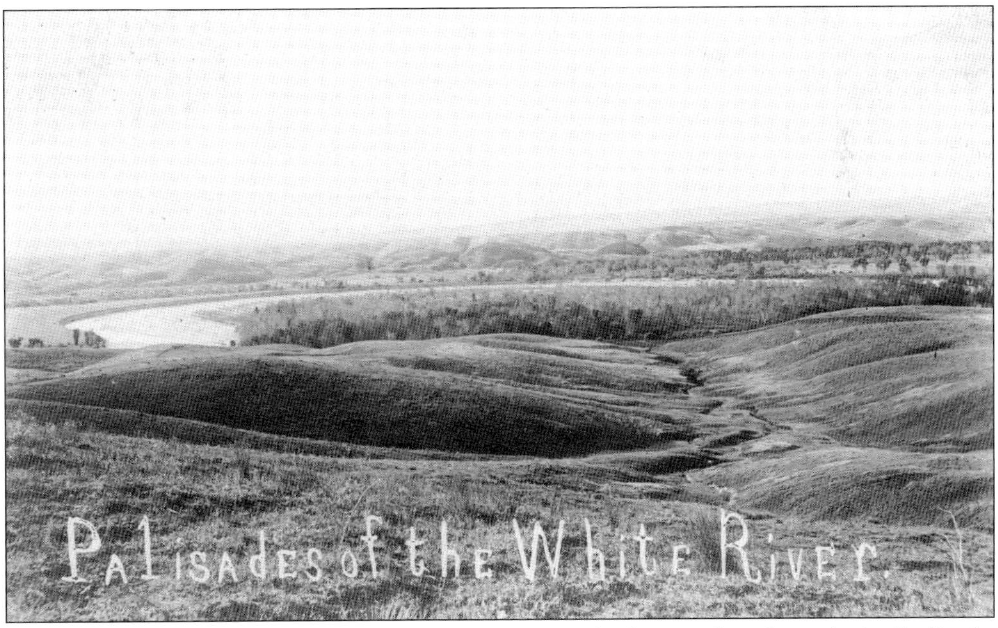

The Kopac brothers photographed the White River, which meanders through the Badlands. The Chicago, Milwaukee & St. Paul Railroad was built through the White River region. Towns sprang up about every 10 to 20 miles to supply water for the steam engines. From Kadoka, the stops were Weta, Interior, Conata, Imlay, Scenic, Creston, and others. Most of these towns disappeared when transportation improved and they were no longer needed.

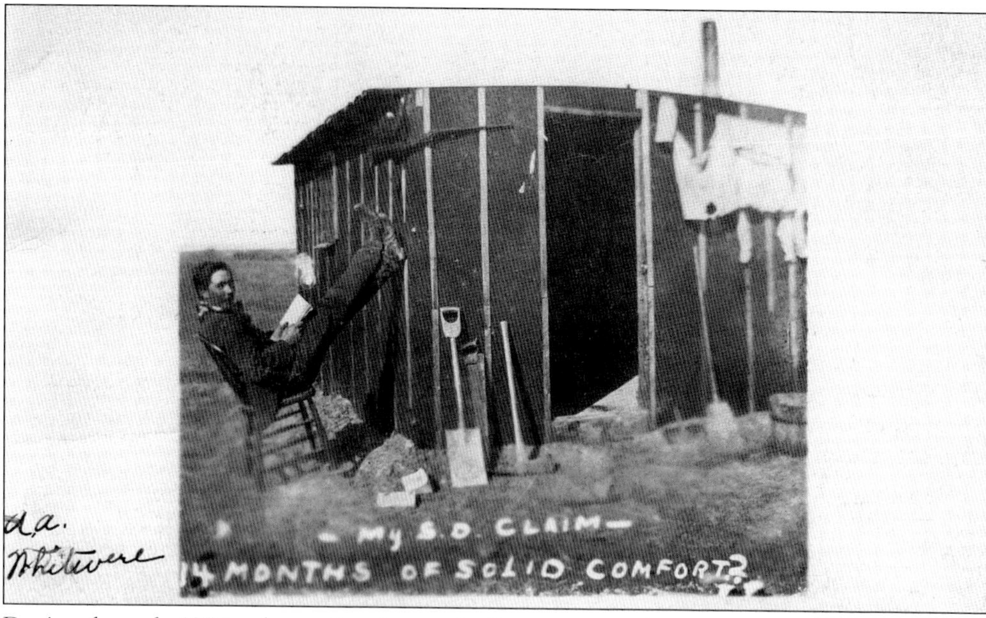

During the early 1900s when railroads were built west across the state, people were on the move to file on homesteads. This is a typical tar paper claim shack built to fulfill the requirements of a residence. Tar paper shacks were hot in the summer and bone chillingly cold in the winter. Postmarked from Rapid City in 1910, this mailed message reads, "Dear folks, just got here and am going on east towards where Spencer people are."

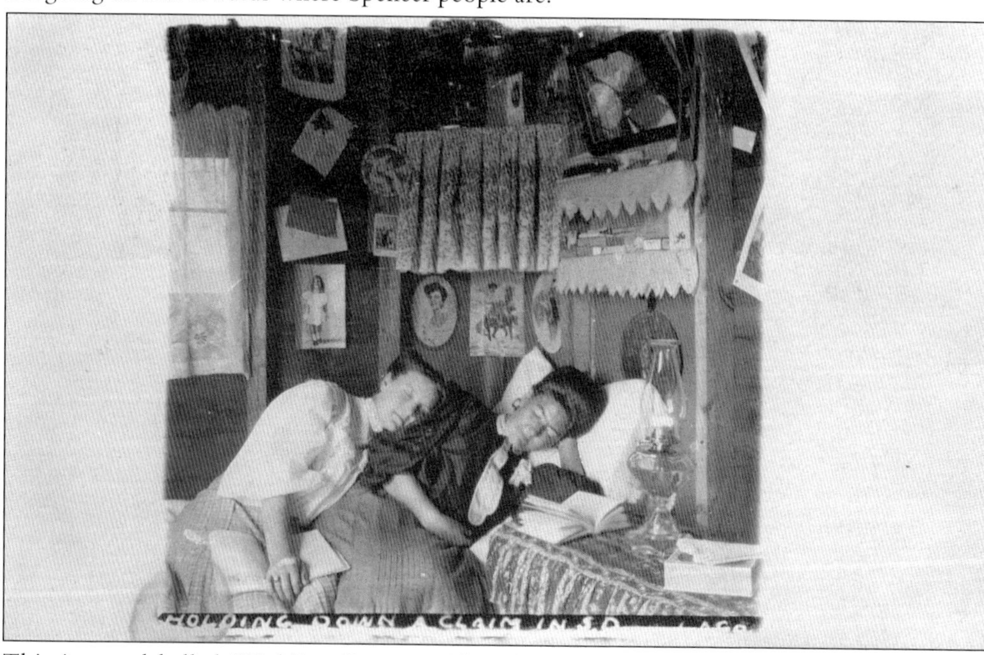

This image, labelled "Holding Down a Claim," implies that meeting the requirements of residency was easy. Homestead life was grueling and subject to the whims of the weather in addition to meeting the requirements of the law such as digging a well, breaking the sod, and showing improvements. Even though the outsides of claim shacks were a bit shabby, the interiors could be fixed up nicely. Not all homesteaders intended to stay; some were mere speculators.

Five

INTERIOR

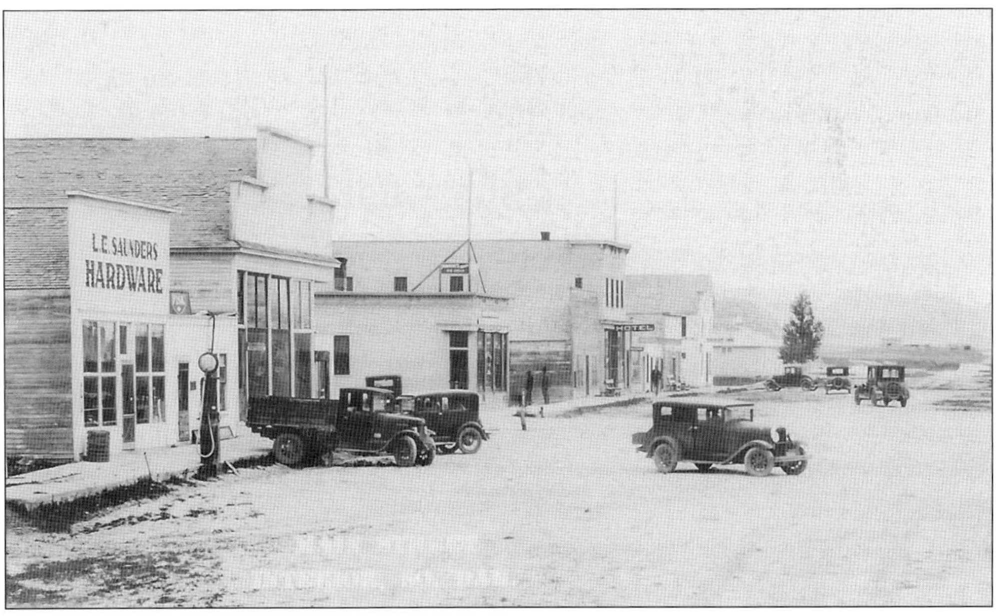

From left to right, the Interior businesses pictured are Saunders Hardware, an unidentified building, the post office, and the Johnson Brothers store. On the next block are the State Bank of Interior and the two-story Burkholder's Hotel. Interior was a promising cattle town in the early years until a series of fires in 1939 and 1941 destroyed the town's businesses. Interior never completely recovered. It is now a ghost of what it used to be.

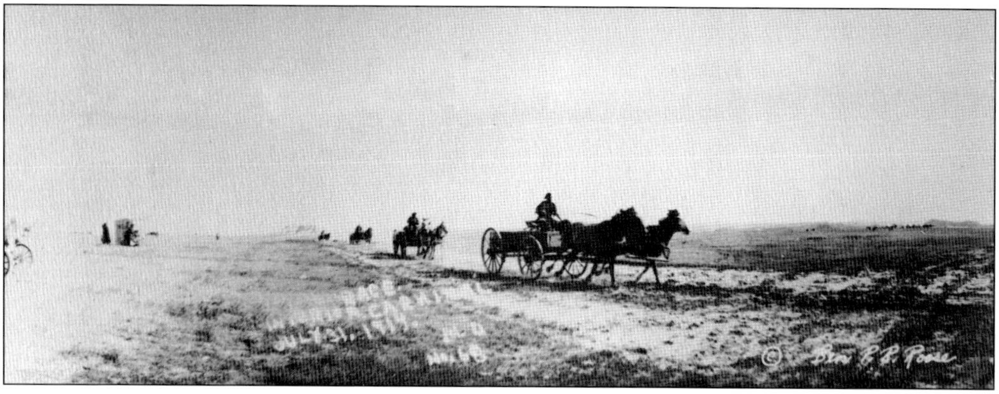

Interior organized annual carnivals before the town became famous for its roundups. Interior was moved from Black, also known as Old Interior, when the railroad came through in 1907. A carnival was organized the next year. Among the events were horse racing, bucking horses, movie shows, and bowery dances. Pictured here, Indian women race wagons at Interior on July 31, 1914. (Courtesy of Keith Crew.)

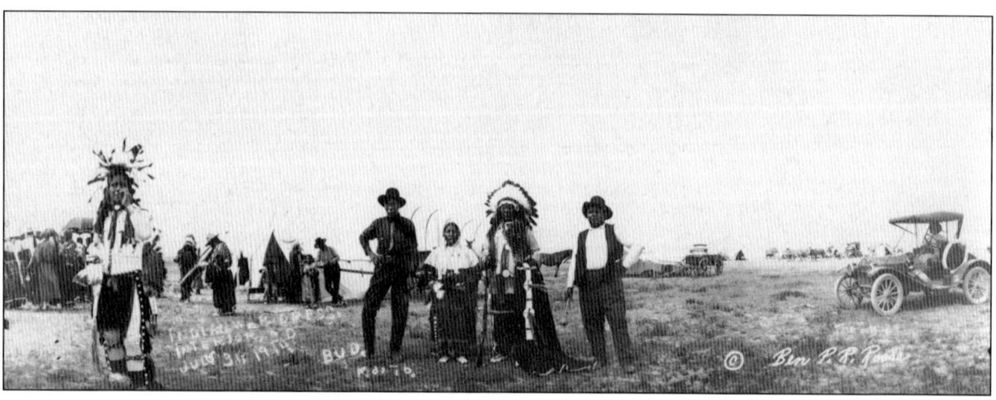

The Native Americans who came to Interior celebrations to dance and participate in the activities camped outside of town. As many as eight steers were usually provided for them to butcher while there. The government issued canvas tents to replace their tepees, desiring that the once nomadic people would settle down and become farmers. (Courtesy of Keith Crew.)

The town of Interior built a special grandstand to seat 3,000 spectators for the roundups. Five hundred tents were erected and five big roundup wagons were brought in to feed the crowd. The Chicago, Milwaukee & St. Paul Railroad brought in famous participants and spectators. The Presbyterian church and water tower can be seen in the distance. (Courtesy of Keith Crew.)

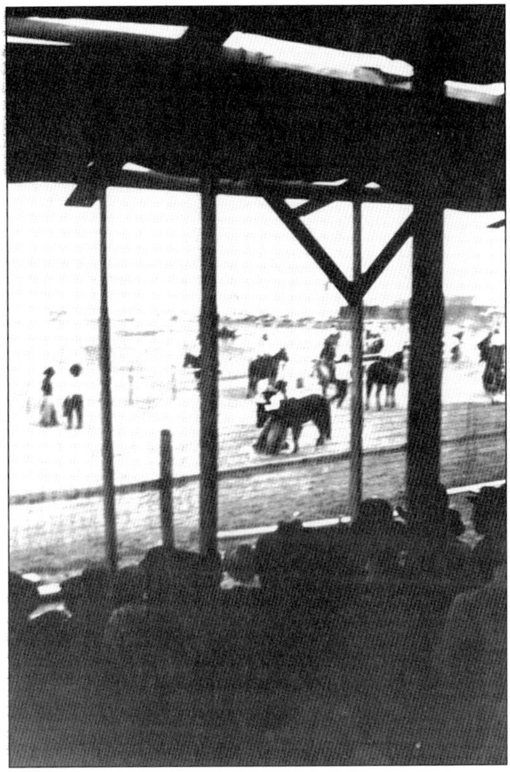

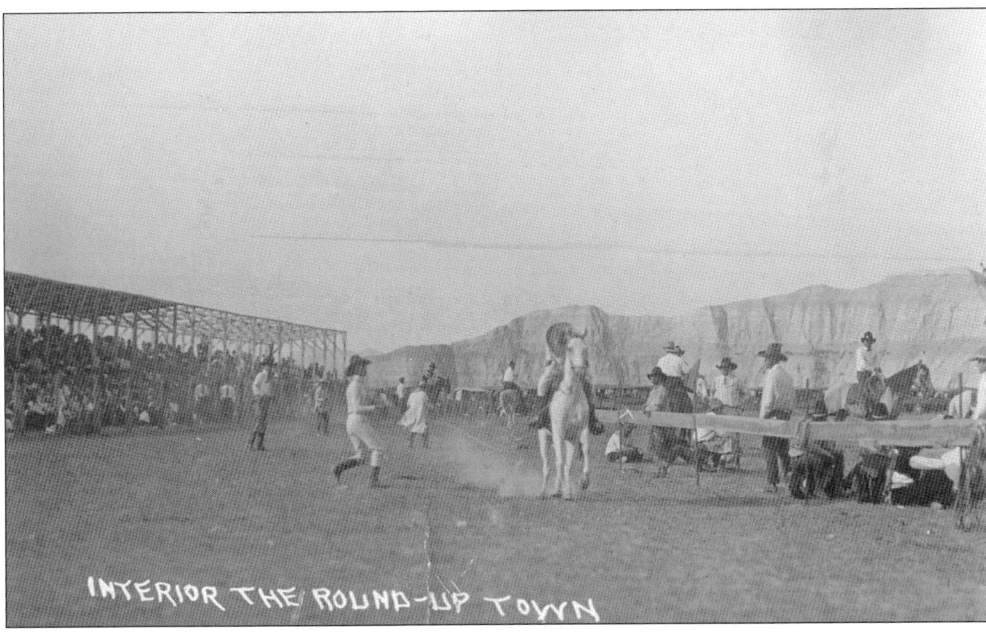

Interior was named the "Round-up Town," although it only hosted five at the most. But during those few years, it drew in famous champion cowboys and cowgirls. In addition, the roundups brought in local Indians, who dressed in their regalia, paraded, danced, and participated in the various events. The trains transported a great number of spectators to enjoy the roundups. (Courtesy of Keith Crew.)

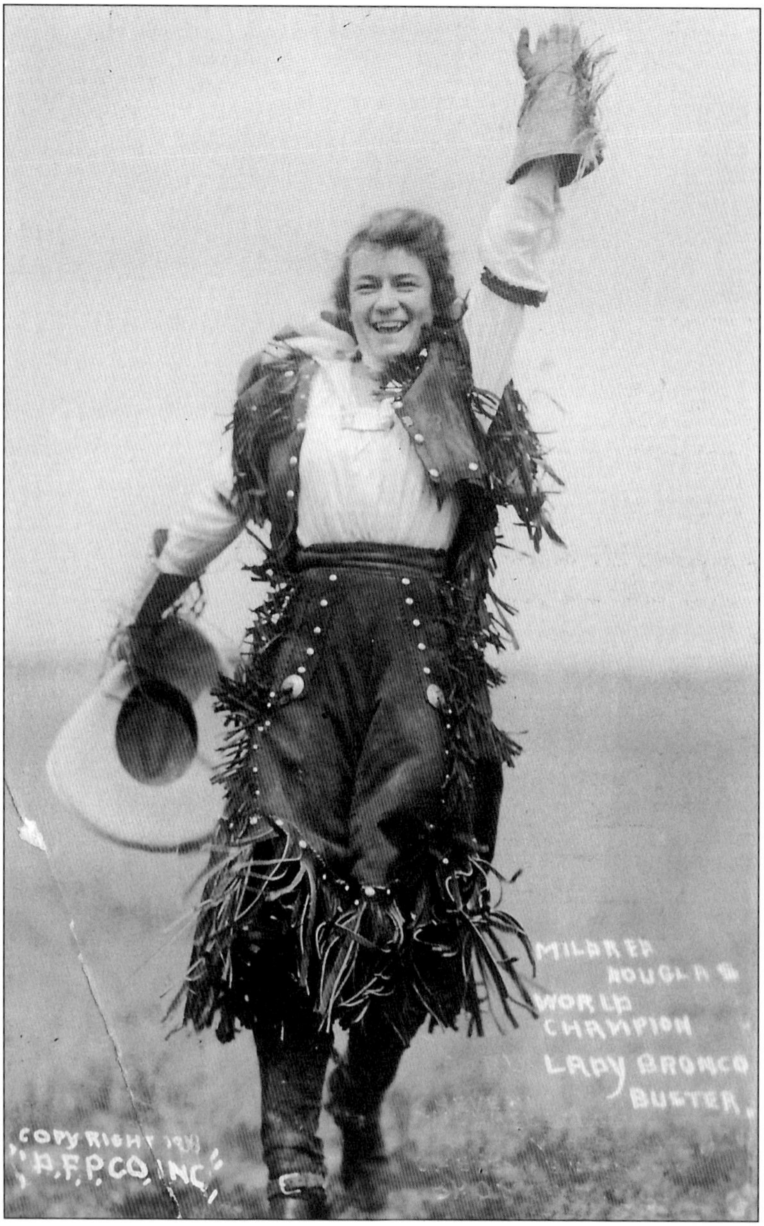

The first Interior Round-up of August 20–22, 1919, featured world champion lady bucking horse rider Mildred Douglas of Prescott, Arizona, appearing in this 1918 photograph. In addition, Milt Hinkle, also known as the South American Kid, was set to perform. Mildred Douglas began her career performing with several different circuses. She also participated in the Miller Brothers 101 Ranch Wild West Show as a rough stock rider in Ponca City, Oklahoma, where she met Tommy Douglas. In 1916, she rode her first bronc, and by 1918, she had won championships in Cheyenne, Wyoming, and Pendelton, Oregon. She was also a trick rider and did trick shooting. In 1917, she went to Hollywood, where she appeared in films and movies with Tom Mix. While there, she married Pat Chrisman. She left Hollywood and joined the Wild West show circuit and was active in rodeo until 1926. At the age of 59, she left the rodeo and became a nurse for the next 20 years.

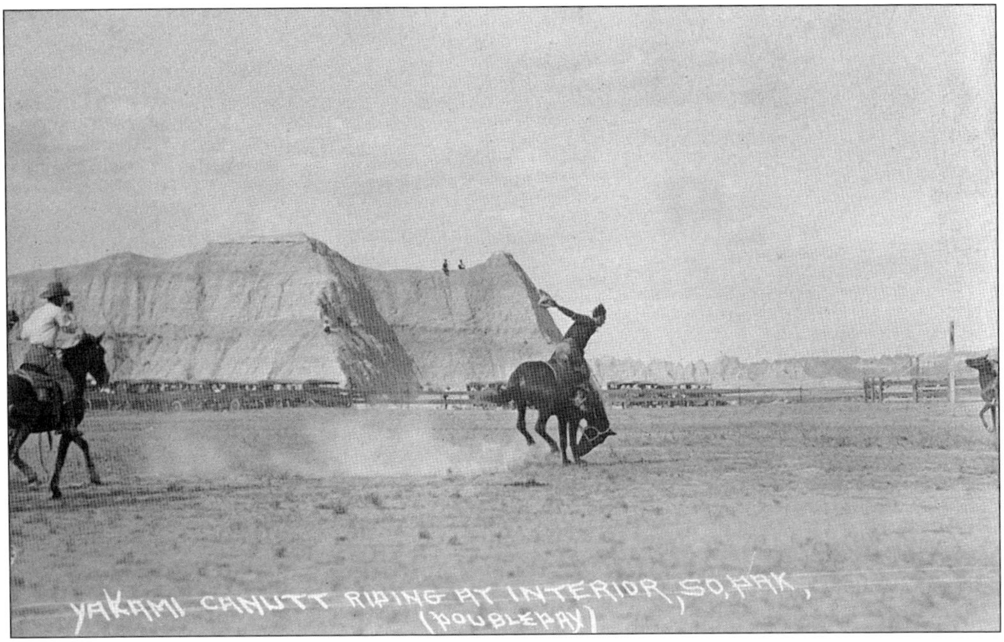

Yakima Canutt appears at an Interior Round-up in 1920. Not only was he a champion bronc rider, he has been recognized as the first legendary stuntman who performed stunts for such greats as John Wayne, Clark Cable, Roy Rogers, and Gene Autry and even staged the chariot race for *Ben Hur.* Canutt appeared in dozens of silent films, thrilling viewers with his daring feats on horseback. (Courtesy of Keith Crew.)

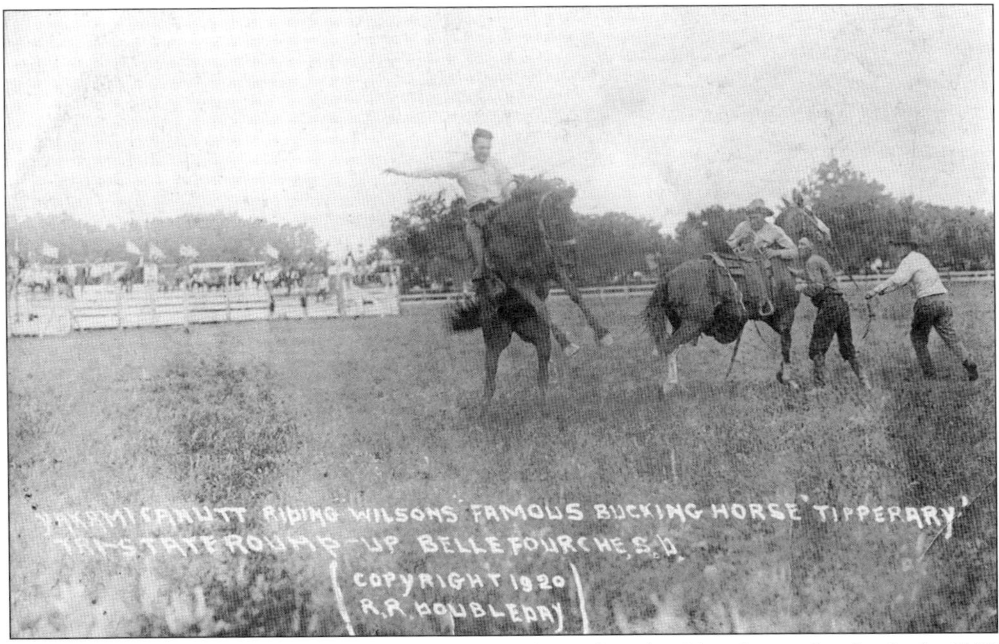

In this image, Yakima Canutt rides Tipperary, a legendary bucking horse that bucked off 80 riders until Canutt made a qualified ride in 1920 at the Tri-State Round-up in Belle Fourche. A year later, he again rode Tipperary in Belle Fourche, South Dakota. Tipperary's rodeo career lasted until 1926. (Courtesy of Keith Crew.)

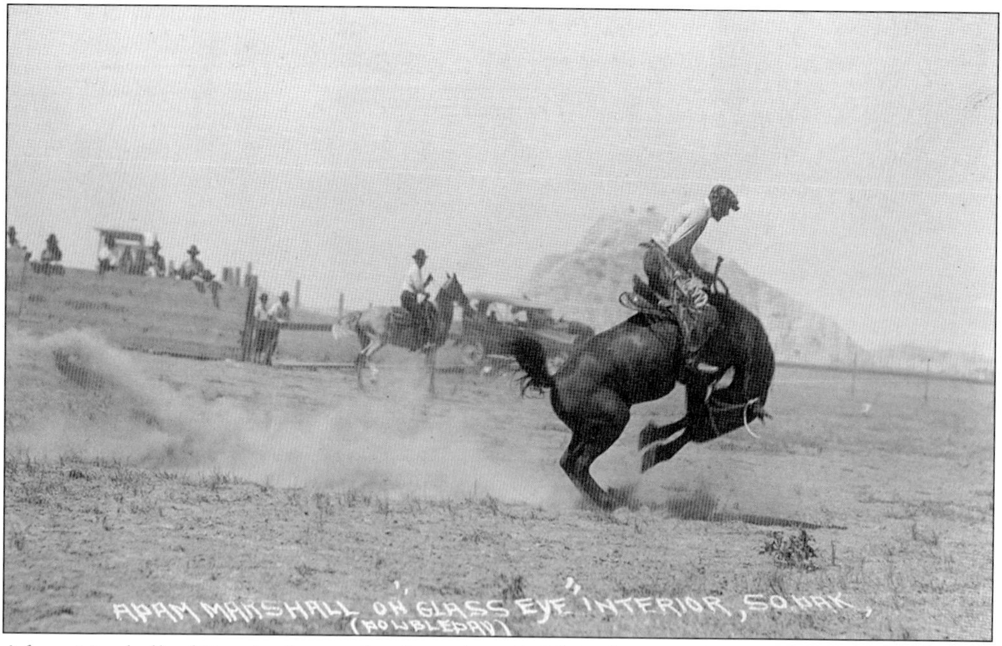

Adam Marshall of Rosebud earned a first-place finish in bronc riding in August 1920 during the second annual Interior Round-up. In this image, he is riding Glass Eye, a horse that earned a reputation for bucking and twisting his body 180 degrees in mid-air and landing in the opposite direction. (Courtesy of Keith Crew.)

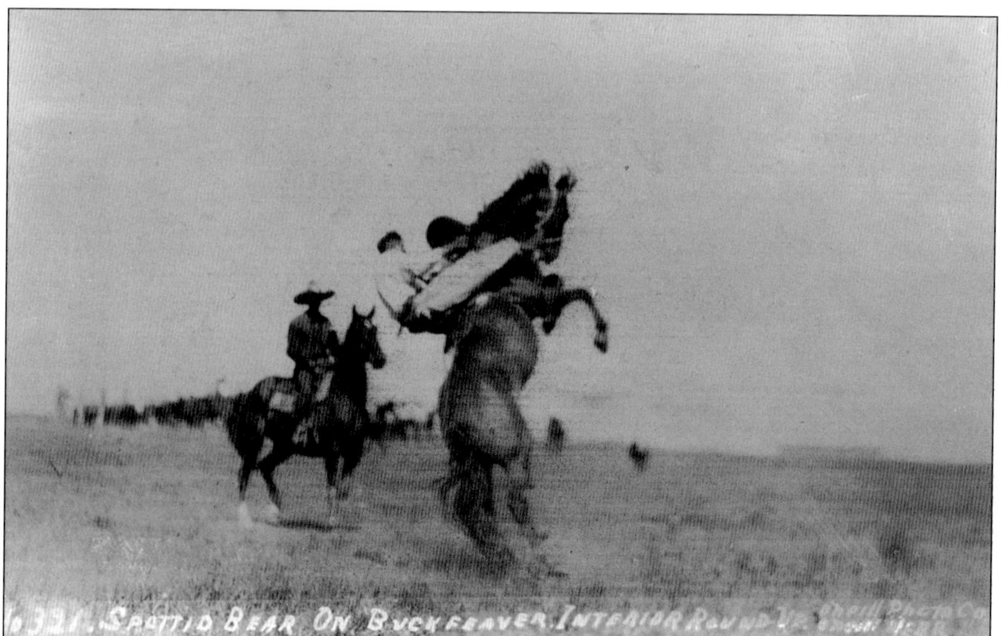

Spotted Bear (his first name is unknown) rode Buck Fever during an Interior Round-up. In 1912, the Lakota planned the first Independence Day celebration on the Rosebud Sioux Reservation in the town of White River, featuring bronco busting and roping contests, a forerunner to the White River Frontier Days, which ran until 1954. (Courtesy of Keith Crew.)

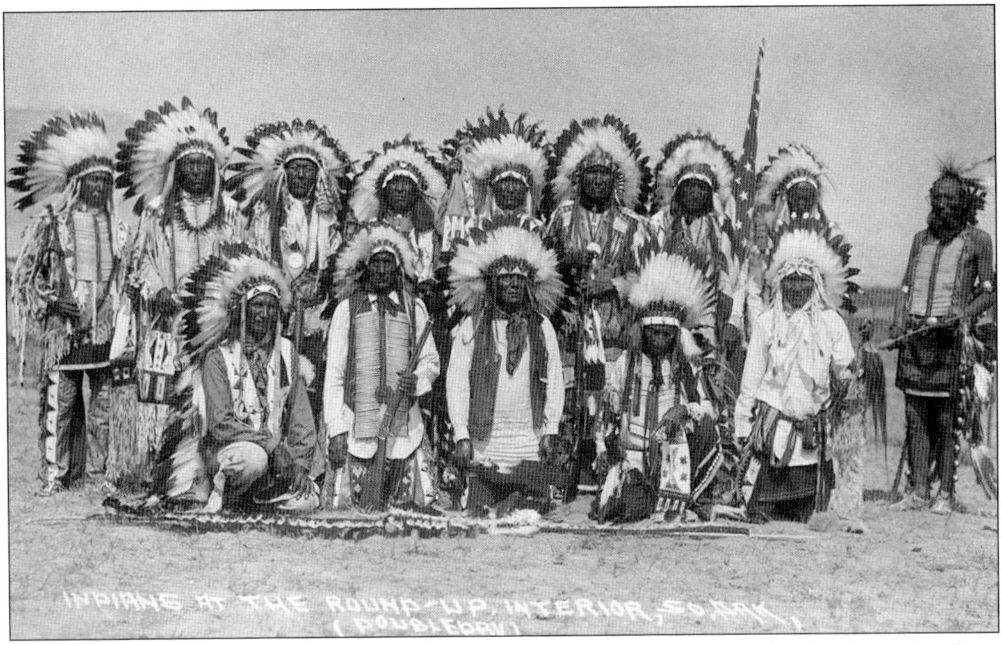

Dewey Beard stands second from left in this group of men, identified by his distinctive bear claw necklace. Although this image is undated, it was probably taken at the 1920 Interior Round-up. It appears that no pictures were taken of the first Interior Round-up in 1919. (Courtesy of Keith Crew.)

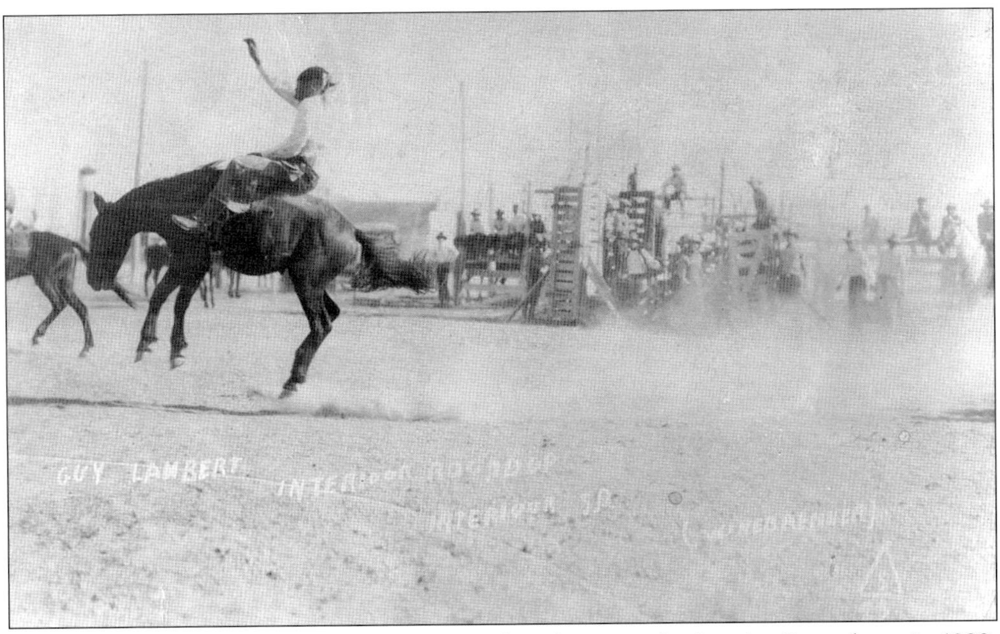

Rosebud reservation cowboy Guy Lambert rides a bronc at the Interior Round-up. In 1922, Lambert took second in bareback riding at the Interior Round-up. Other Native Americans participating were Ed Arcoren, Alex Larvie, and Yellow Thunder. Iron Crow and Jake Herman were entered in calf roping. Approximately a dozen native riders took part in Interior's 1920 roundup. (Courtesy of Keith Crew.)

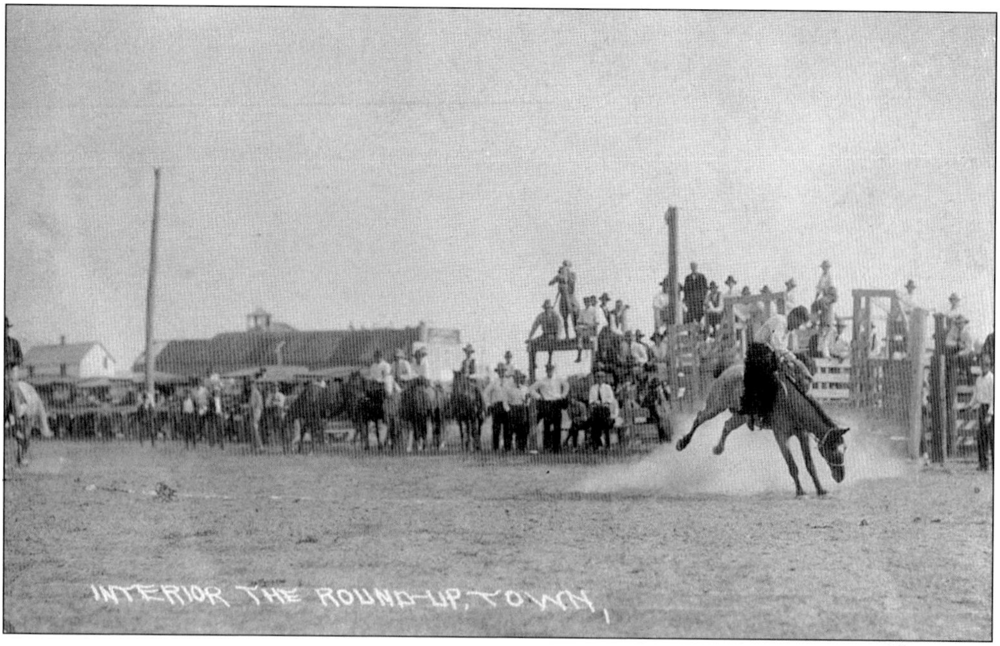

Above, an unidentified man rides a bronc in this undated image. Many locals participated in the Interior Round-ups. Support from the audience is apparent as the men at the chutes cheer him on. Another cowboy tries his luck on a bucking bronc in the image below. Rodeos are still popular in Interior and are usually held on an annual basis. Several men and women in the area have become well known on the rodeo circuit. (Both, courtesy of Keith Crew.)

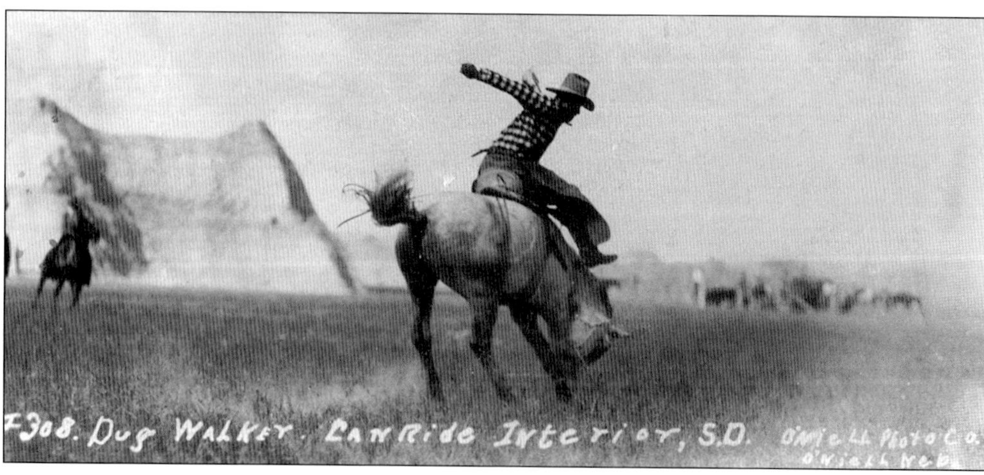

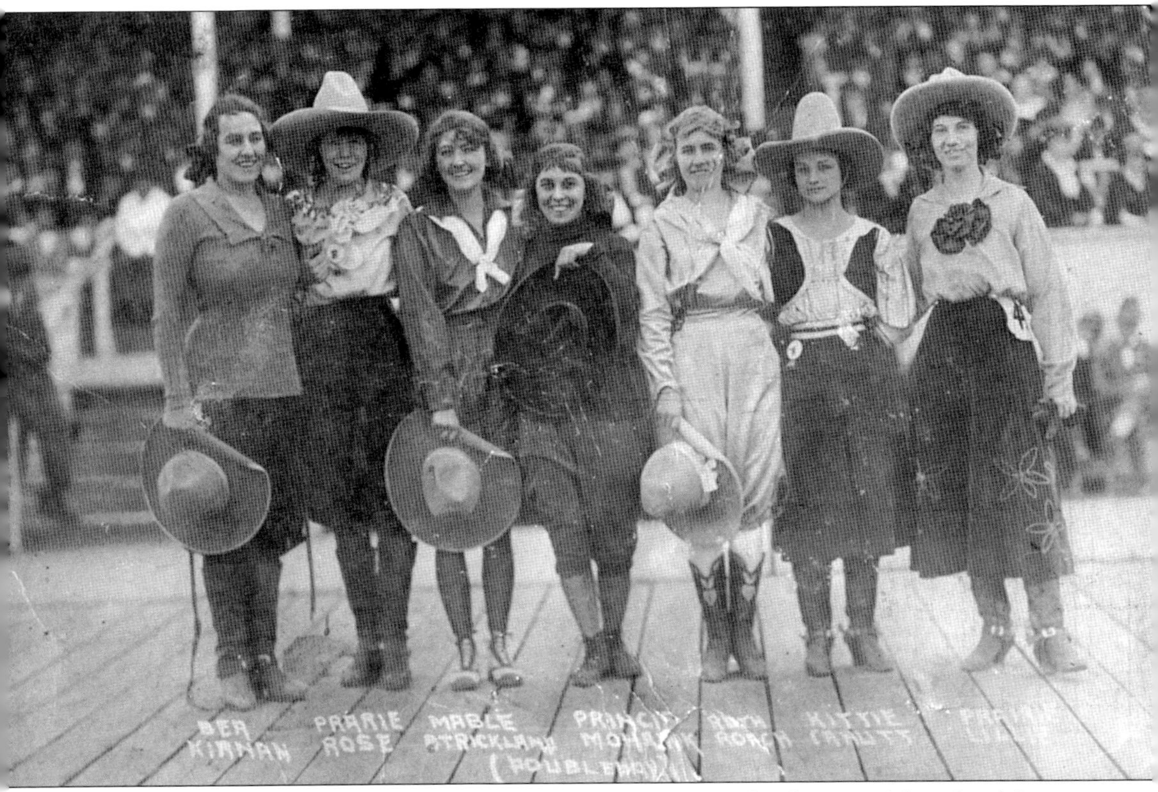

Appearing in this 1921 Ralph Russell Doubleday photograph of rodeo cowgirls at Pendelton are Ber Kirman, Prairie Rose, Mable Strickland, Princis [*sic*] Mohawk, Ruth Roach, Kittie Canutt, and Prairie Lillie. Several of these cowgirls also appeared in Interior Round-ups. In 1920, Kitty Canutt received first place in ladies' bronc riding; Princess Mohawk claimed second place. Myrtle Cox, not pictured, won third. Also not pictured are Esther Quiver, who placed first in the ladies' Indian race, and Spotted Horse (first name unknown), who placed second. Other women could have participated in Interior Round-ups, but no additional names are known. (Courtesy of Keith Crew.)

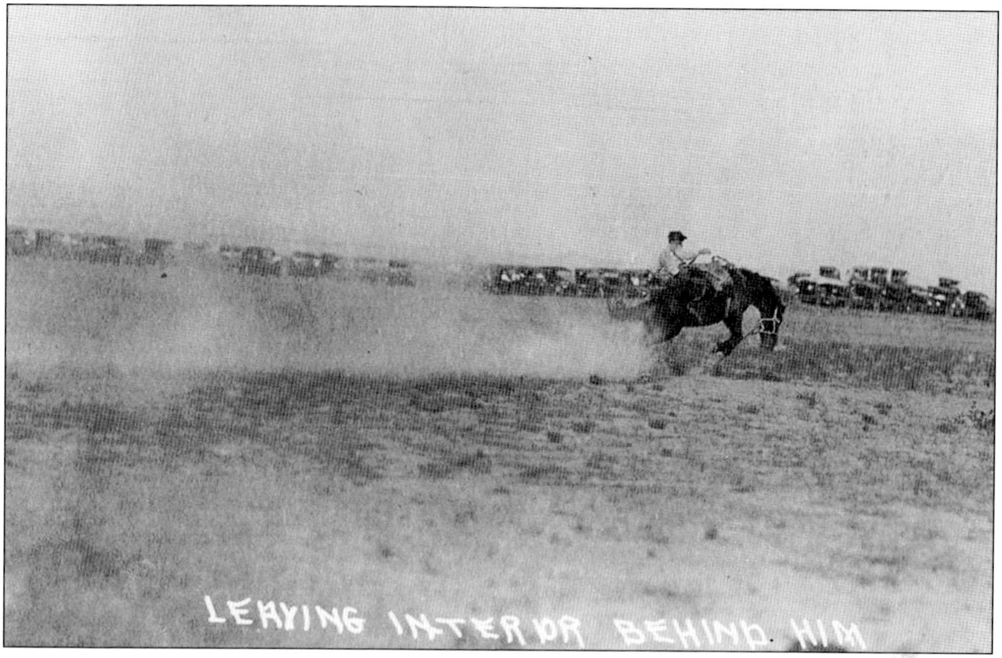

An unidentified cowboy rides a bronc on this undated postcard. Cars in the distance have lined up to watch the action. The photographer was from the O'Neill Photograph Co. in O'Neill, Nebraska, perhaps indicating a different year than the photographs taken by R.R. Doubleday in 1920. (Courtesy of Keith Crew.)

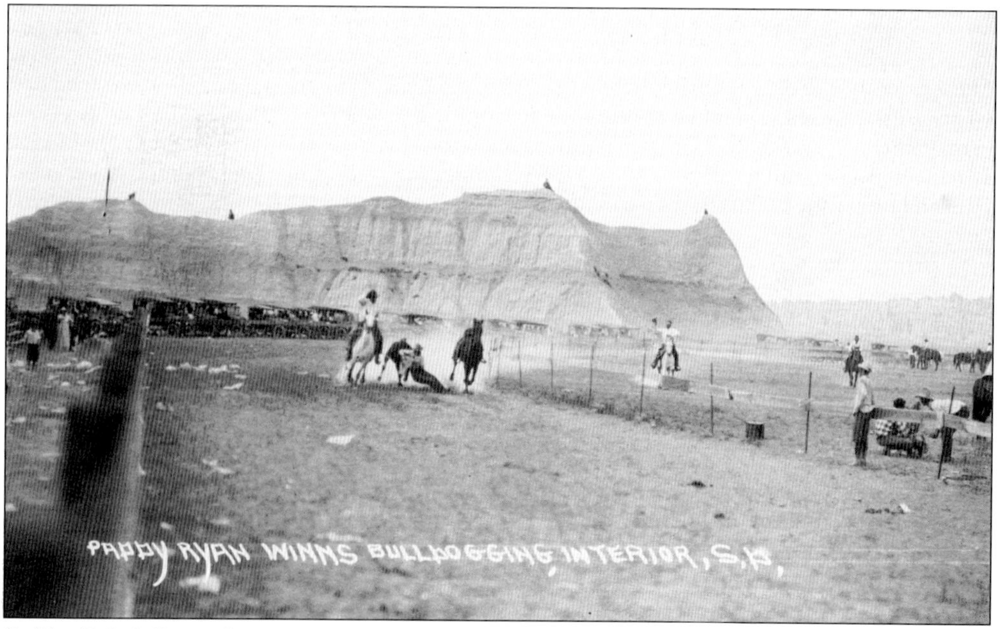

Paddy (John) Ryan from Ismay, Montana, won first in steer wrestling at the 1920 Interior Round-up. He entered his first rodeo in 1916 in Miles City, Montana. Over the course of his career he participated in almost every event, but bronc riding and bulldogging were his favorites. Ryan was a top bronc rider and won most of the shows he entered. Jack Wells, from Kadoka, came in second.

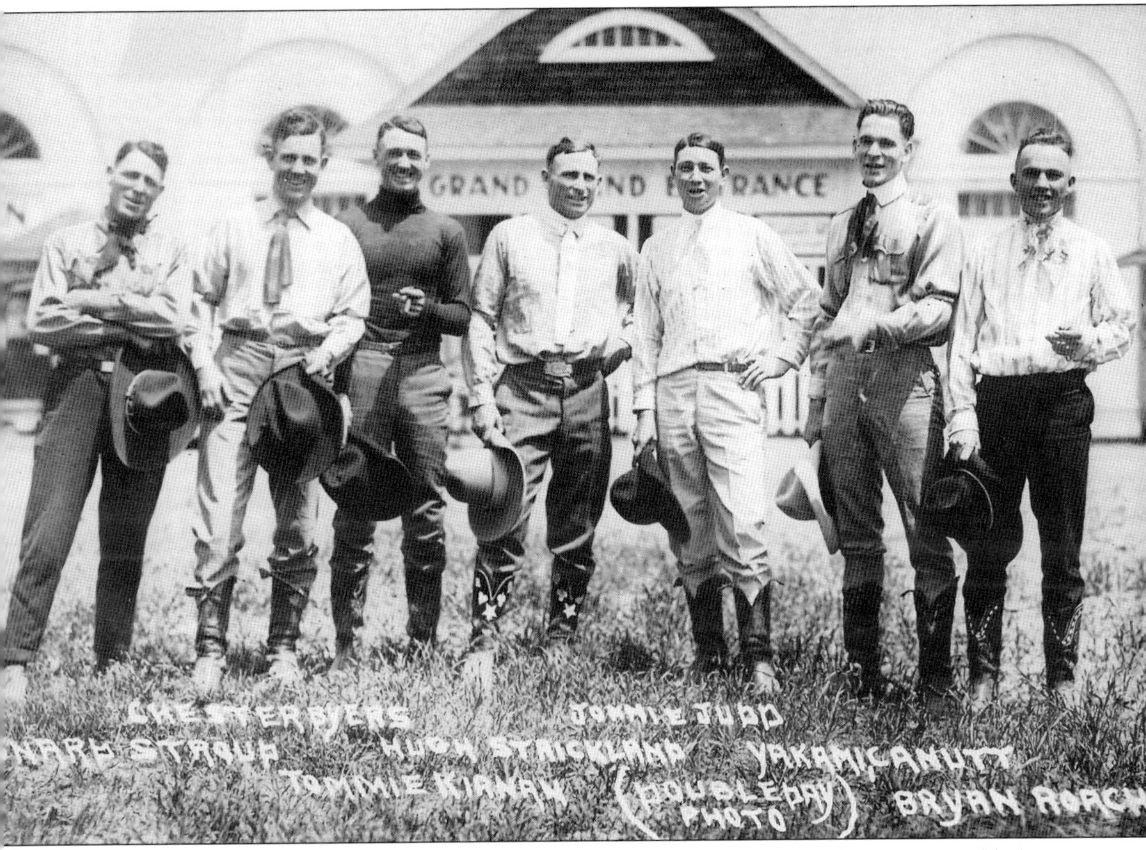

These famous rodeo men of the early 20th century pose for a photograph by R.R. Doubleday, a famous rodeo photographer of the day. Performing in the 1920 Interior Round-up were Leonard Stroud, trick rider; Chester Byers, rope tricks; Yakima Canutt, saddle bronc; and Hugh Strickland, steer roping. Two wives, Mayme Stroud, known for her trick riding, and Minnie Canutt, also performed. Besides participating in the Interior Round-up, the husband-and-wife team of Stroud also appeared at the Haakon County fair in Philip, South Dakota, with their own string of horses in August 1920 as trick riders. They were advertised as jumping a horse over a large automobile containing five passengers, the only horse in the world performing this feat. In addition, Mayme Stroud was billed as the champion woman trick rider of the world. (Courtesy of Only Classics.)

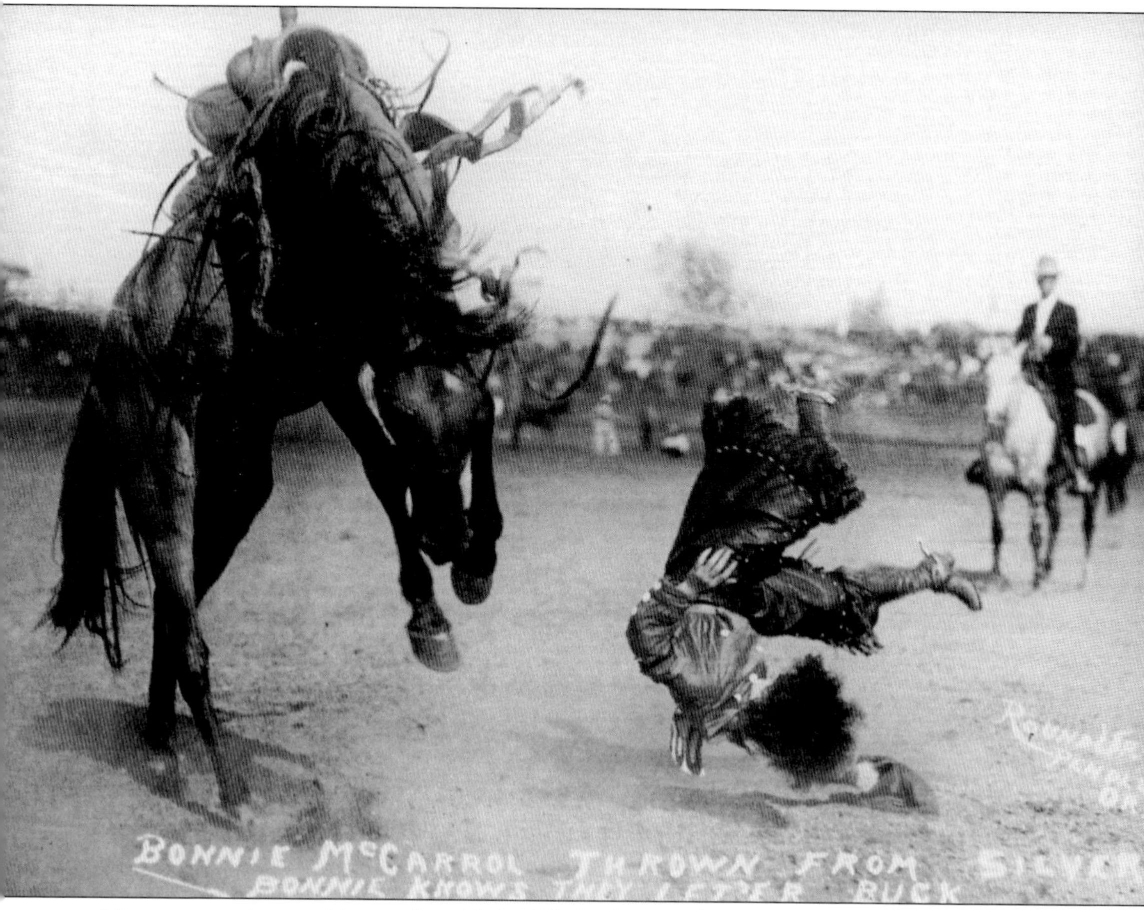

Most women bronc riders rode with hobbled stirrups; the stirrups were tied together under the horse. Doing so supposedly made the bucking horse easier to ride, but was potentially dangerous. In this image, Bonnie McCarrol, who rode that way, was thrown from Silver at the Pendelton Round-up in Oregon in 1915. She was unable to free herself immediately from the stirrups, and when she finally did, she was thrown violently to the ground. Fourteen years later, this popular bronc-riding champion was trampled to death in another Pendelton bronc-riding event in 1929. After her tragic death, the Pendelton Round-up committee dropped bronc-riding as a women's sport. At least seven other women bronc-riders had suffered fatalities earlier, but McCarrol's death hastened the end of bronc riding as a woman's rodeo sport, being dropped at other roundups after 1941. Other factors contributing to this decision were the scarcity of stock during World War II and the dwindling participation of women.

Six

Kadoka

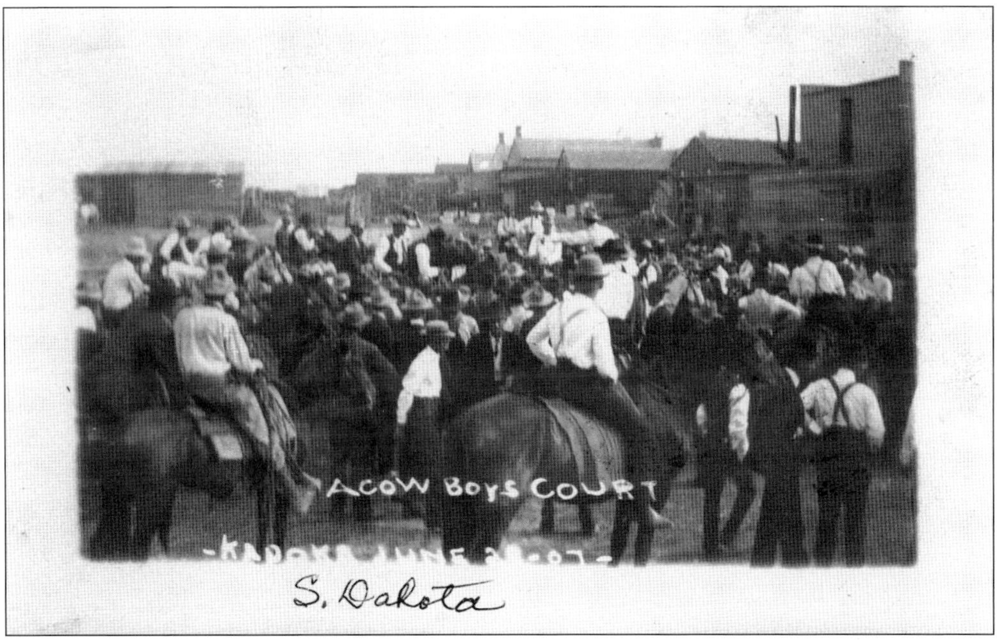

Lots for the town of Kadoka, derived from the Lakota word *Hodoka,* meaning "Hole in the Wall," were platted in 1906. In June 1907, this group of cowboys and farmers assembled on the streets of Kadoka for an unidentified important event. In 1908, the town of Kadoka was incorporated and continued to grow and develop, becoming the county seat with the dedication of the Jackson County Court House in 1915.

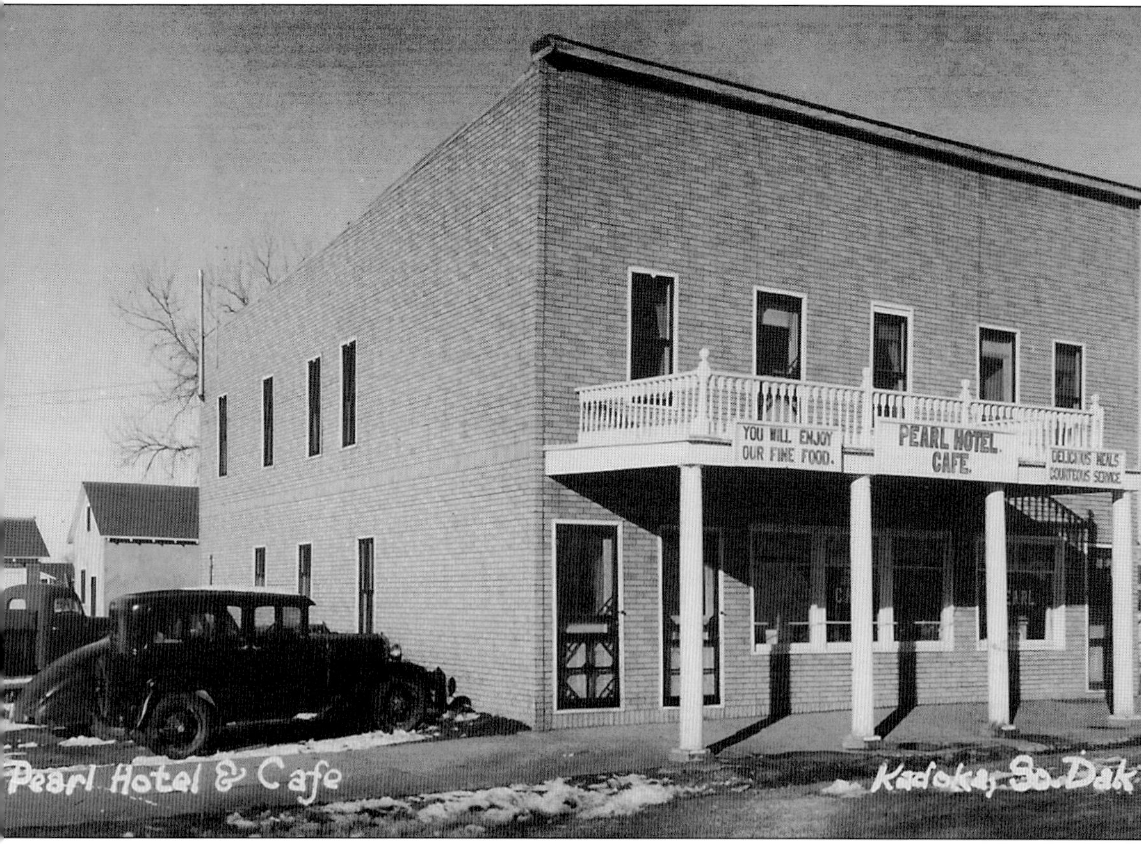

In August 1906, Jack Jones built a restaurant in the north part of Kadoka and called it the Pearl Restaurant. When the first town lots owned by the Milwaukee Land Co. were put up for sale, Jones purchased one on April 5, 1907, and moved his restaurant to the newly purchased lot on the southwest end of main street across from the newly completed Milwaukee Depot. At the new location and still on its moving timbers, the restaurant staff served the first meal to the passengers and crew of the inaugural passenger train through Kadoka. The Pearl Restaurant was soon enlarged and became the Hotel Pearl, which continued to provide meals and rooms to the traveling public. Jones added a balcony and an eight-foot-wide cement walk connecting the hotel with the depot. In 1910, a two-story addition on the north side was added. The Hans Boock family purchased the hotel in 1924. The Pearl Hotel, as it is now known, is listed in the National Register of Historic Places.

At one time, there were seven saloons in Kadoka, but after the railroad was completed and businesses were built, the number dwindled. In 1907, Kadoka had many businesses, including a lodging house, the Pearl Restaurant, a real estate office, Webb's lunchroom, F.E. Reidinger land agent, Hotel Robinson, a millinery, a hardware store, a harness stop, and the Kadoka House. The tents in the distance may indicate a celebration. The Yanky Robinson Circus came to town in August 1907. (Courtesy of Bonnie Riggins.)

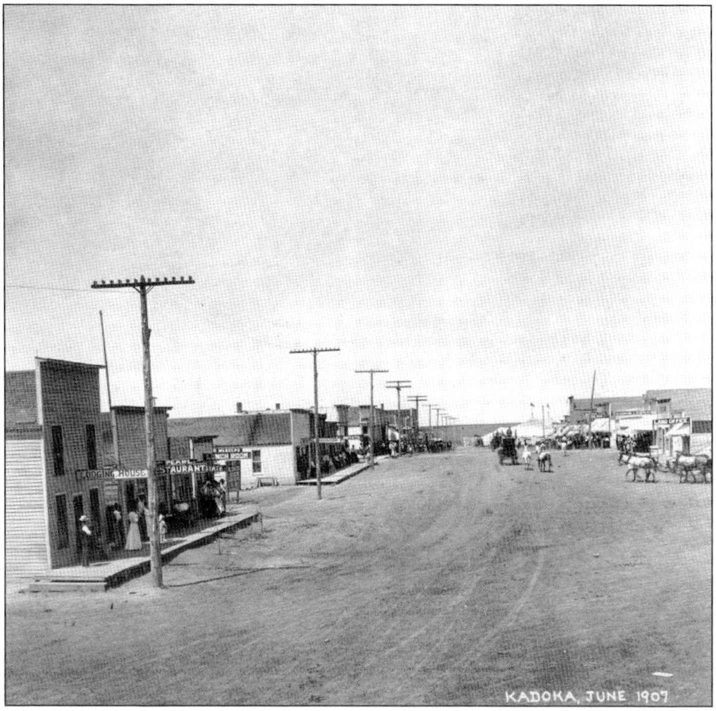

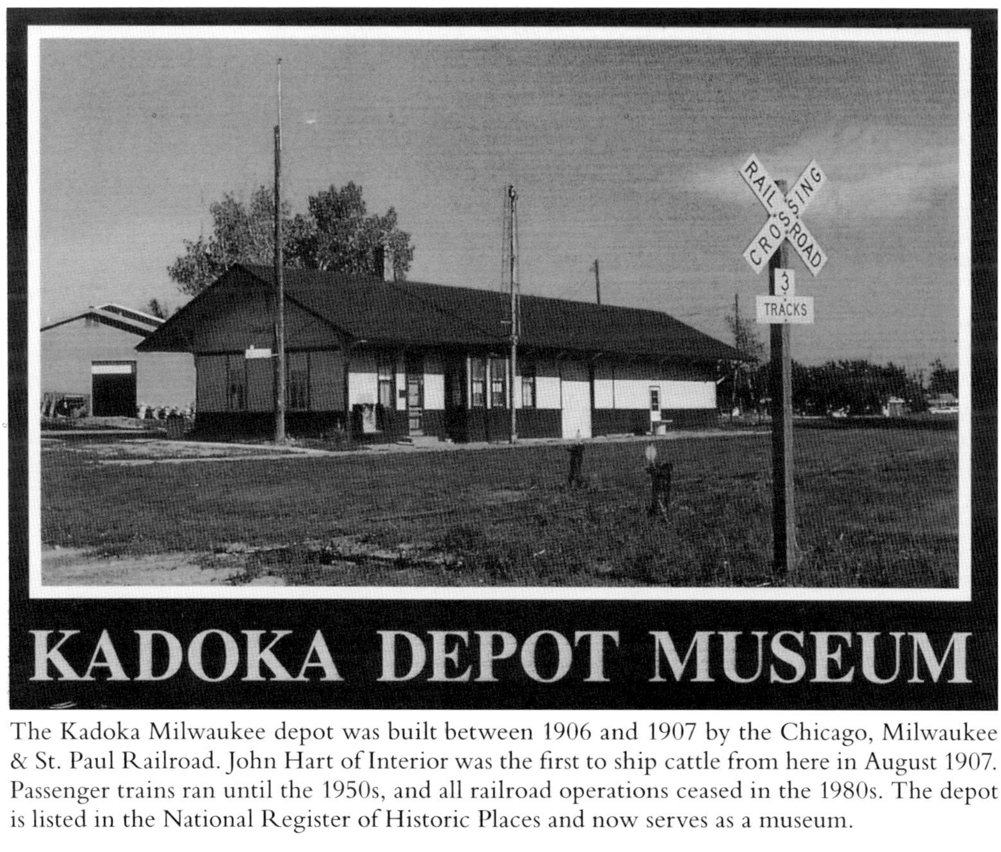

The Kadoka Milwaukee depot was built between 1906 and 1907 by the Chicago, Milwaukee & St. Paul Railroad. John Hart of Interior was the first to ship cattle from here in August 1907. Passenger trains ran until the 1950s, and all railroad operations ceased in the 1980s. The depot is listed in the National Register of Historic Places and now serves as a museum.

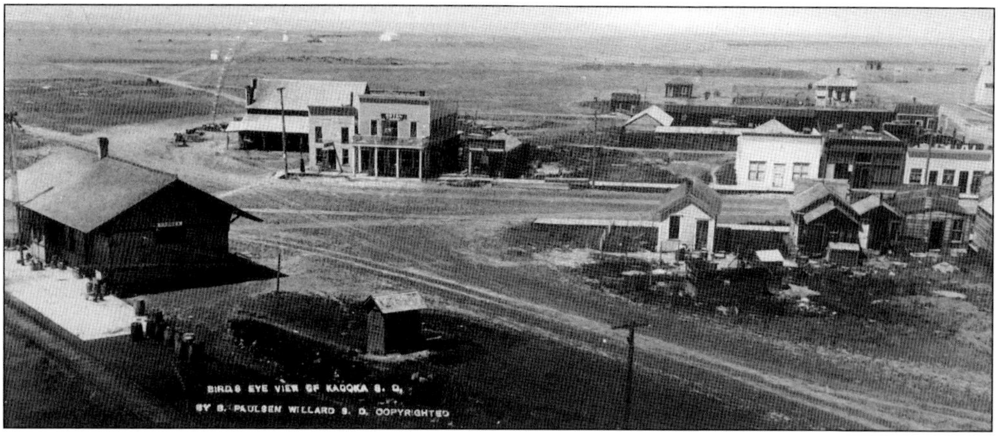

In the above image, the Kadoka depot is pictured across the street from the Pearl Hotel. The Lawrence Lodging House was south of the Pearl but was later moved away. Tuck Biddle's Circle L Livery stable is behind the Pearl. The Presbyterian church and parsonage are at upper right. By 1909, many businesses had been established and included three churches, two banks, two lumberyards, four general stores, a drugstore, a butcher shop, a harness shop, two hardware stores, two implement houses, three livery barns, two blacksmith shops, a clothing store, a bakery, three hotels, two newspapers, four real estate dealers, a millinery, and a grocery. The depot and the Pearl Hotel have both been preserved. Below, the Kadoka schoolhouse takes a prominent place on the north end of town. Kadoka's Main Street is at far left. (Both, courtesy of the Kadoka Depot Museum.)

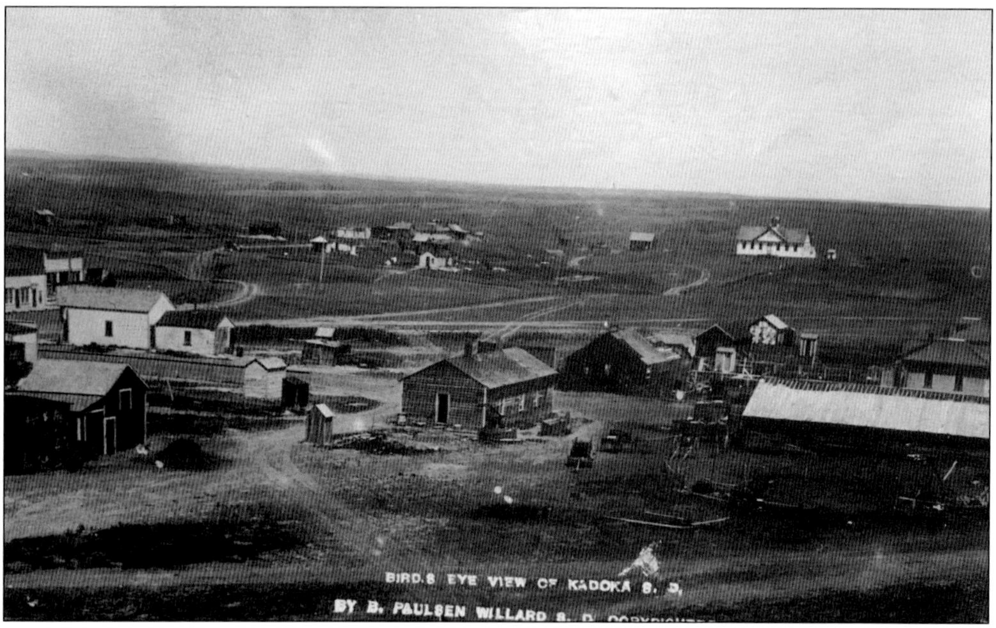

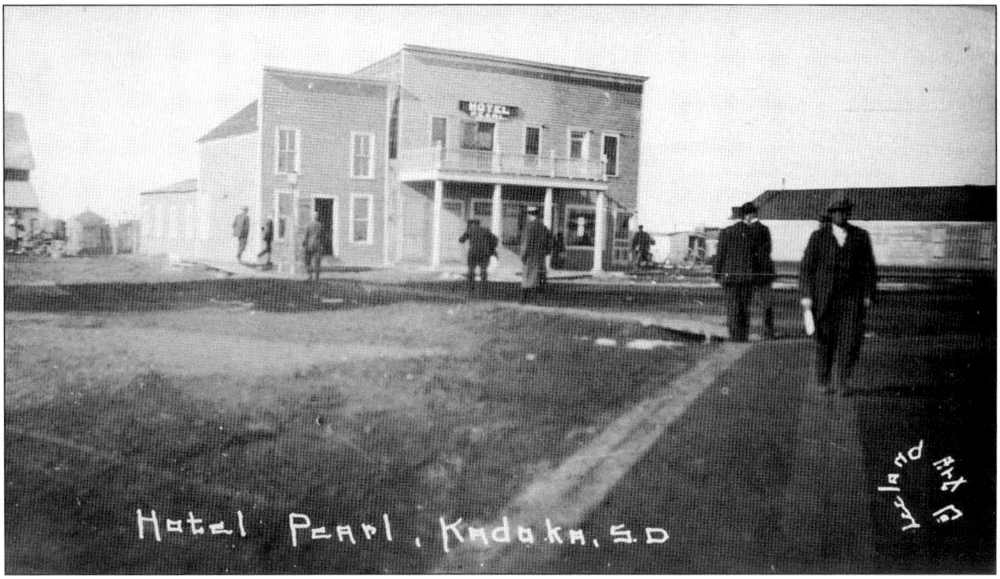

The Pearl Hotel served a noon meal to the train passengers and crew. It was the duty of a kitchen staff member to watch for the train from the hotel's balcony and then hurry downstairs to tell the cook the train was coming. The meal was quickly placed on the table, as the passengers had only 20 minutes to eat. The meal of roast beef and trimmings was constant each day, and was served family style.

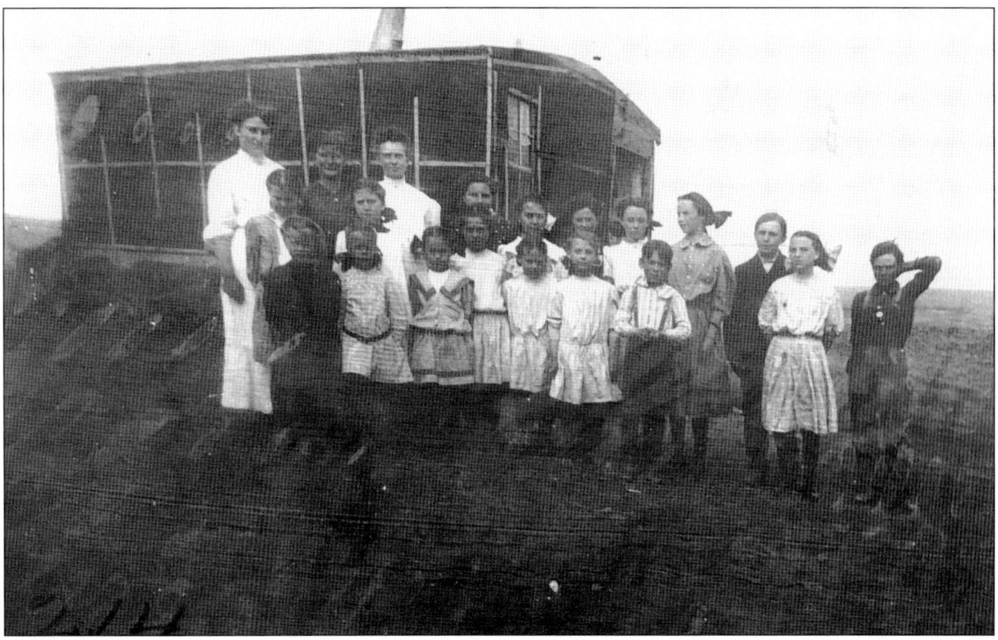

This tar paper schoolhouse was similar to many of the first schools established in the area. This one was known as the Nellie Webster School in 1908. Only a few students have been identified. They are Lucy Fields, Mary Halbrook, Ernest Schultz, Herman Schultz, and Nellie Webster (one of the teachers). (Courtesy of the Kadoka Depot Museum.)

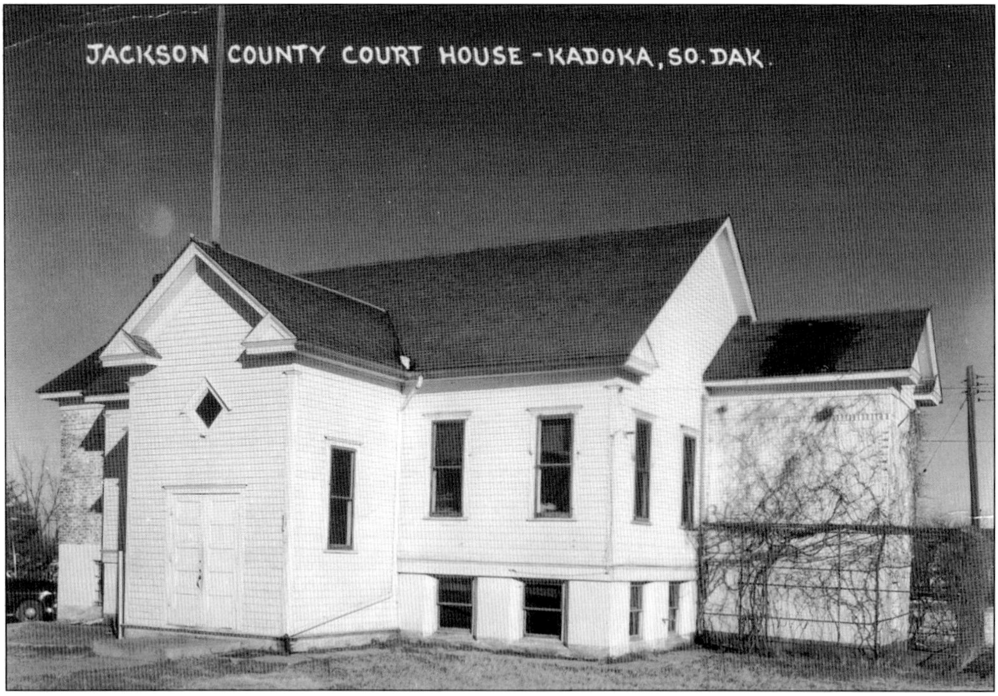

In 1914, Stamford, Belvidere, Kadoka, Weta, and Interior campaigned for the county seat when a new Jackson County was formed. Kadoka won the election by a large margin. The Commercial Club constructed a building and turned it over to the county to use for its courthouse. On July 28, 1916, a dedication was held for the new building. (Courtesy of Bonnie Riggins.)

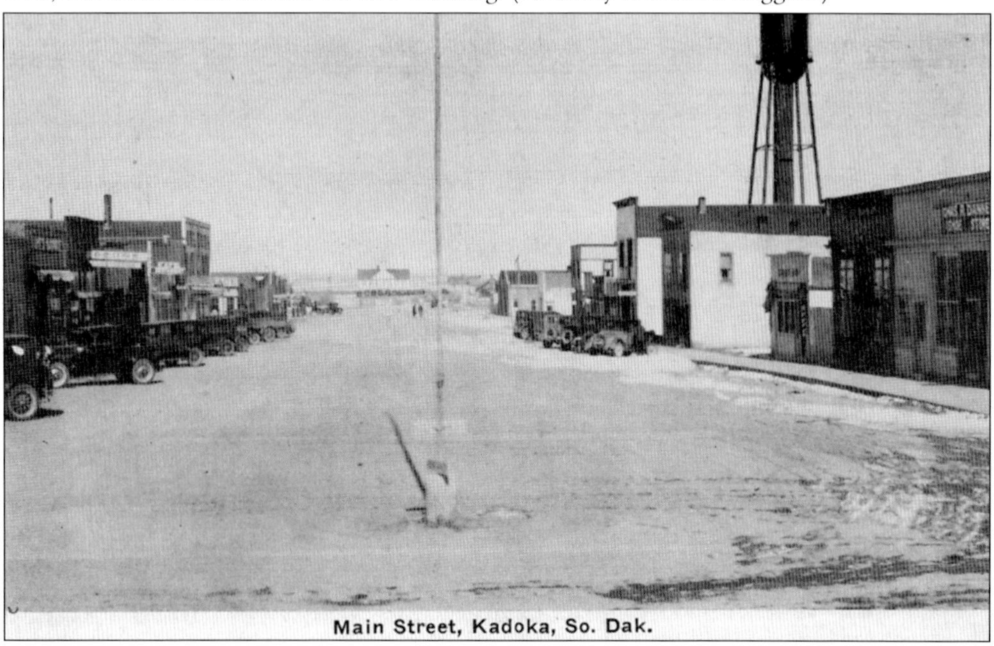

A flagpole without the flag is seen in the middle of Main Street in Kadoka. The street was dirt until it was graveled in 1926 and re-graveled in 1931, eventually becoming hard surfaced. Cars line the street. At some point, the flagpole was removed.

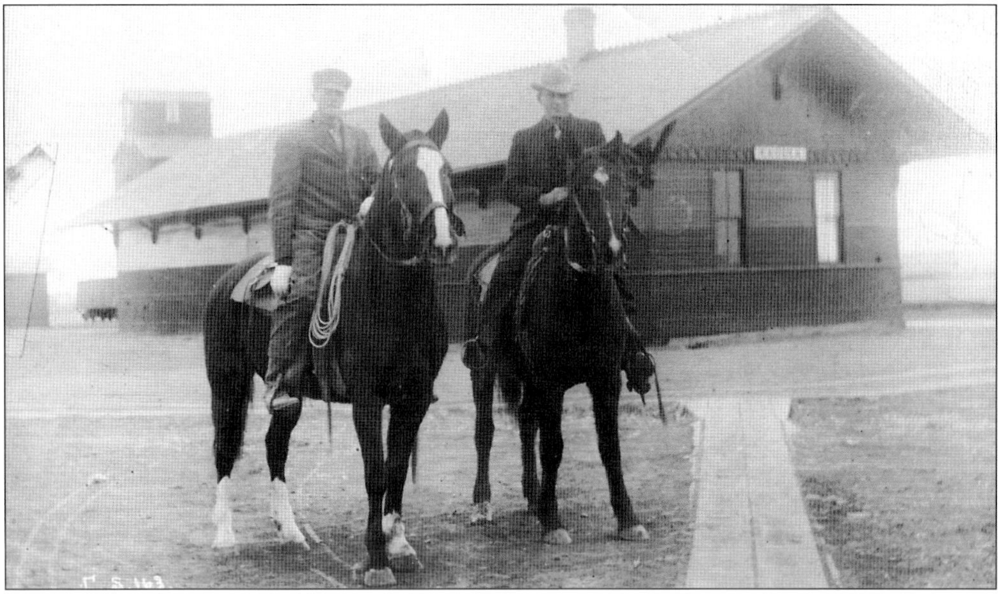

Two men on horses pause by the depot. Note the cement sidewalk that connects the depot with the Pearl Hotel. In 1916, boardwalks were condemned and businesses and residents were encouraged to replace them with cement. Jack Jones was the first businessman to install a cement sidewalk.

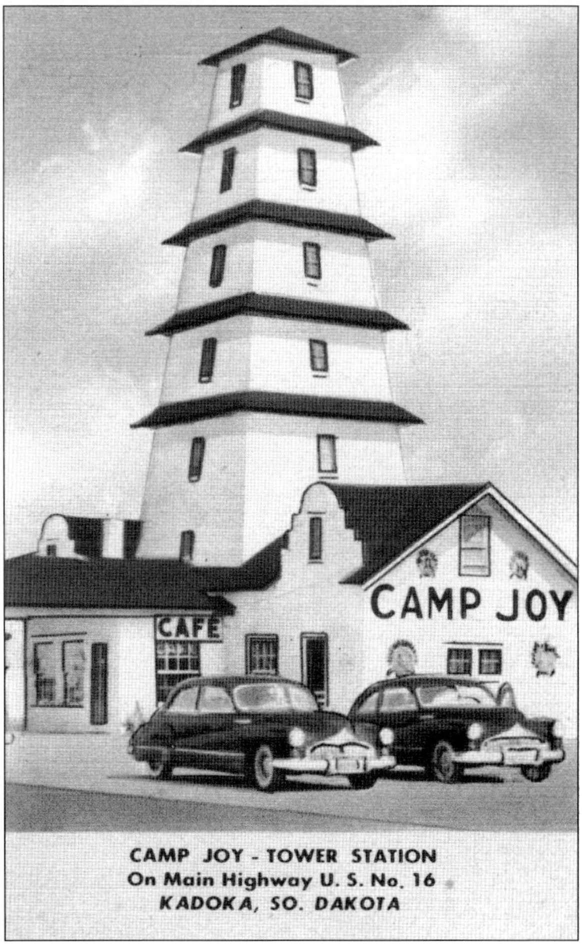

Peter and Matilda Simon built Camp Joy, the first cabin camp in South Dakota, in 1926. The camp consisted of a row of cabins and a pagoda tower and gas station. The Simons built a second set of cabins known as Dreamland and a service station across Highway 16 from Camp Joy. These cabins were built around a dam with an island known as Pete's Dam.

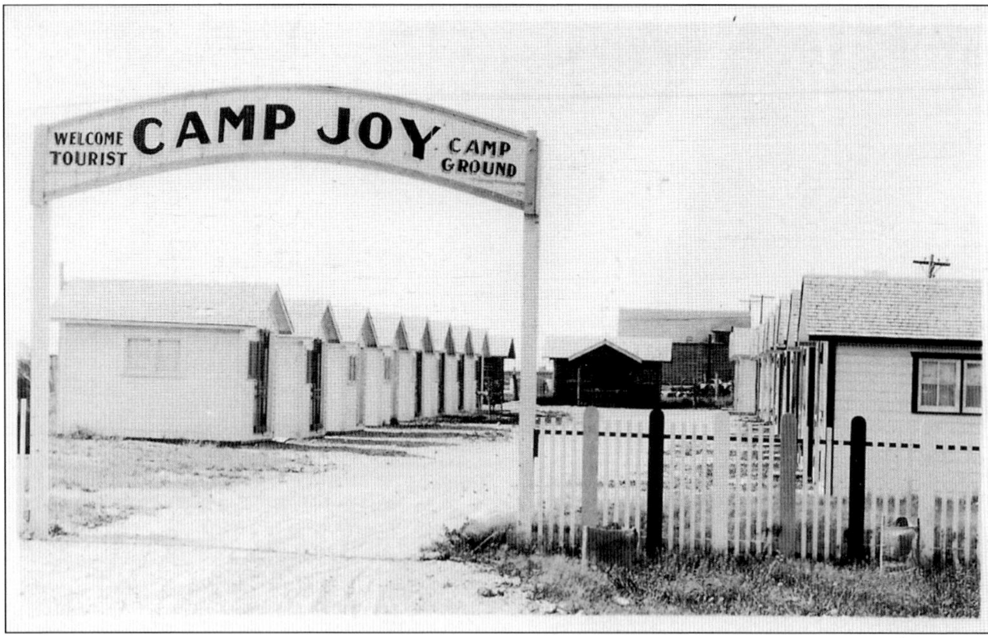

Kadoka was a popular place for tourists to lodge overnight. As many as 40 cars came inquiring for a cabin every evening. By 2:30 every afternoon during tourist season, the motels and cabins would be full. Pictured are the Camp Joy cabins. The Simons sold Camp Joy to Jim Whitford, who acquired the name "Turkey Jim" because of the turkey dinners he served at the camp. The station and tower were later destroyed by fire.

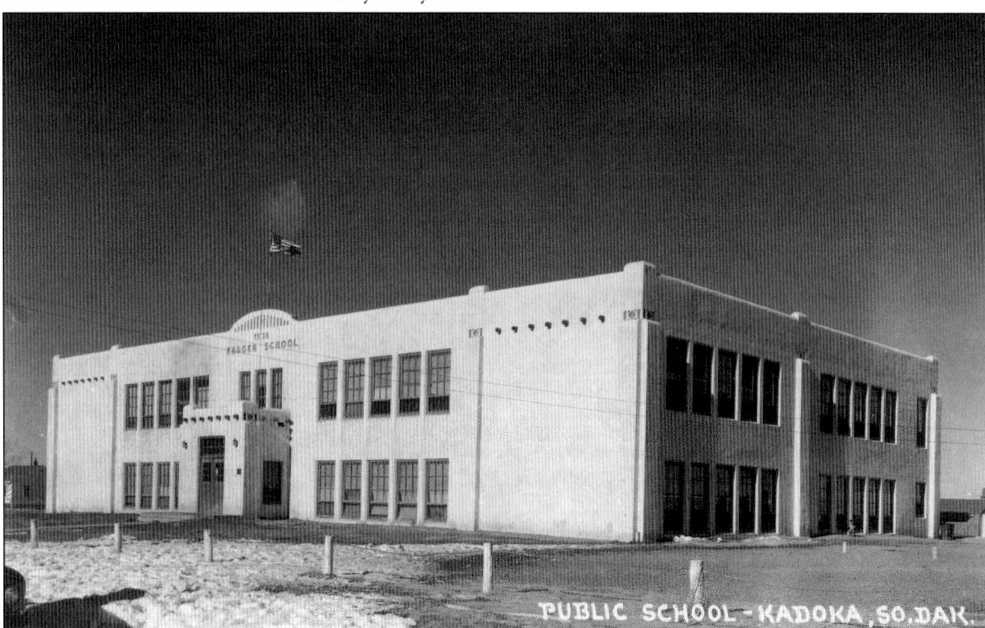

In September 1937, Kadoka voted for a new public school building. The total cost was projected at $61,000. The district was slated to pay $20,000, with the federal government covering the rest. On September 5, 1939, the building was completed and school opened with 127 students in attendance. C.B. Gilchrist served as superintendent. (Courtesy of Bonnie Riggins.)

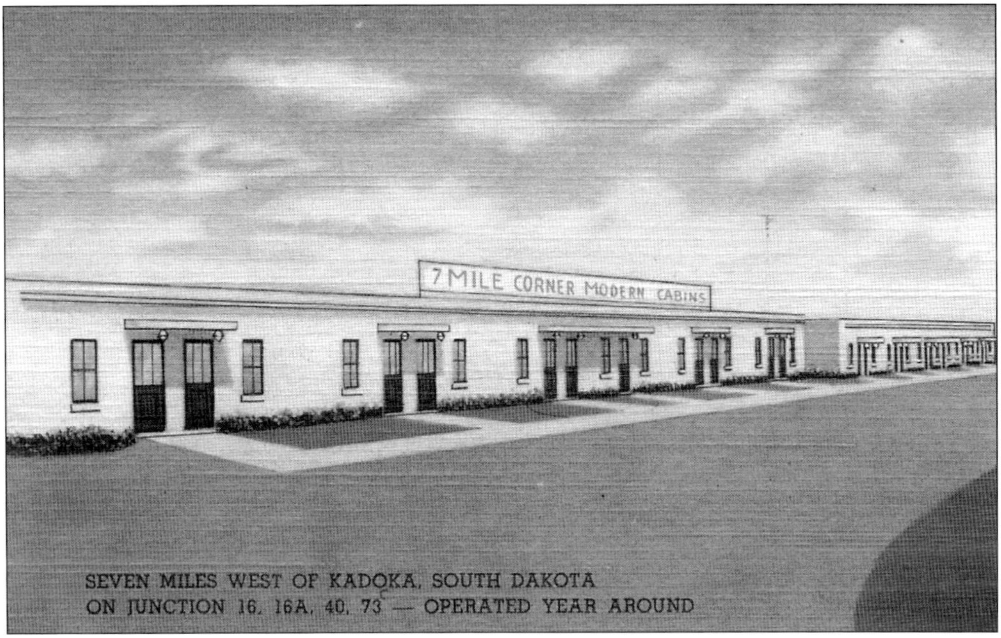

Seven Mile Corner was located seven miles west of Kadoka at the junction of Highways 16, 16A, 40, and 73 before I-90 was constructed. It was advertised as a town of its own with 20 modern cabins, fireproof buildings, private baths, single and double cabins, and automatic heating and air conditioning. Seven Mile Corner advertised a café, garage, service station, and souvenirs. Nothing of the once-busy corner remains today.

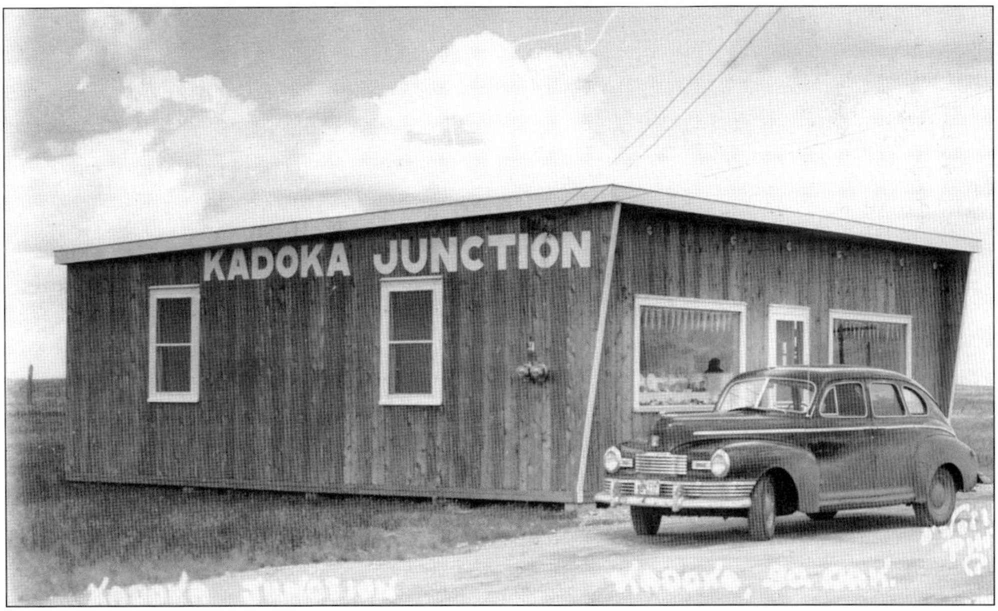

Bill and Allene Goins established Kadoka Junction in 1946. It is pictured when it was located at Seven Mile Corner, before it was moved to the town of Kadoka from the junction of Highways 73 and 16 several years later. Bill and Allene Goins employed many locals during Seven Mile Corner's duration. (Courtesy of Bonnie Riggins.)

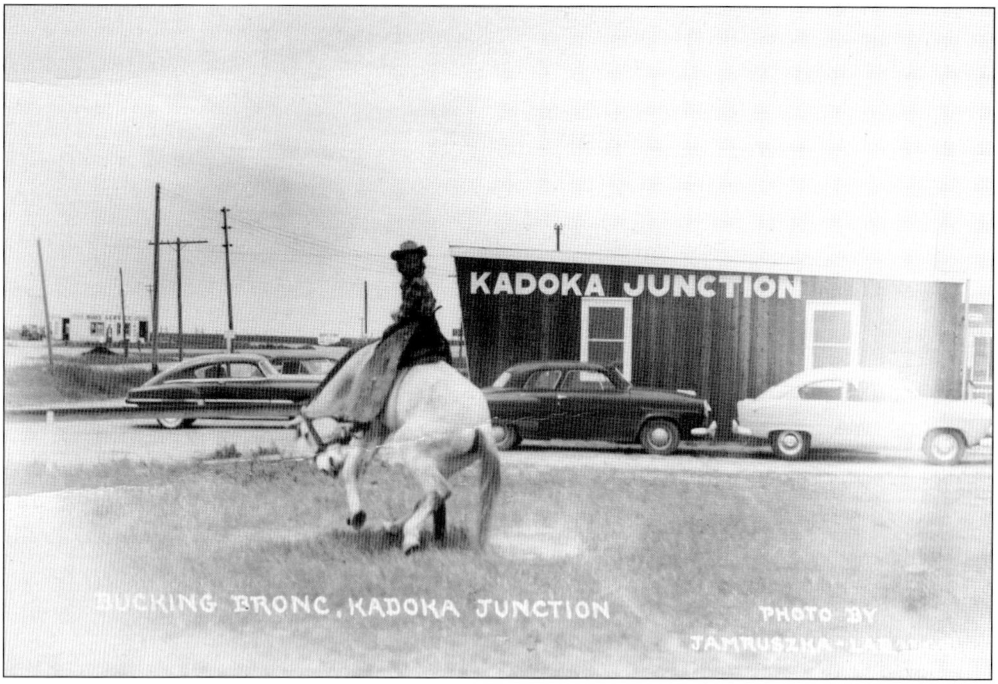

A stuffed horse at Kadoka Junction was a tourist attraction both at the junction when it was located at Seven Mile Corner and when it was moved to Kadoka. This young lady is outfitted for a ride. Bud Alden's Service Station is visible at left. (Courtesy of Bonnie Riggins.)

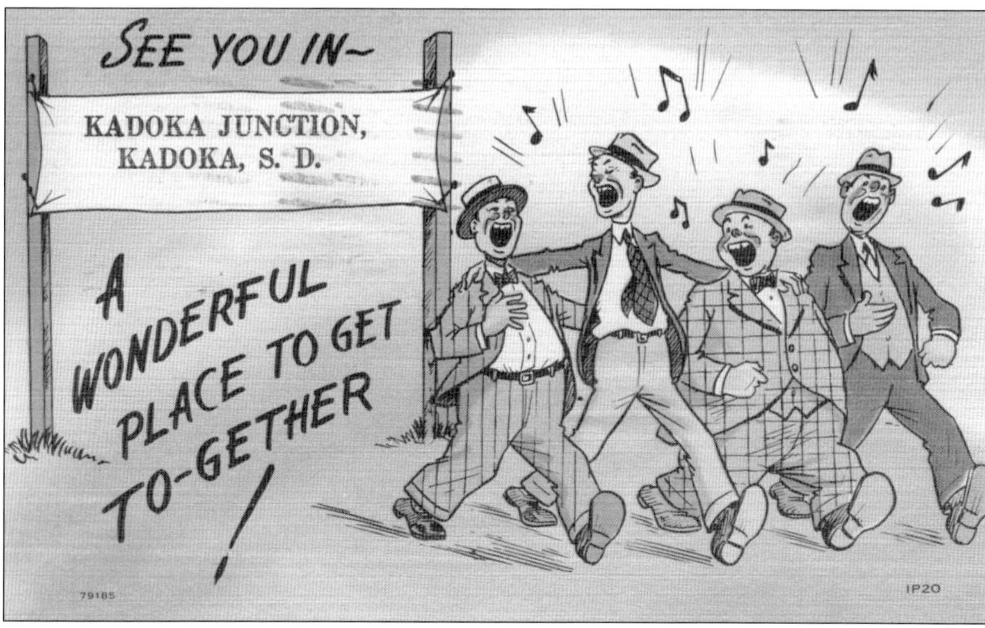

Kadoka Junction used this tourist postcard, postmarked in 1951, to advertise its location. It was a popular stop for food and gasoline along Highway 16 to the Badlands and Black Hills. The sender wrote, "Saw a good rodeo. There was a lot of boys and girls riding in the parade with their horses."

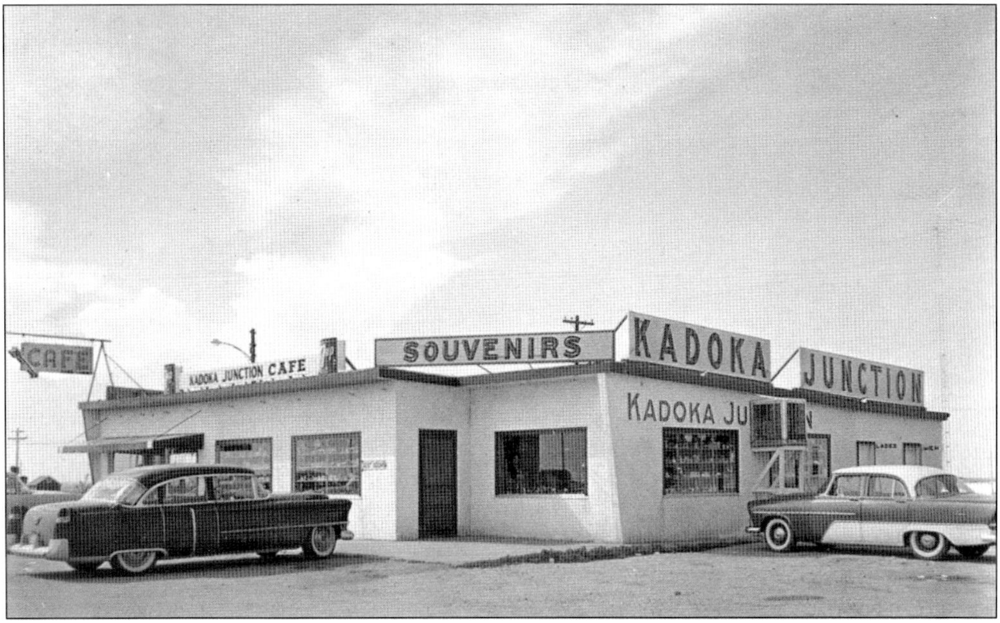

When the Kadoka Junction business was moved from Seven Mile Corner, Bill and Allene Goins added on to the original structure, advertising it as a large gift and souvenir store and modern café. A chicken dinner cost $2.15; breaded shrimp, $2.25; pie, 45¢; hamburger, 50¢; and a side of French fries, 30¢. The business was liquidated in 1987, and the building was sold and eventually torn down.

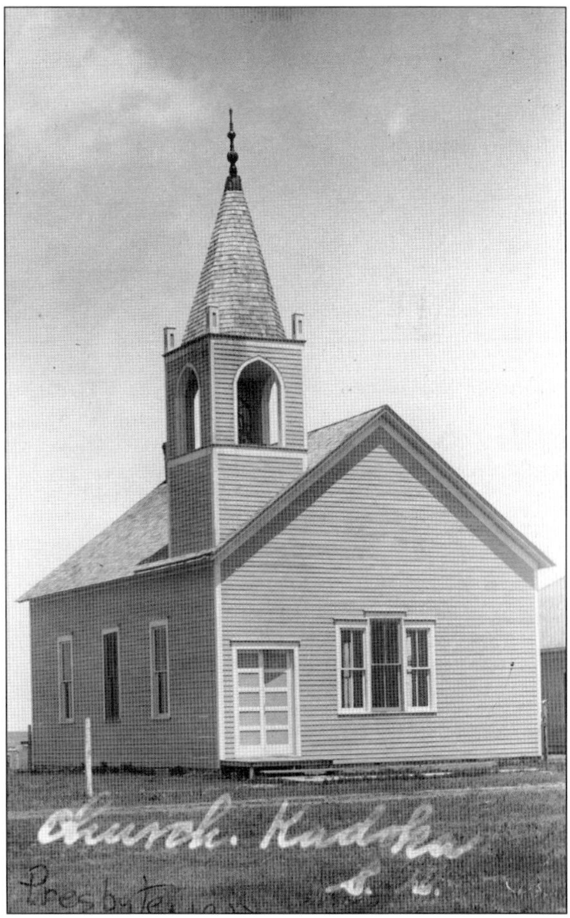

Rev. David S. Brown began worship services in Kadoka in 1906 in homes and various business buildings. He organized a Presbyterian church with 60 members in June 1907, followed by the building of Kadoka Presbyterian Church in the fall of 1907. A basement was dug between 1939 and 1940 to accommodate increasing church activities. (Courtesy of Bonnie Riggins.)

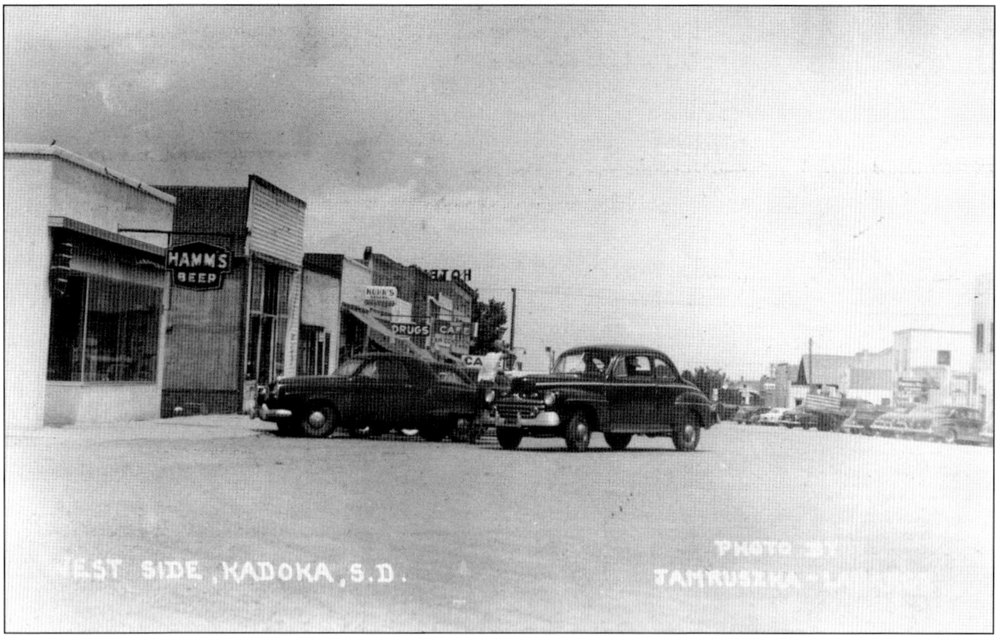

Pictures of Kadoka's Main Street have been updated over the years. On the west side of Kadoka, the businesses pictured here are Bill Goins's pool hall, a vacant building, the post office, Kuhn's general merchandise, a drugstore, Kerlin's market, a tourist café, and the Dakota Hotel. (Courtesy of Bonnie Riggins.)

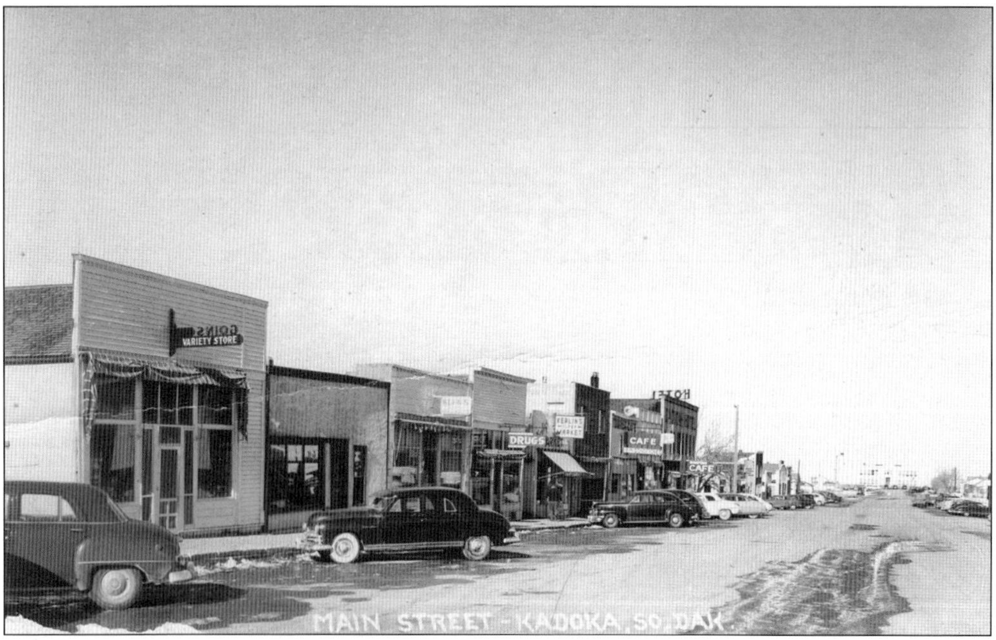

Taken in the early 1950s, this photograph shows the businesses on Main Street: Bill Goins's variety store, the post office, Kuhn's, a drugstore, Kerlin's market, a tourist café, the Dakota Hotel, a bar, Red Mill Café, Hal Stewart men's clothing, the State Theater, Rudy Petterson's building, Hemmingson's auto, the Carlyle residence, Helen Collins's beauty shop, and a gas station. (Courtesy of Bonnie Riggins.)

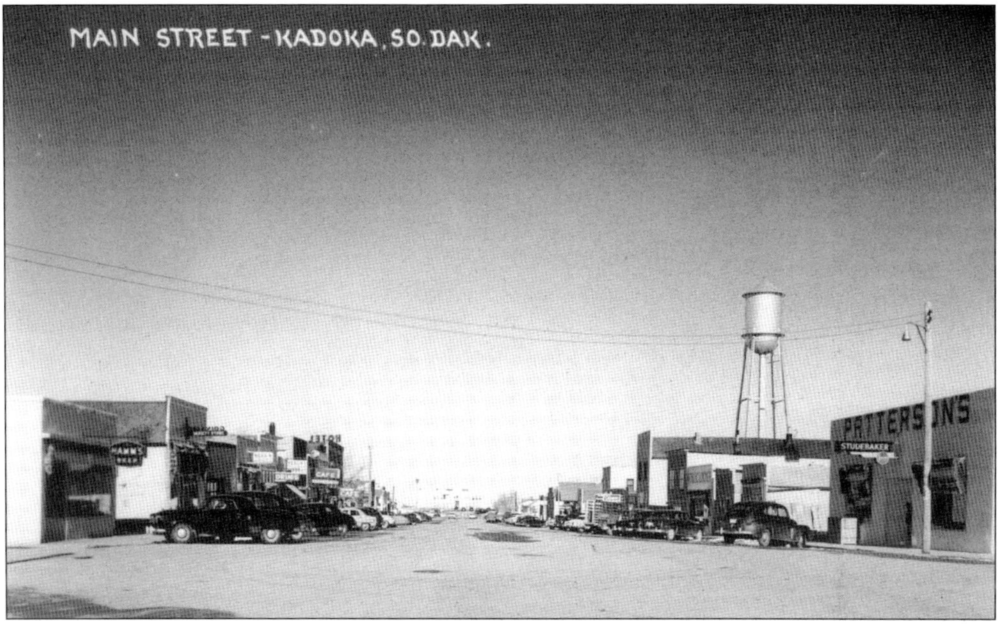

Kadoka Main street businesses, from north to south on the east side, include a building containing the sheriff's office, a recruiting office, and a conservation office; the Tidy Inn; the *Kadoka Press*; Doc Sundet's office or possibly the photograph shop; Marshall Wells hardware; Burkholz apartments; public lockers; and Brown Barbershop. (Courtesy of Bonnie Riggins.)

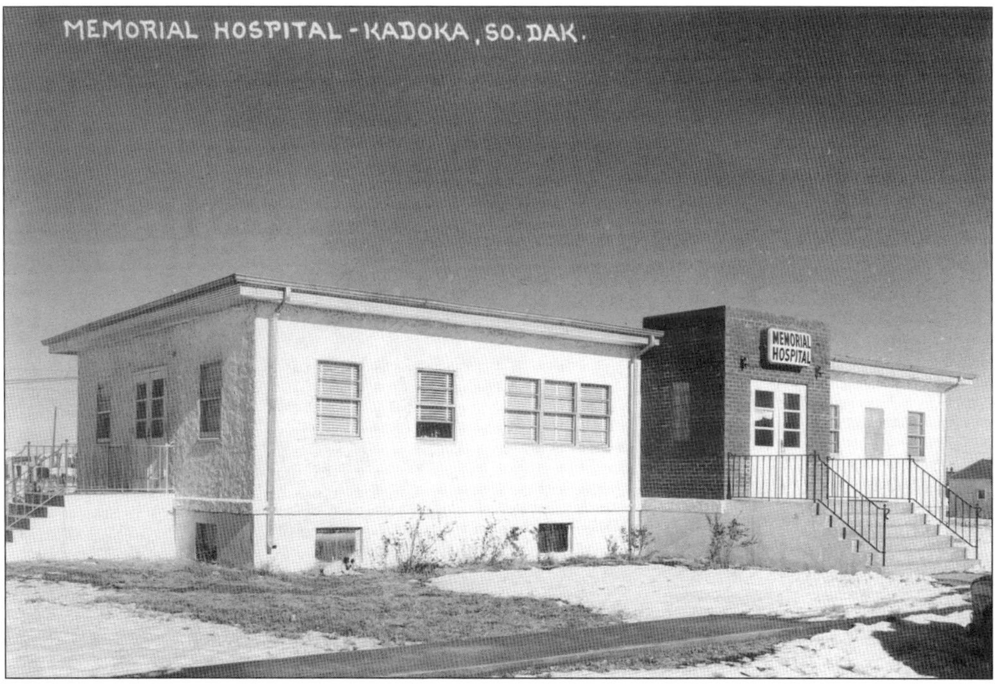

Dr. Daniel was the first doctor to establish a facility for patients in his office building. Marie Olney offered her home for patients, and Alice McRae Kjos operated a hospital in the former Corrington house. A new Memorial Hospital was built between 1950 and 1951 and added onto between 1963 and 1964. (Courtesy of Bonnie Riggins.)

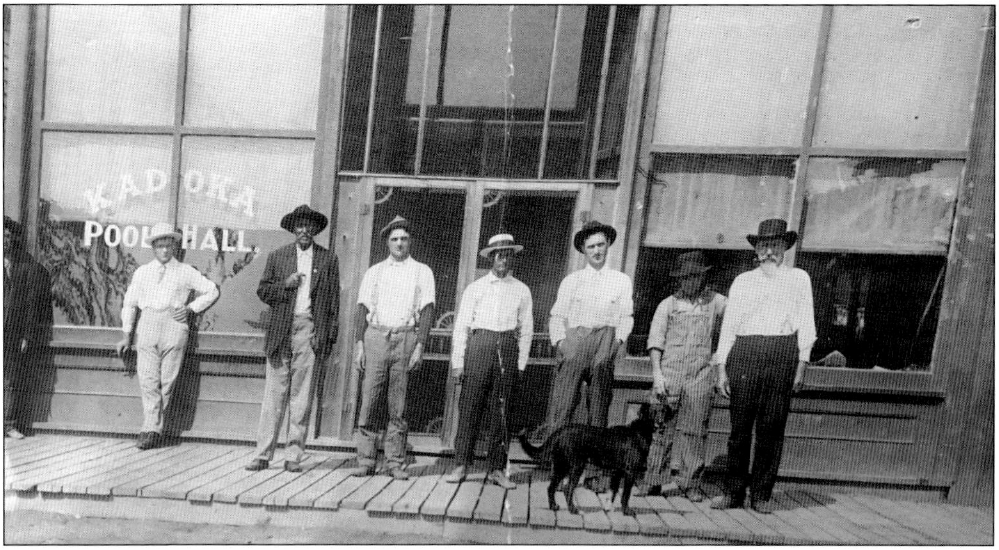

As in most early towns, pool, billiards, and card rooms were popular. Tuck Biddle operated a pool hall until 1918 when he and his wife, Laura, moved. The Kadoka Pool Hall changed owners over the years. Some of the owners were Frank Reidinger, George Hutton, J. Vandermuelin, a Mr. Hutchinson, Sid Parkinson, Bill Shroll, Leo Barrett, and Bill Goins. (Courtesy of the Kadoka Depot Museum.)

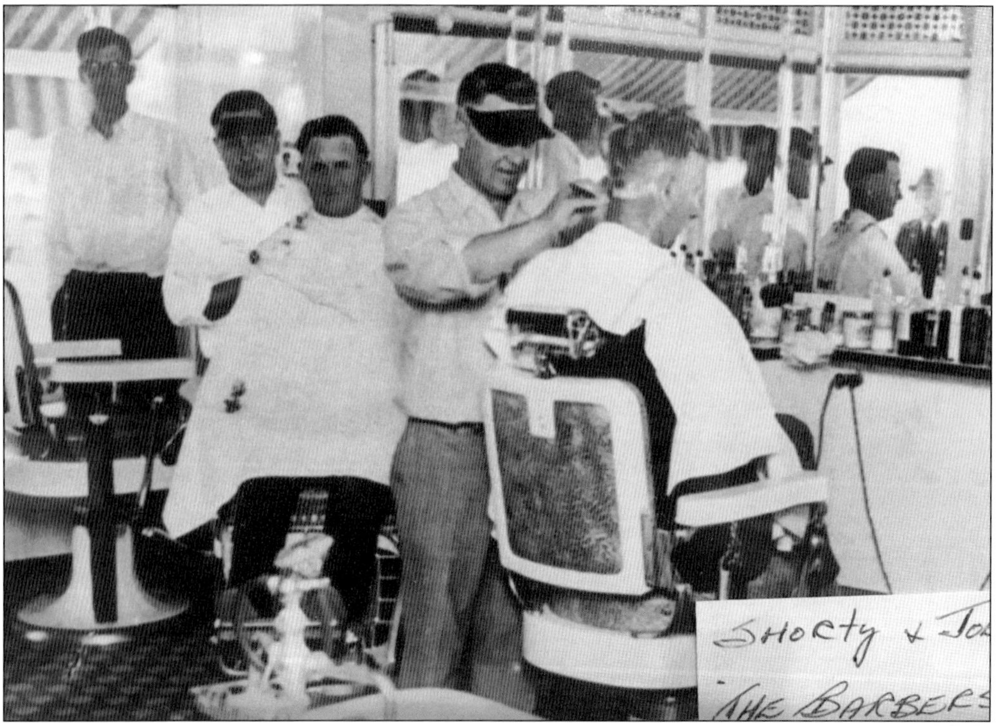

Pictured in a Kadoka barbershop are Joe Brown and Shorty Anerud. Joe Brown married Eloise Trimble in 1917 and ranched until 1929, when he began to barber in Kadoka. Joe Brown Jr. operated his father's barbershop until he became state fire inspector. (Courtesy of the Kadoka Depot Museum.)

When Kadoka was first established, hundreds of reservation Indians pitched their tepees outside of town and came to Kadoka to trade. They also participated in parades, fairs, and celebrations. Jim Whitford invited them to dance in full regalia at Camp Joy when he owned the tourist camp. (Courtesy of the Kadoka Depot Museum.)

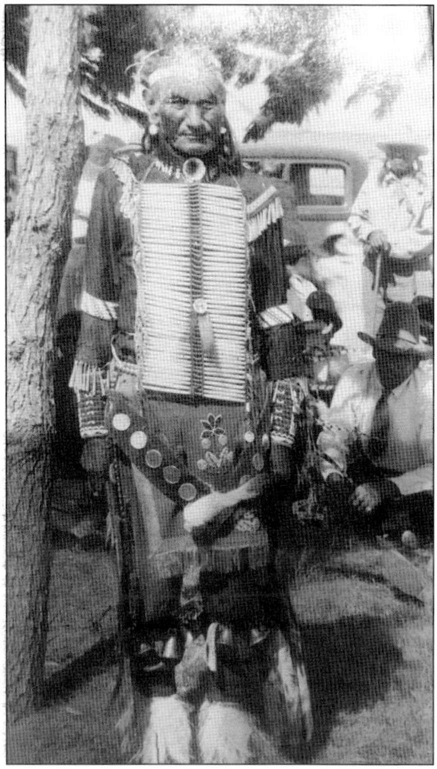

Mike Mednansky purchased this store in 1929 in which he repaired harnesses and shoes. Others who operated similar businesses over the years were J.A. Frazer, Iver Arnsten, Charlie Danner, and Herschel Brugman. (Courtesy of the Kadoka Depot Museum.)

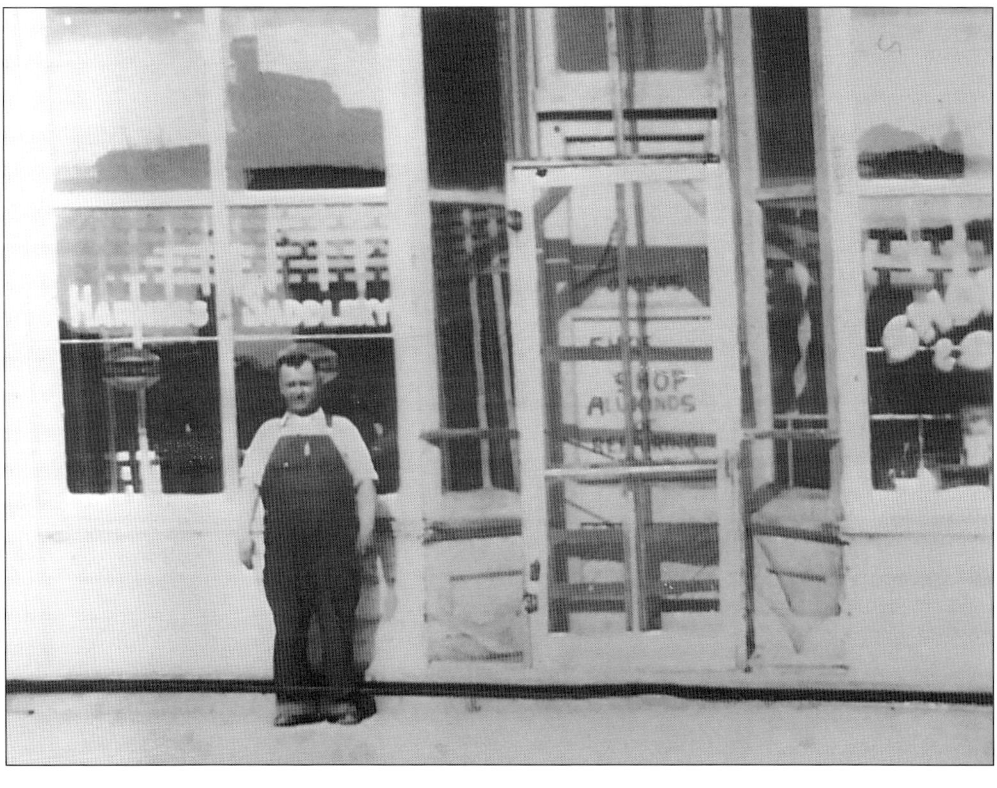

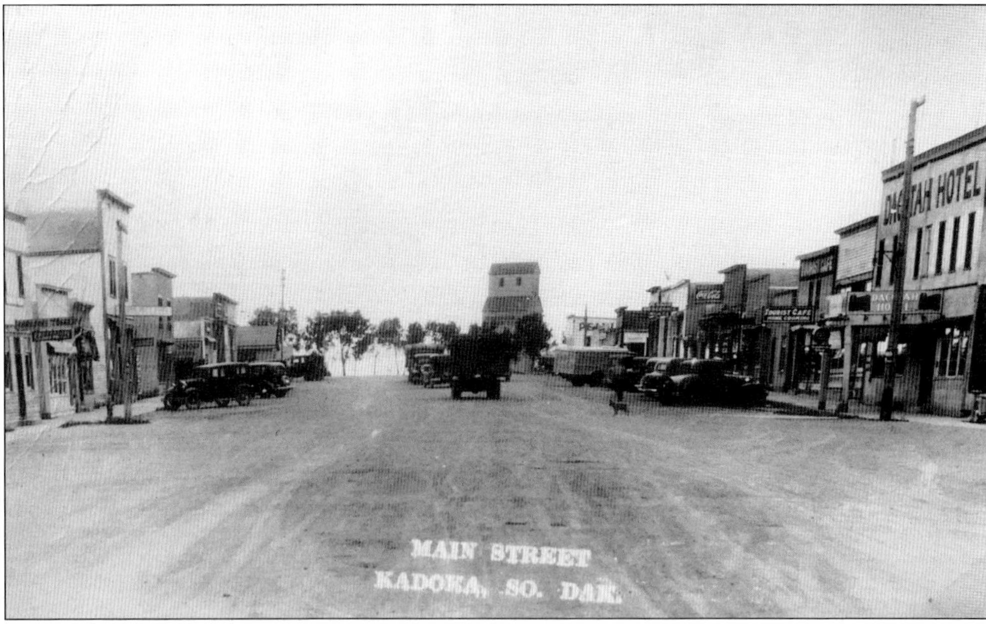

On the right side of Main Street in Kadoka, looking south in the 1930s, are the Dacotah Hotel, a tourist café, Simon's grocery and meats, the Pearl Hotel, and an elevator. The Dacotah Hotel, which was a landmark in Kadoka for a number of years, burned in 1965. (Courtesy of the Kadoka Depot Museum.)

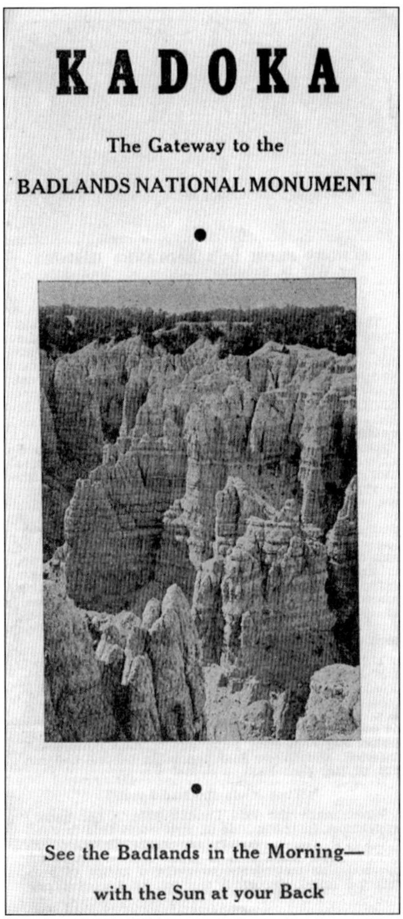

Camp Joy sponsored this Badlands brochure during the height of tourism. Today, Kadoka does not host as many tourists as in the past. A few people still stop by for gas or food, and some for evening accommodations. Since the late 1960s, I-90 has limited tourist visitation to the town.

Seven

Wall

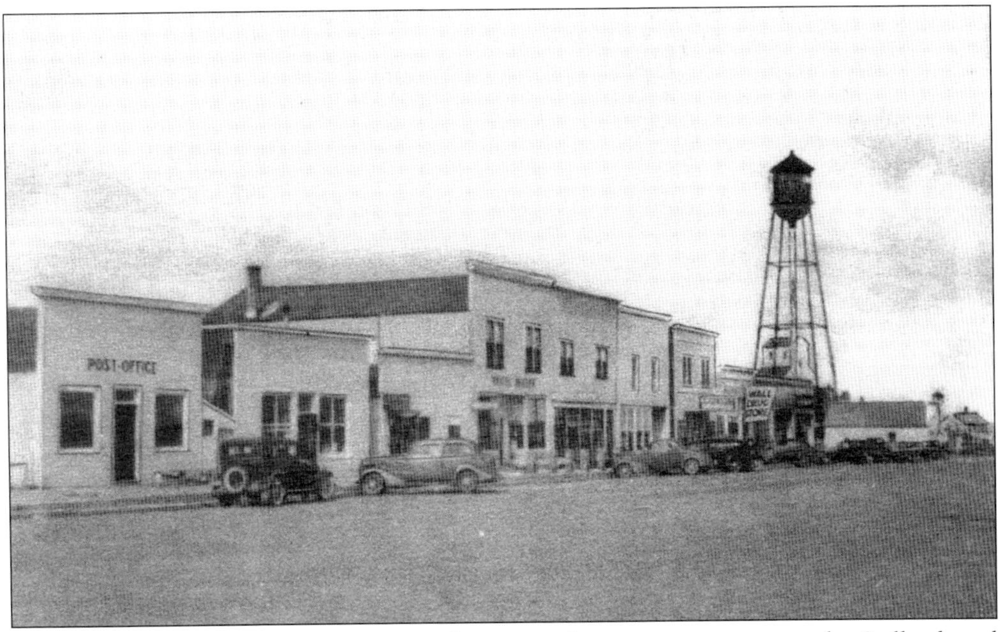

The City of Wall, established in 1907, is known as the western gateway to the Badlands and was named for the Badlands Wall, which forms a 60-mile barrier on the north rim that hinders travel between the upper and lower prairies. Town lots were sold on July 10, 1907, and the first through train, the Chicago Northwestern, operated from Pierre to Rapid City.

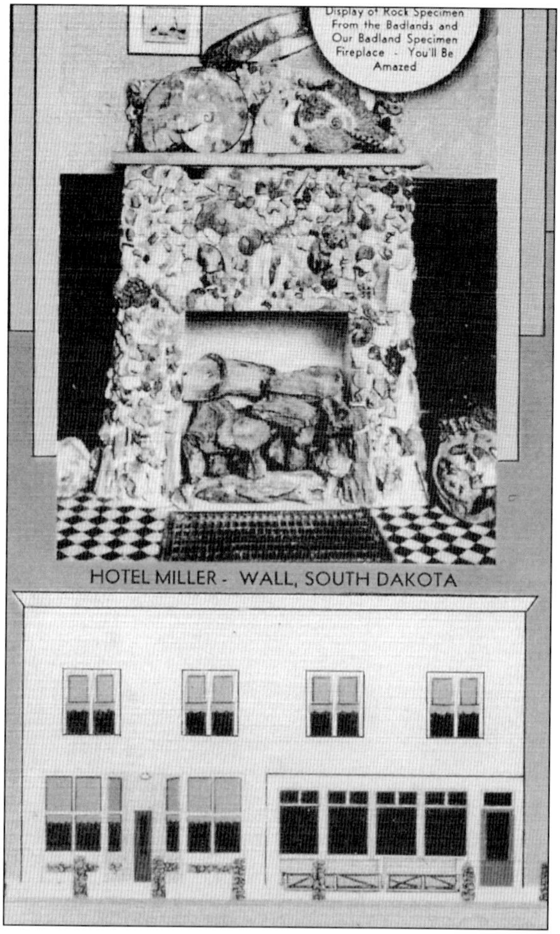

In 1912, William and Hulda Miller leased their farm and established a general store, a hotel, and a café. The Hotel Miller accommodated 43 guests and hosted a few celebrities during its years of operation. Among them were Amos and Andy; Gumbo Lil, who owned land south of Wall; and Senator Norbeck, who probably stayed there when working on promoting the Badlands. The Hotel Miller advertised clean beds, pure water, choice meals and lunches, hot and cold water, and baths and showers, all at reasonable rates. The 1949 blizzard filled Wall with snow, partially burying the Hotel Miller. The Cactus Café now occupies the spot where the hotel once stood.

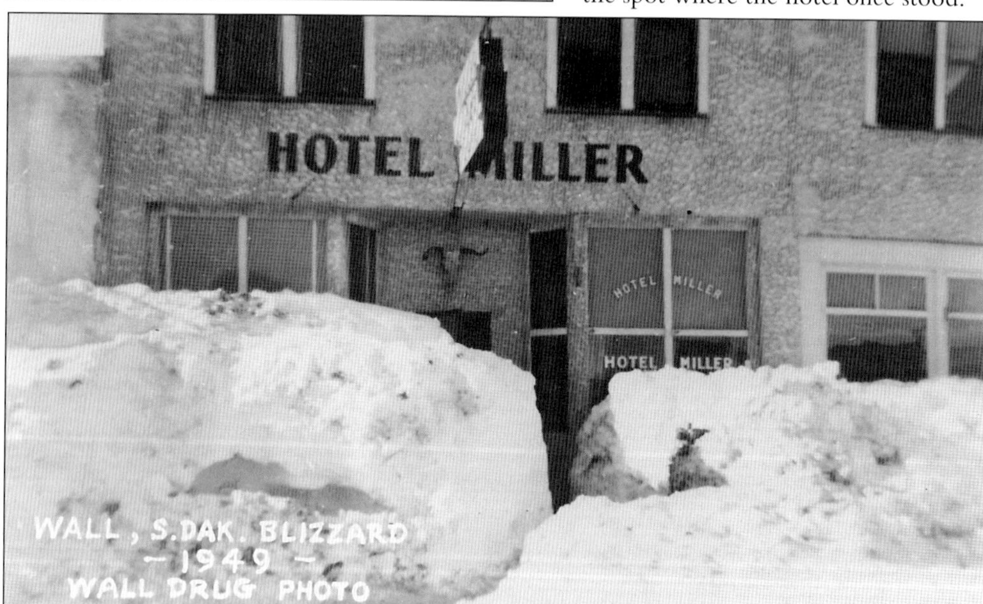

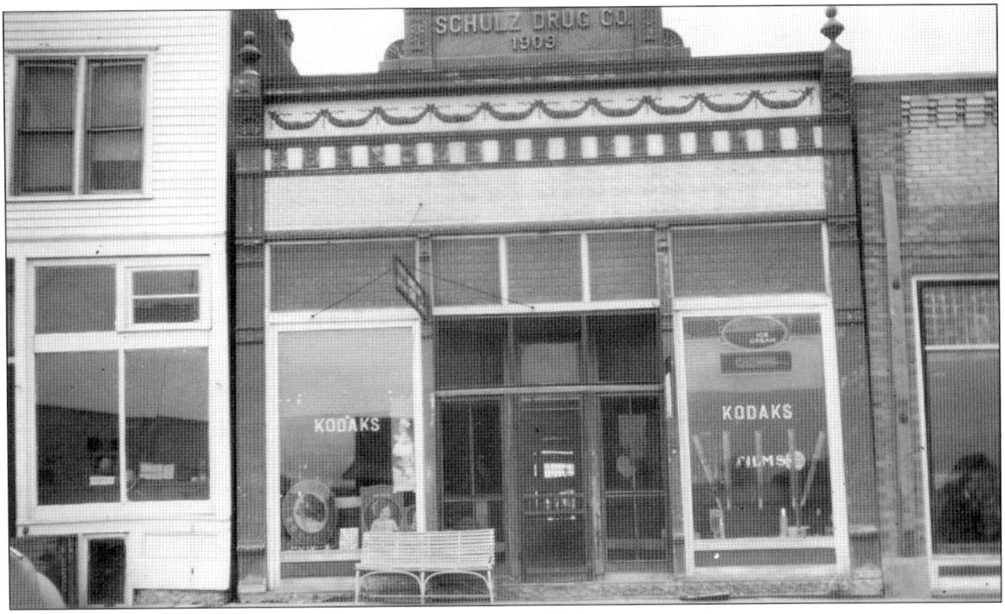

Pictured is the Shulz Drug store, established in 1909. The store advertised ice cream, candies, and Kodak film. The bank is at right, and down the street to the left is the Hotel Miller. This is the drugstore that Ted and Dorothy Hustead purchased in 1931 with hopes that they could make a go of it. They were uncertain about their move from Canova, South Dakota, to Wall, which seemed to be in the middle of nowhere. A busy highway ran right by this small town in the late 1920s, but business was slow during the Depression years.

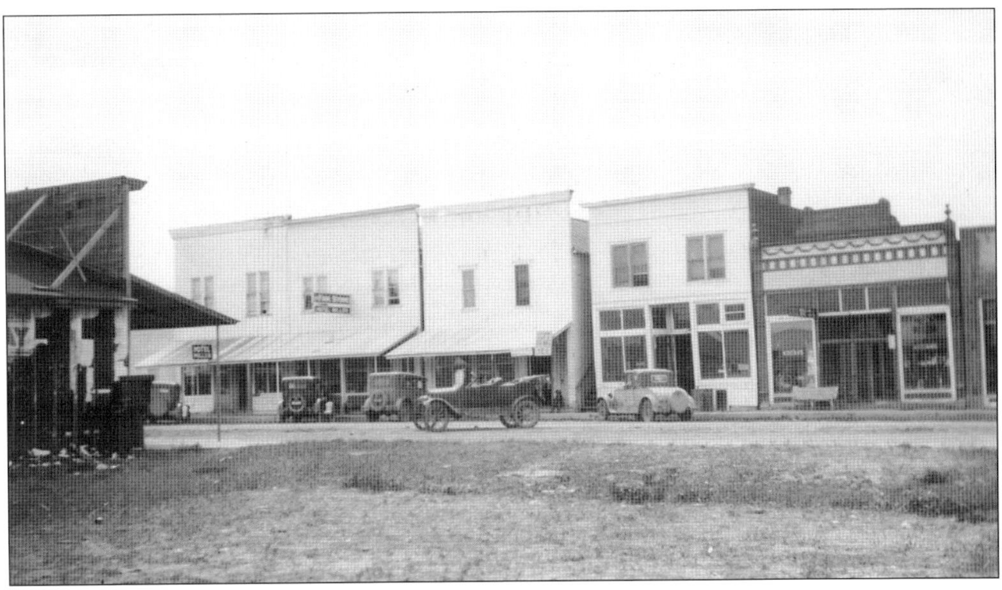

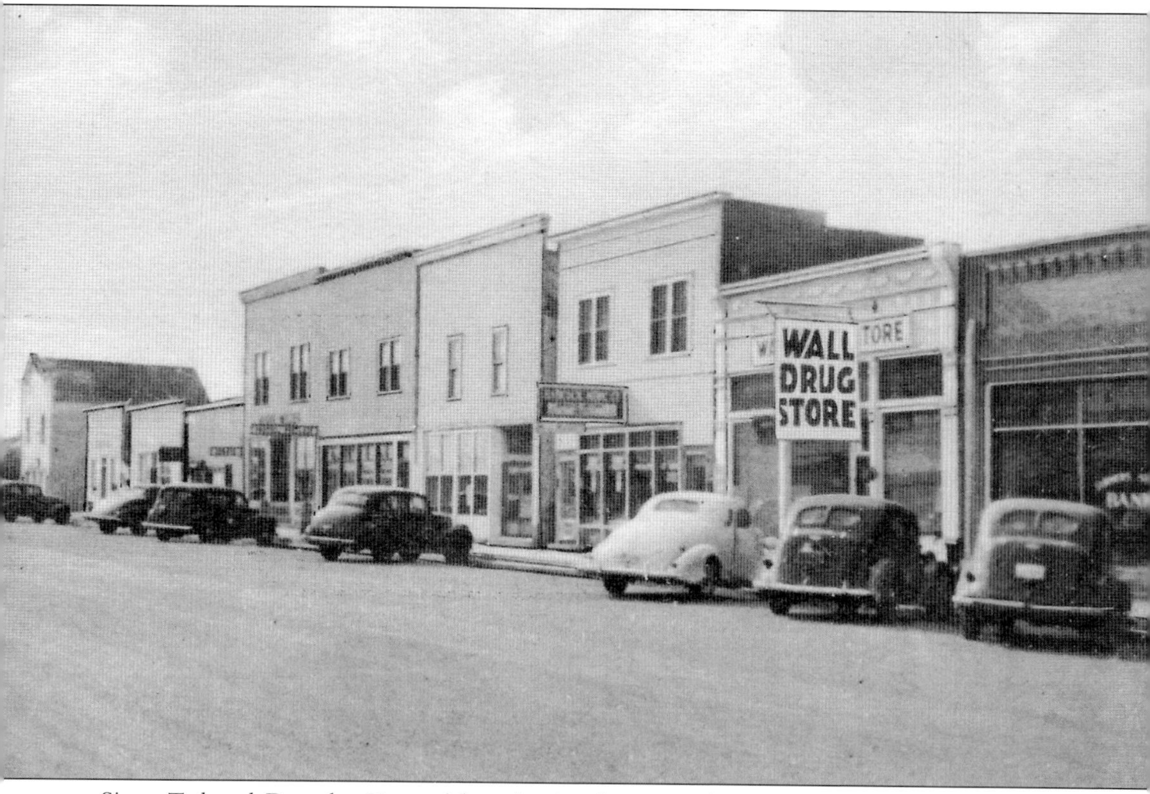

Since Ted and Dorothy Hustead bought the drugstore during the Depression and extreme drought, the couple had a tough time of making their business work. After five years, they were about to give up and move until one hot day during the summer when Dorothy came up with an idea of how to get the traveling public off the nearby road and into the town of Wall and their store—she suggested that they should offer free ice water to the thirsty travelers. Skeptically, they put up signs and placed them along the road. Much to their surprise, the idea worked. People were pulling off the road for free ice water, and many of them bought a few other items while they were there. The following summer, the Husteads hired eight girls to help out at the store. (Courtesy of Wall Drug.)

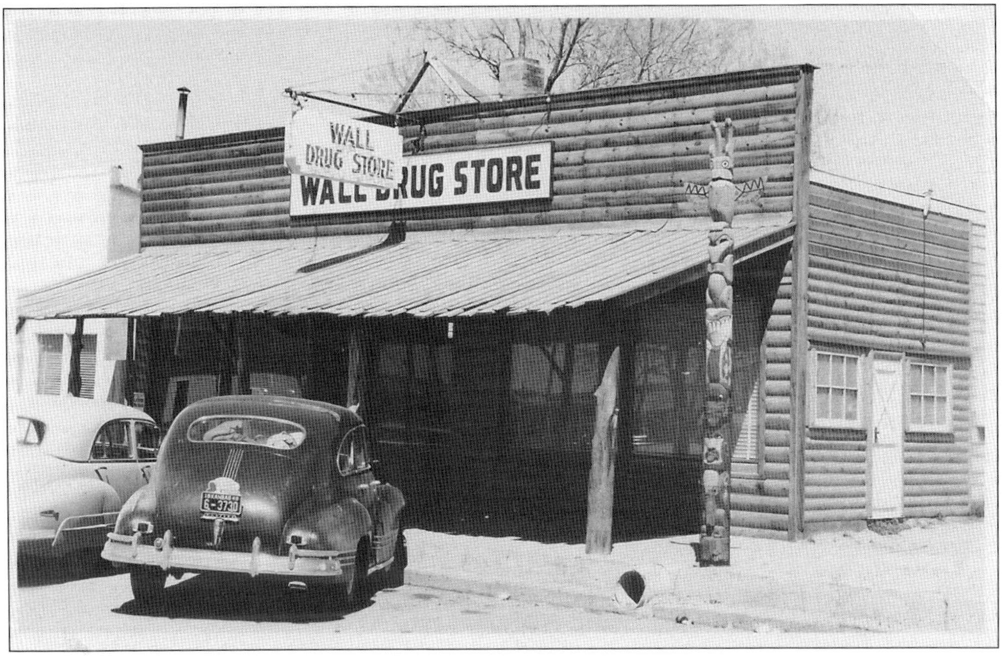

The Husteads moved their business to another building. They had been living in the back of the drugstore, which proved to be drafty and cold. When the Odd Fellows Hall came up for sale across the street, they purchased it. The business also grew in size, incorporating neighboring stores that closed their doors due to the economic conditions. Ted and Dorothy's descendents continue to offer free ice water plus a whole lot more for the traveling public. On a good summer day, Wall Drug draws in up to 20,000 visitors and estimates that it gives away 5,000 glasses of ice water during the tourist season. (Both, courtesy of Wall Drug.)

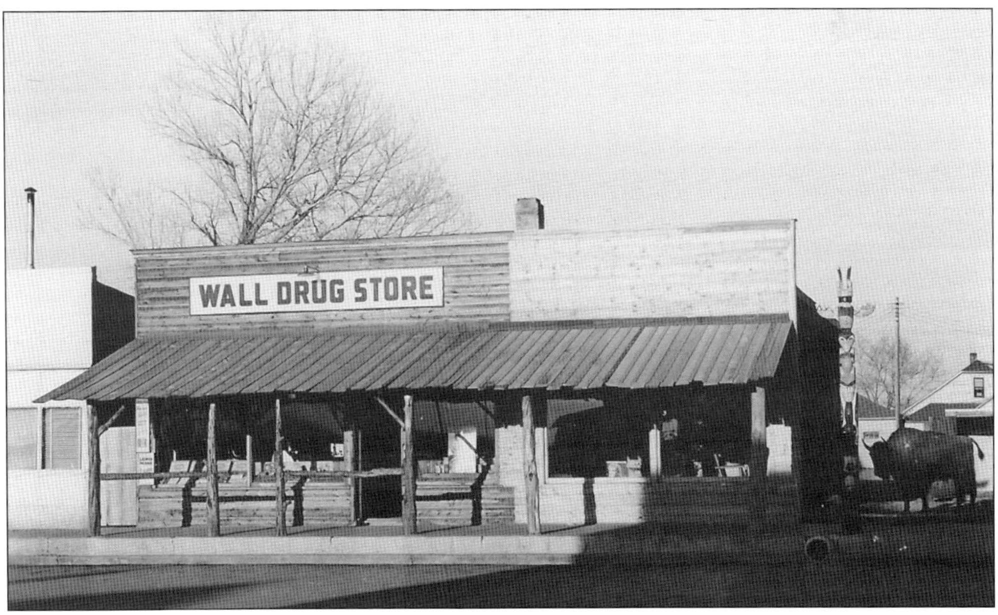

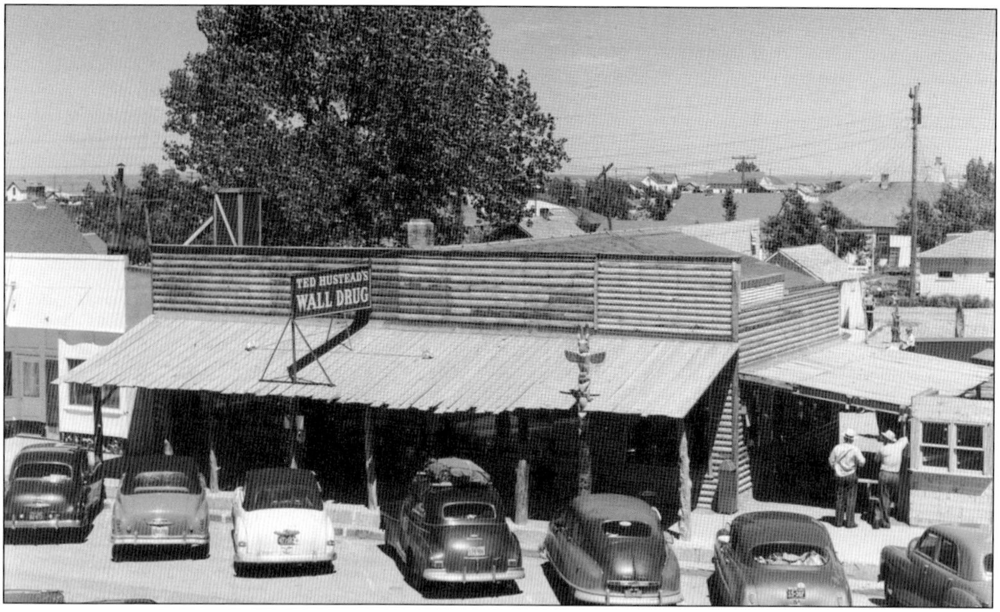

The automobiles date these images to the 1950s. Wall Drug expanded as the tourists increased, offering more for them to see and enjoy. It has been 20 years since Dorothy Hustead made up a slogan to entice travelers off the road into Wall: "Get a soda . . . Get root beer . . . Turn next corner . . . Just as near . . . To Highway 16 & 14 . . . Free Ice Water . . . Wall Drug." In 1954, Wall Drug occupied this small building, but it was a busy one. The rustic front carried over through the many additions to the drugstore. A totem pole was added. A fireworks store is located next door in the image below, taken by Canedy's Camera Shop. (Both, courtesy of Wall Drug.)

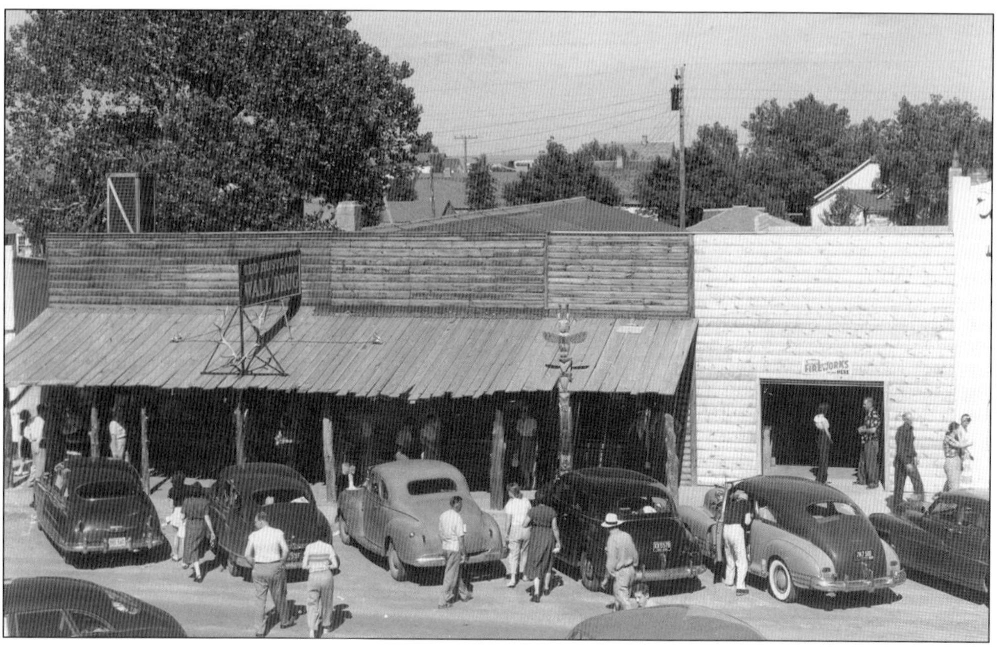

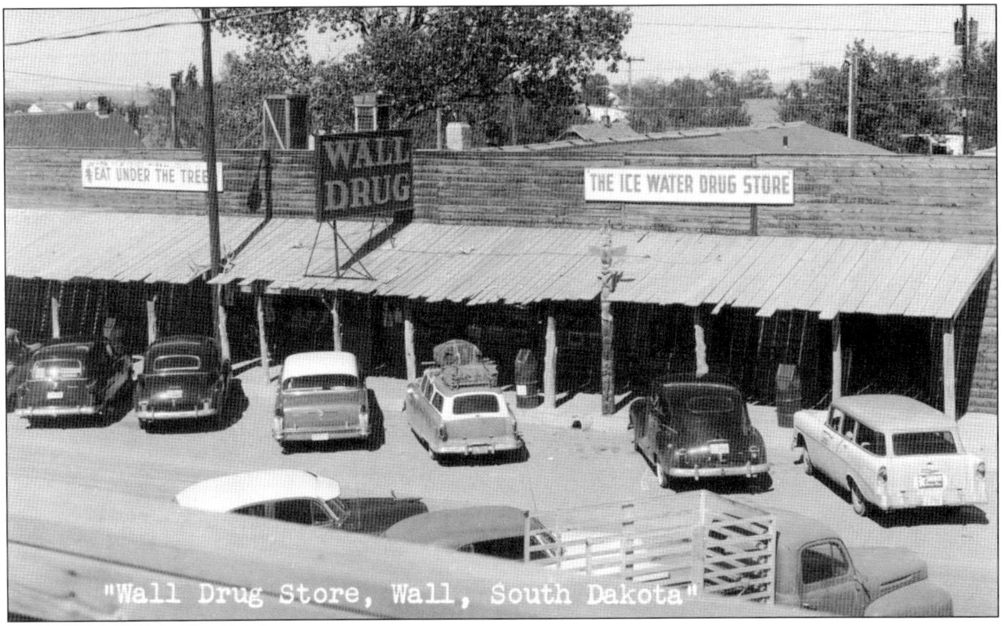

Tourists inundate the town of Wall during tourist season. There are two reasons they divert from I-90. Wall is at the west entrance to the Badlands, and Wall Drug is located here. Wall Drug's advertising signs along I-90 and other highways draw tourists in to see what they could be missing. The free ice water does not pull them in as it used to when traveling was a hot and dusty affair, but there are other attractions today. Artwork, historical photographs, singing cowboys, good food, souvenirs, and a facsimile of Western culture all entice them for a stop. Of course, there are also T-shirts and Wall Drug donuts!

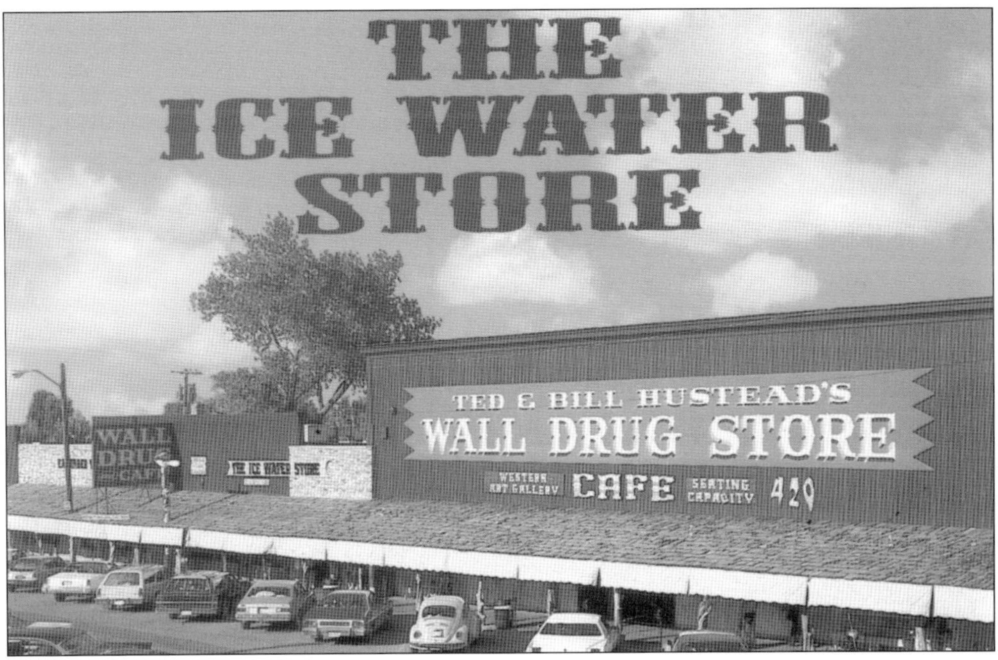

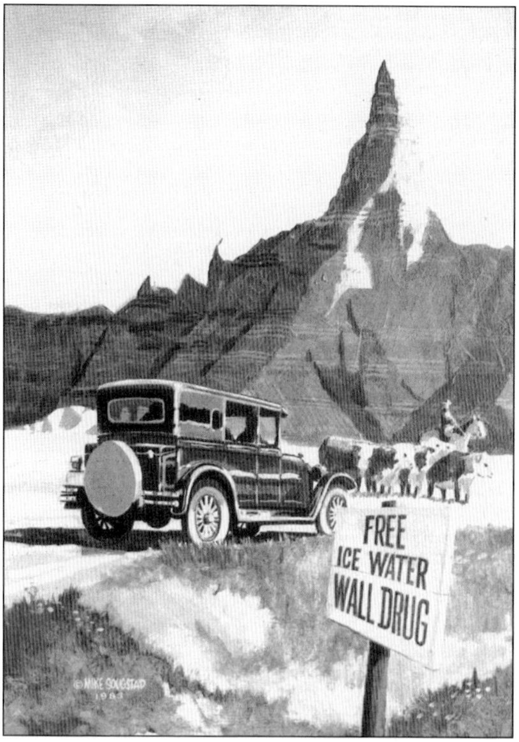

Mike Sougstad painted this picture to depict early tourists about to visit Wall Drug. The free ice water sign was Dorothy Hustead's idea to get tourists to pull off the road and visit the town of Wall. Because of it, Wall Drug is now known around the world. (Courtesy of Wall Drug.)

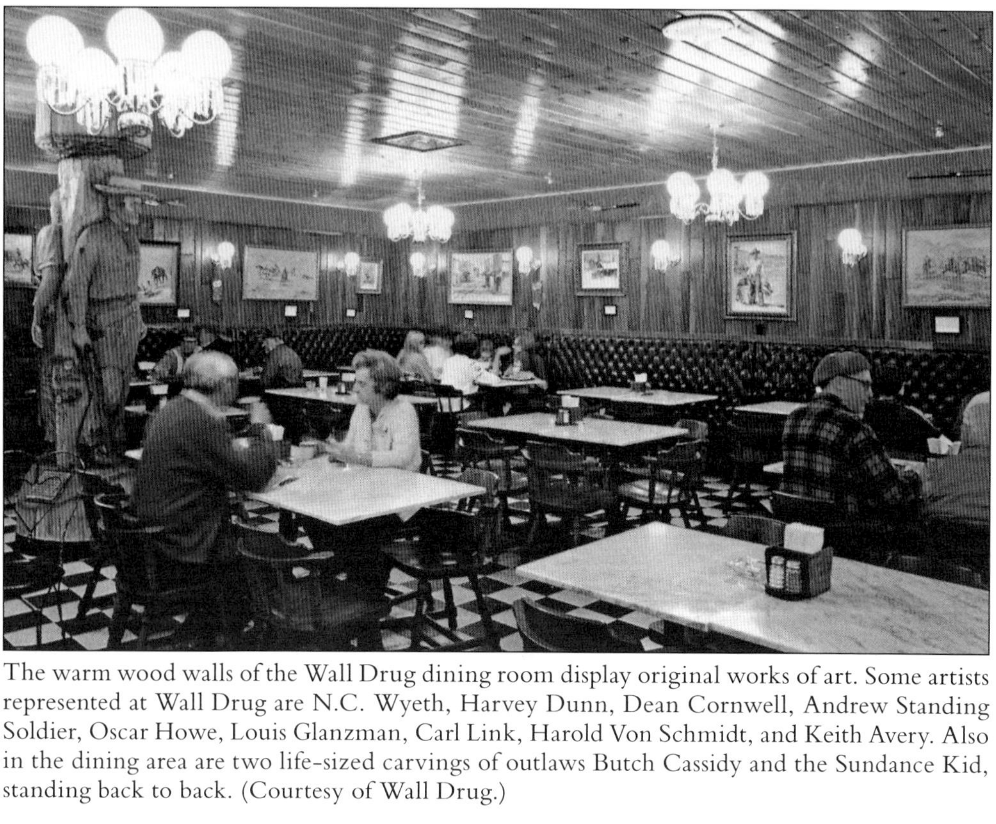

The warm wood walls of the Wall Drug dining room display original works of art. Some artists represented at Wall Drug are N.C. Wyeth, Harvey Dunn, Dean Cornwell, Andrew Standing Soldier, Oscar Howe, Louis Glanzman, Carl Link, Harold Von Schmidt, and Keith Avery. Also in the dining area are two life-sized carvings of outlaws Butch Cassidy and the Sundance Kid, standing back to back. (Courtesy of Wall Drug.)

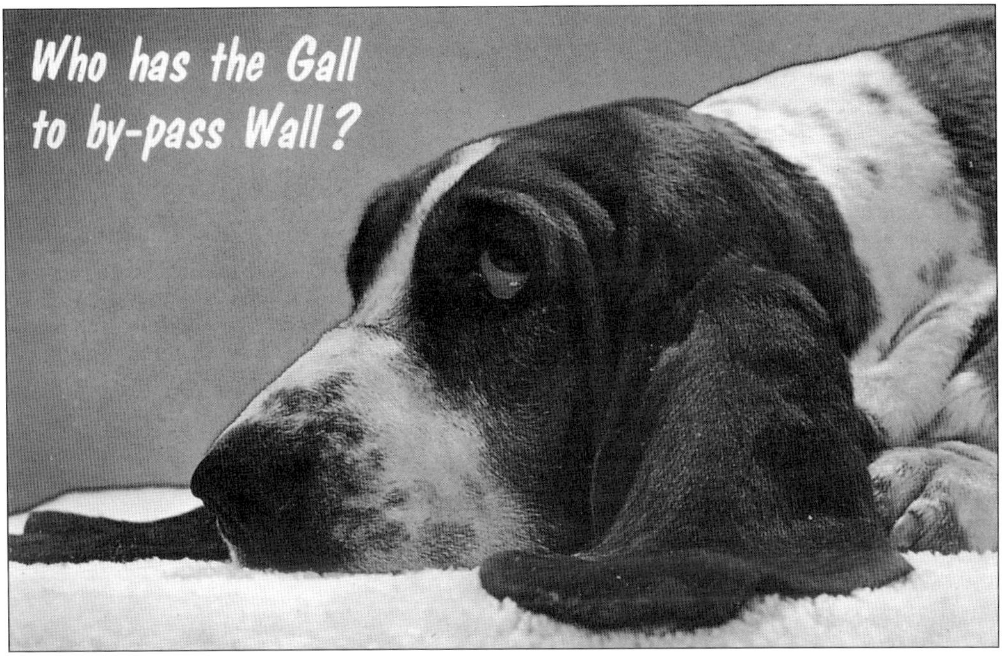

Wall Drug advertises on the reverse side of the postcard above that "Wall Drug is at the Gateway to the Badlands National Park and just off I-90, the main highway to Mount Rushmore. Wall is where you learn, 'How the West Was Fun!' " Wall Drug carried this motto through various displays and activities in their "backyard." The backyard is one big photo opportunity, including a giant jackalope, a Mount Rushmore replica, mining and panning experiences, the shooting gallery arcade, and a life-sized animated T-rex. The jackalope pictured below is claimed to only lay one egg every three years, hence its scarcity. Could it be real? (Both, courtesy of Wall Drug.)

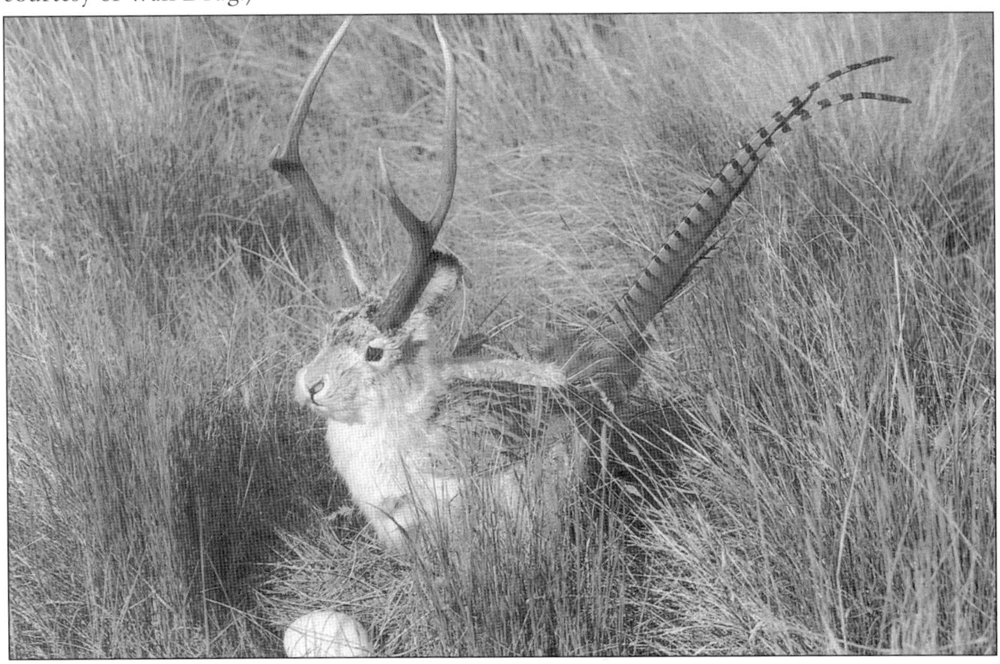

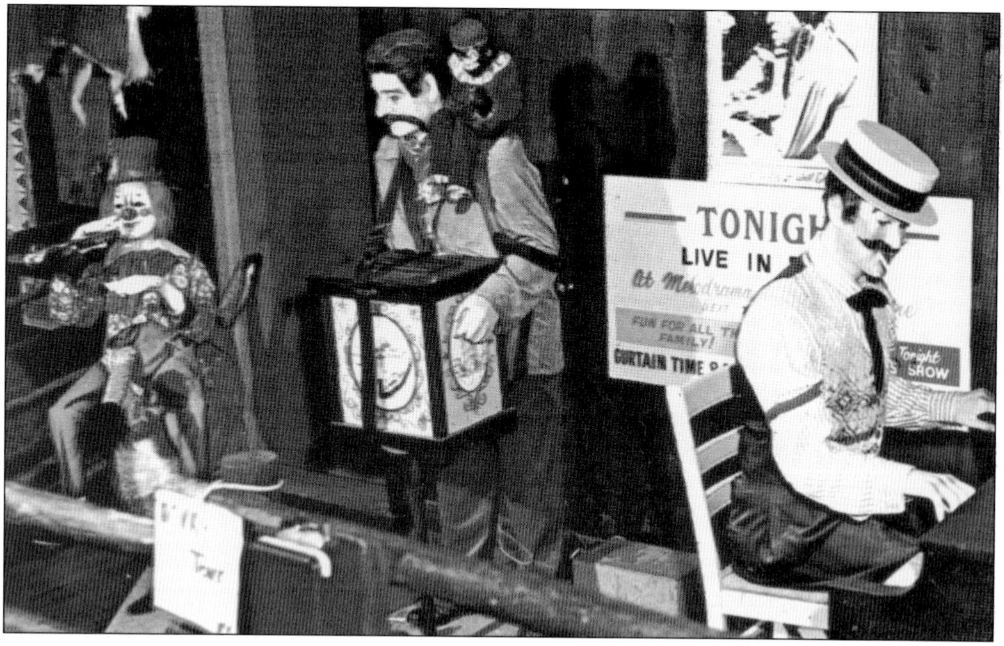

Attractions in Wall Drug's backyard have changed over the years, with many updates including the shooting gallery pictured above. Around the perimeter are spouting water fountains, a jackalope, a giant rabbit, a stagecoach, a bucking horse, and a covered wagon. A mining and panning experience, toy emporium, and food are available inside at the Prairie Food Parlor. There is also an outstanding collection of historical photographs that the Husteads have collected. The main street of the Wall Drug Mall suggests a typical Western town, complete with a traveler's chapel. Cheyenne River rock paves the indoor street. Native timber and old brick were used to create an Old West feeling outside the shops. (Both, courtesy of Wall Drug.)

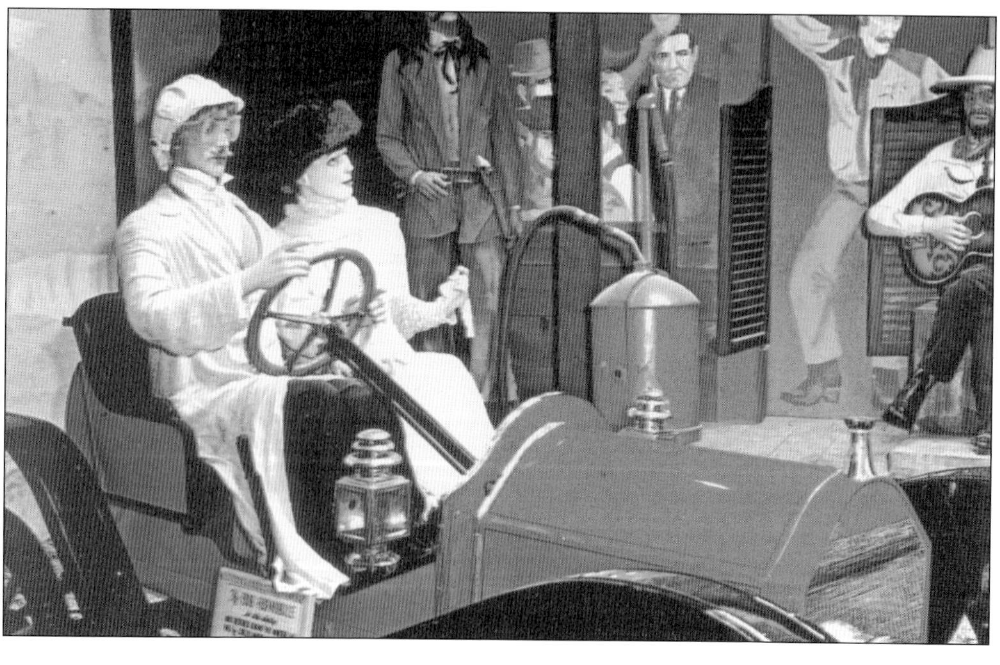

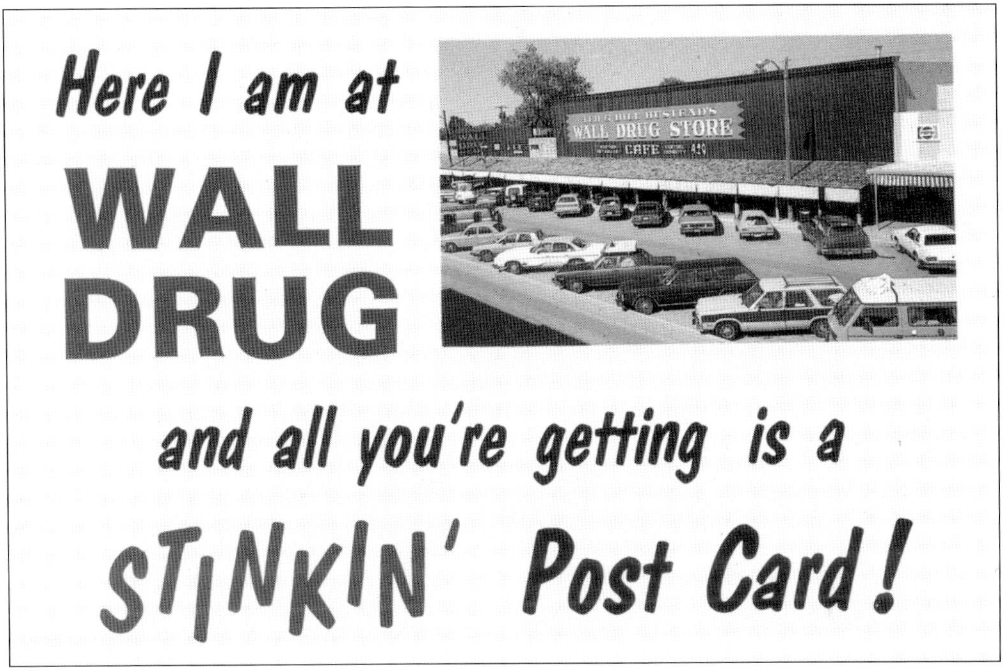

Businesses could order postcards such as the one above and personalize them by changing the name and image. Tourists fill Main Street during the season. Not only is ice water still free, but coffee is a bargain. The postcard below states that 5¢ coffee is available; it still sells for a nickel today. The message on the reverse reads, "Like these two . . . After 4,000+ miles, none of us can stand tall, either!" The illustration was taken from an original drawing by Gerald Farm of Farmington, New Mexico. (Both, courtesy of Wall Drug.)

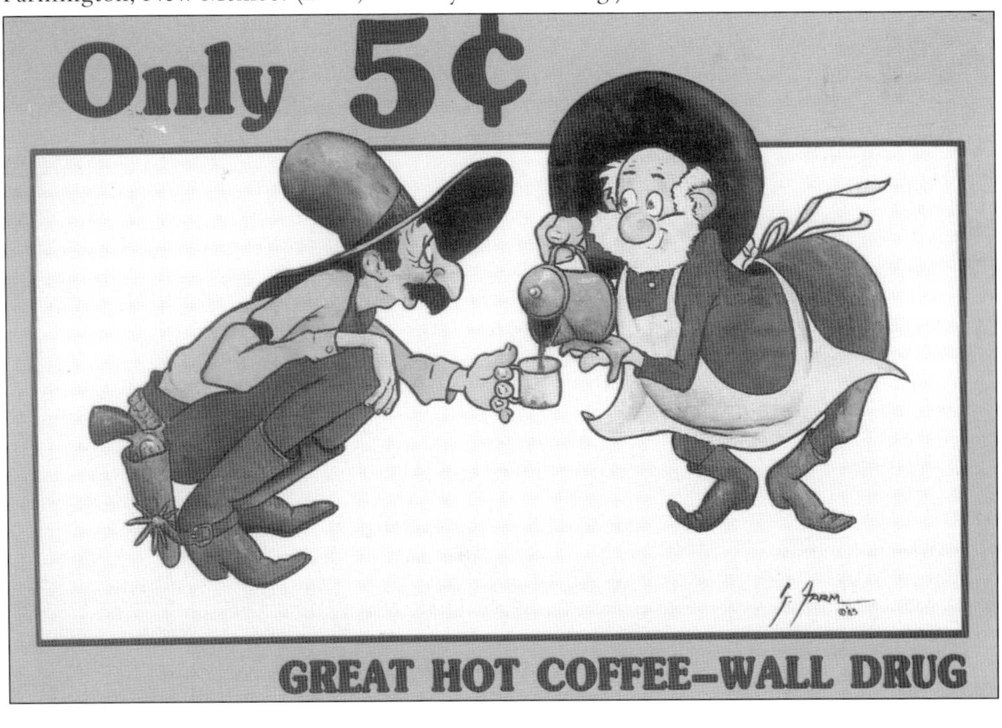

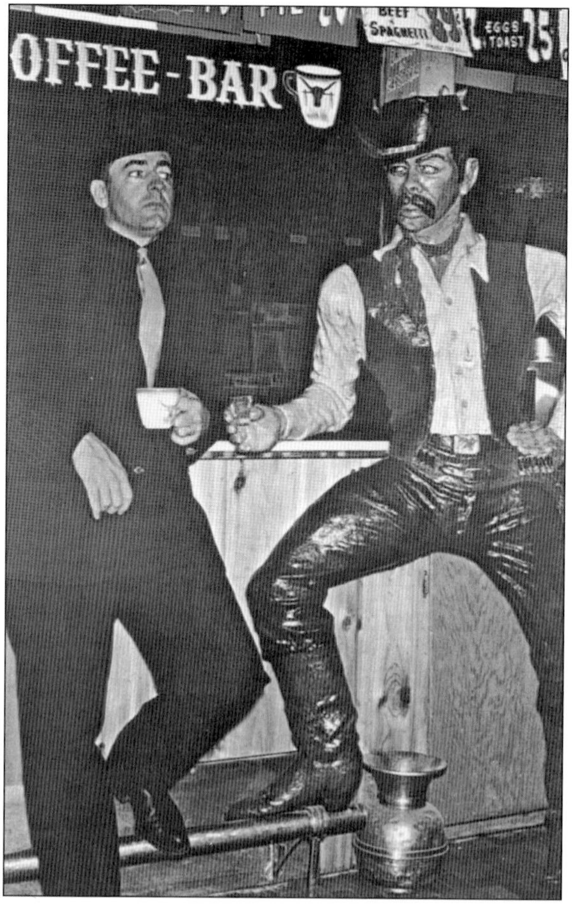

A visitor poses with 5¢ coffee at the Silver Dollar Bar along with one of the many life-sized carvings in Wall Drug. Nearby, Butch Cassidy and the Sundance Kid are carved from a 187-year-old cedar tree. Many tourists and locals stop to take a picture with their favorite. Ranching was an important part of Badlands history and is still ongoing today. Area brands have been burned into wood that is displayed around the perimeter of the dining area. Below, the girl kissing an old-timer is one of many who stop to have their picture taken with him at Wall Drug. (Both, courtesy of Wall Drug.)

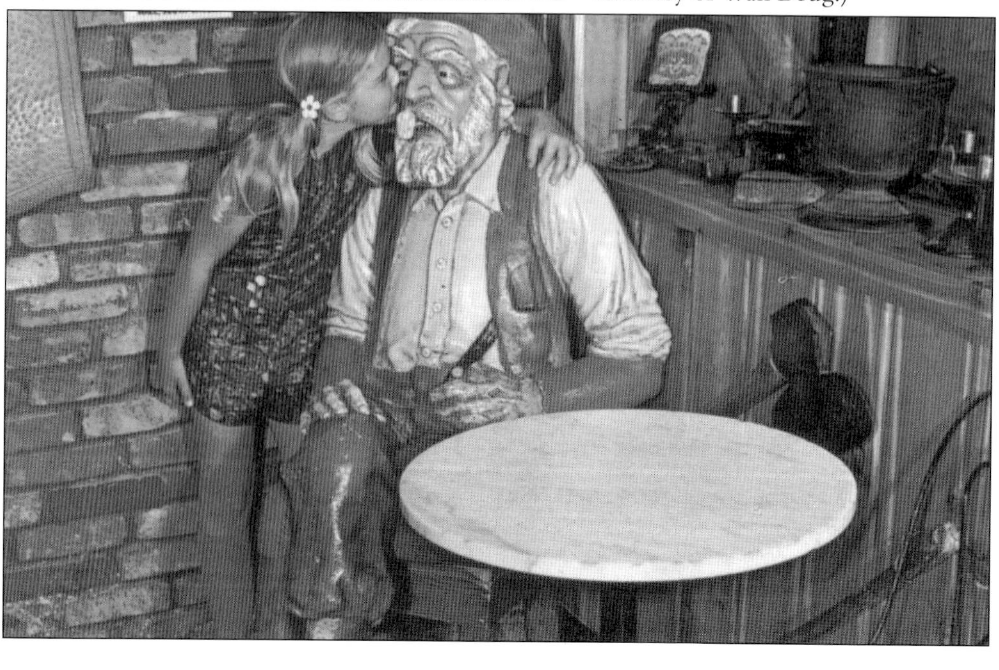

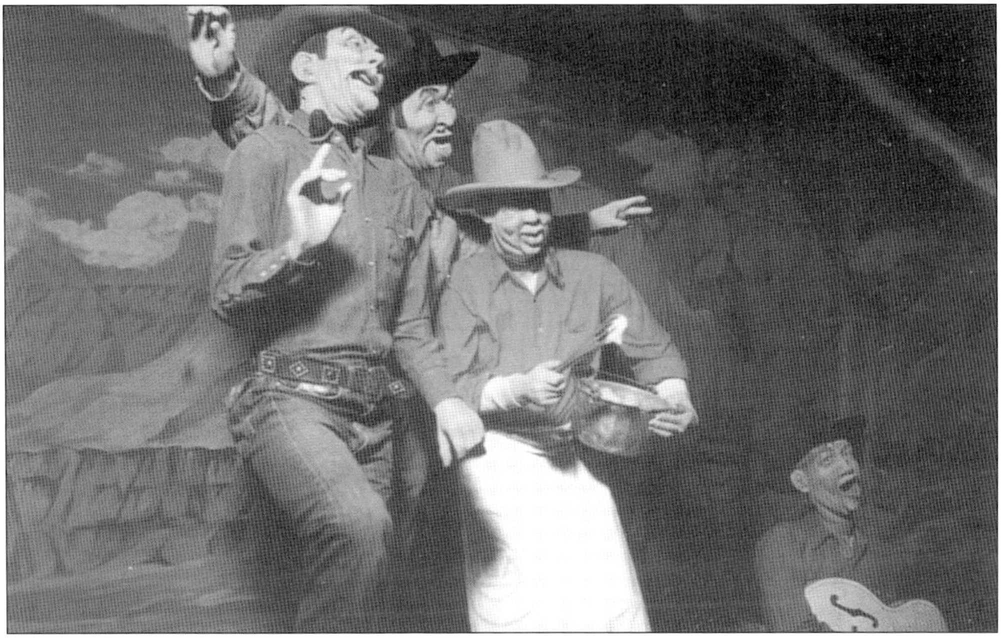

The picture above of the Chuck Wagon Quartet shows the cook stirring up a batch of biscuits. Singing cowboys have long been a feature of Wall Drug. Ted Hustead's Cowboy Orchestra can be seen playing at the front of Wall Drug, while the Chuck Wagon Quartet is at the back of the store. The chuck wagon was a necessity, especially during roundups. It was well stocked with food that a cook would prepare with a whole lot of imagination on his campfire. Beans, potatoes, bacon, and later, canned goods often were the menu for a hungry group of cowpokes. And there was always strong coffee. (Both, courtesy of Wall Drug.)

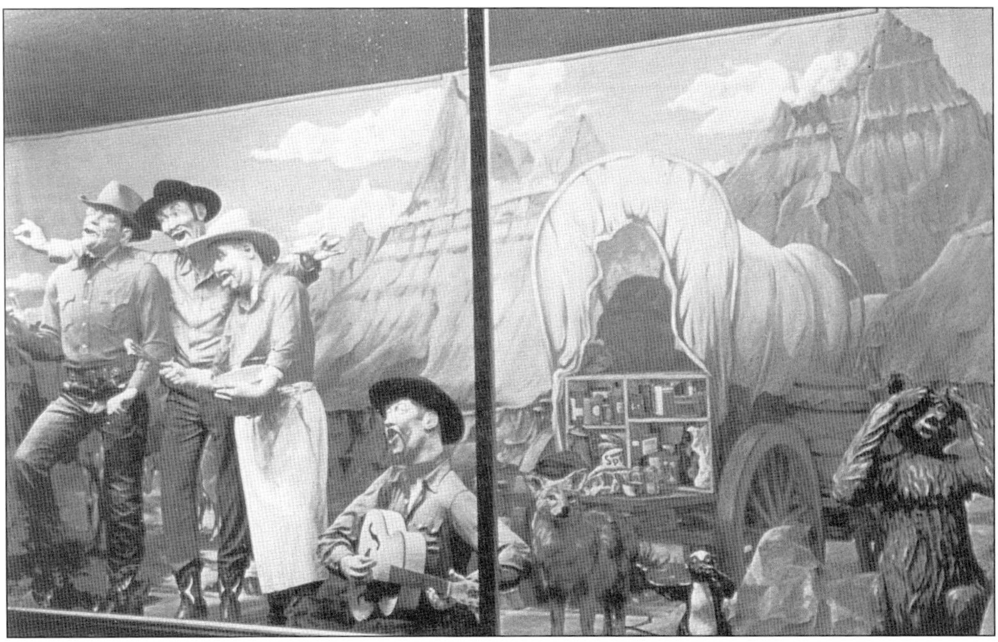

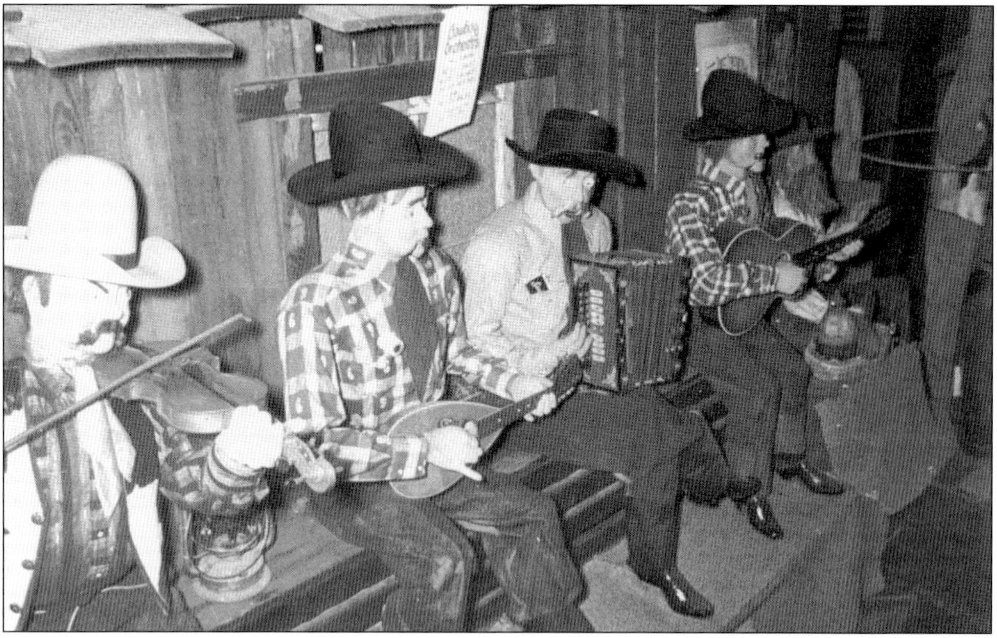

The Cowboy Orchestra plays in the front part of Wall Drug every 10 minutes. Ted Hustead's cowboys play Western songs while one twirls a rope and the hound dog scratches fleas. Music was an important form of entertainment in the wide, open spaces where isolation could wear on a person. Those who could play an instrument were gathered together, and an impromptu band was formed to provide music for dancing. Sometimes the furniture was moved out of a soddy, or claim shack, to make room for a dance floor. Women brought food and children, who fell asleep before the dancing was over. The band often played all night and into the wee hours of the morning. (Both, courtesy of Wall Drug.)

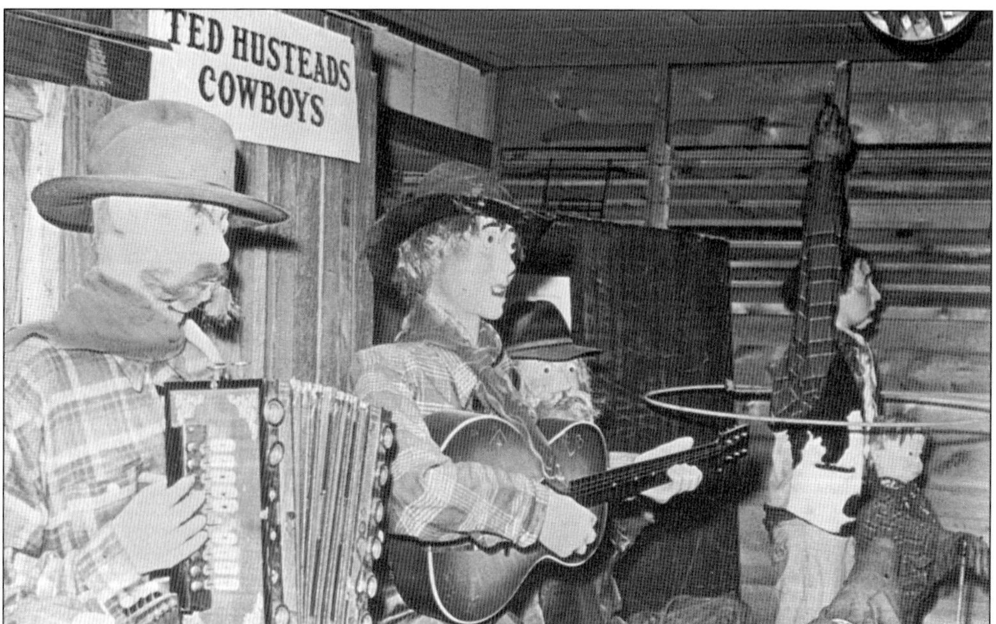

Eight

Ghost Towns

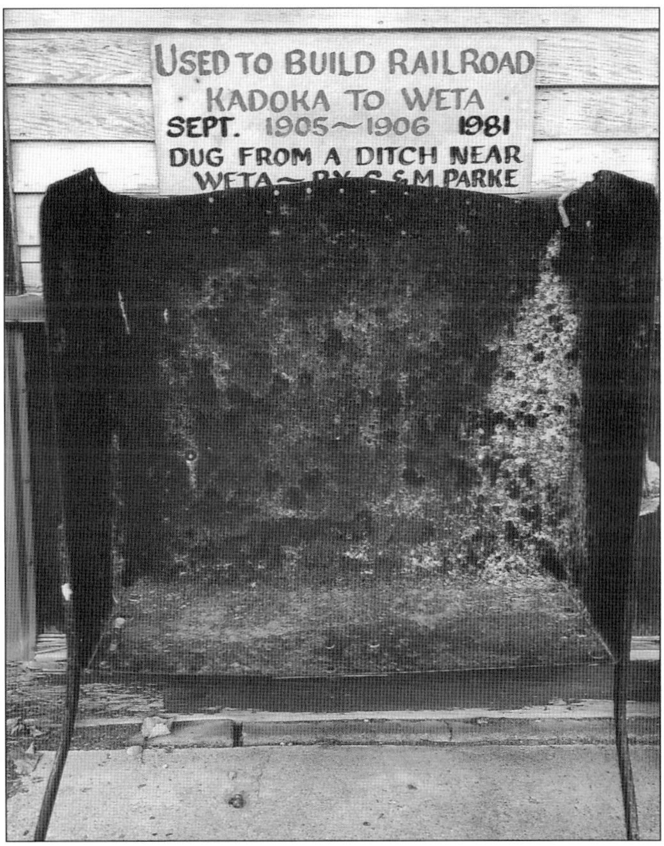

A series of towns sprang up to provide water for the steam engines as the Chicago, Milwaukee & St. Paul Railroad was being built on the lower prairie near the White River. North of the Badlands Wall, the Chicago Northwestern was also laying tracks. Scrapers like this one were used to build the railroad grades. This chapter includes towns built along the tracks. Most have become ghost towns.

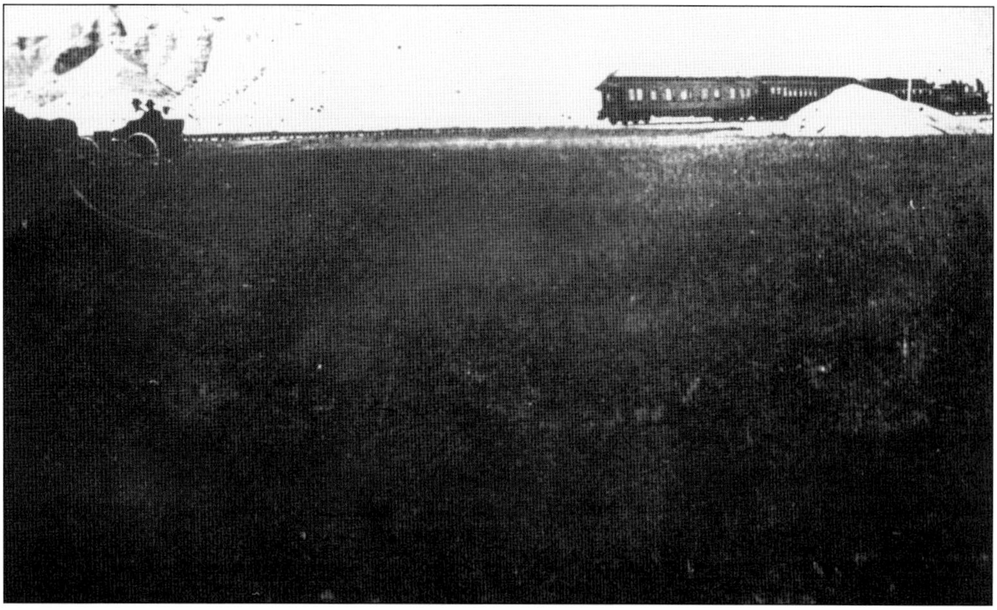

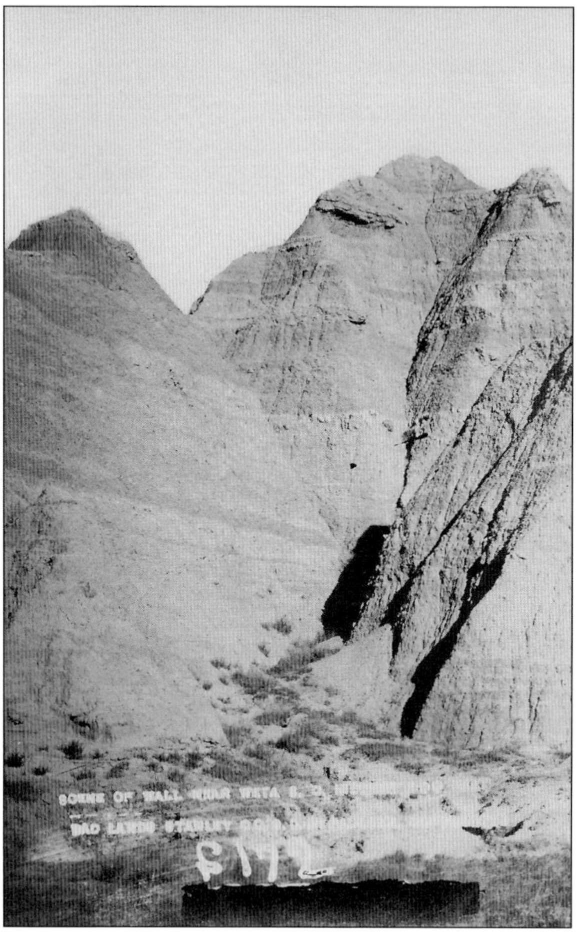

A Chicago, Milwaukee & St. Paul train enters the Badlands. The railroad had extended its line from Chamberlain to the Badlands area in 1907. To the north, the Chicago Northwestern also sold town lots and a line of towns grew. Most of these railroad towns faded into the landscape over the next 30 to 50 years. At one time, these towns were important to the settlers who moved into this unsettled country

This section of the Badlands Wall, considered an obstruction to travel, was photographed near Weta in the early 1900s. The Chicago, Milwaukee & St. Paul built below the wall and reached Weta in 1907, bringing an influx of homesteaders with it. Cattle were also trailed from great distances to be shipped to market on the trains.

Water was a problem in the Badlands. People who lived near the White River could dig wells, but those homesteaders who did not hauled water in barrels. To supply water for the steam engines, the railroad built the Weta dam. Water was pumped from a pump house to a water tank west of the depot, which was located at the south end of Weta's Main Street. Area residents hauled water from the water tank or from a brick cistern with a pump in the center of Main Street. Schools, churches, and businesses were established rapidly; however, the 1930s drought years accelerated Weta's demise. The post office closed in 1936, the depot was sold to Jackson County and moved to Kadoka next to the telephone office, and other buildings were either moved off or dismantled. (Right, courtesy of Bernard and Barbara Herber; below, courtesy of the Kadoka Depot Museum.)

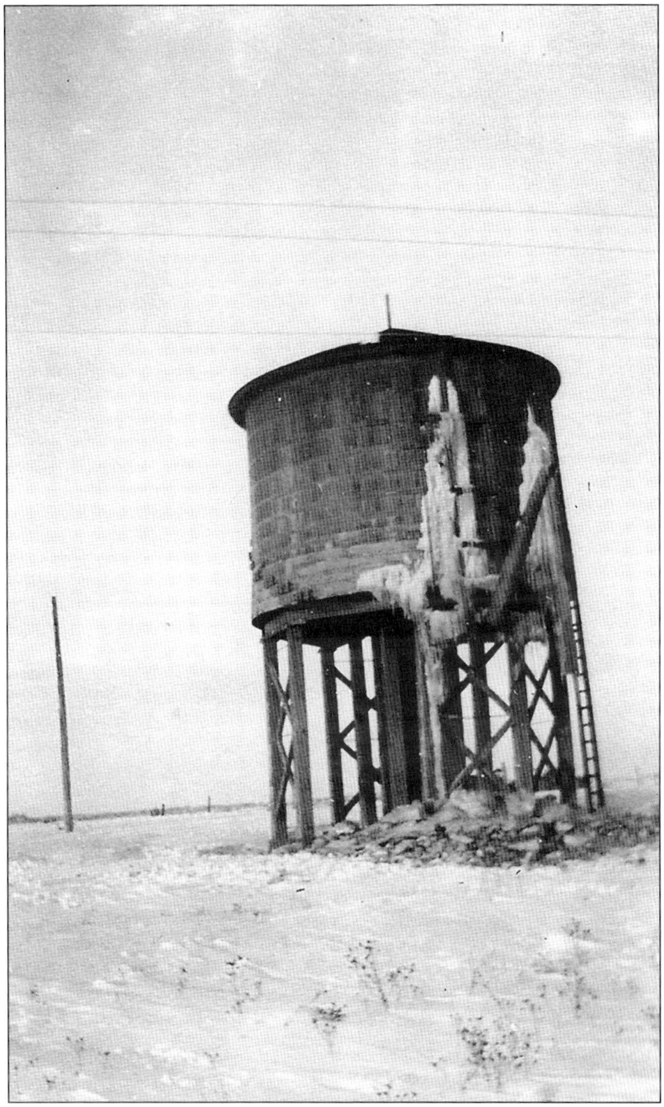

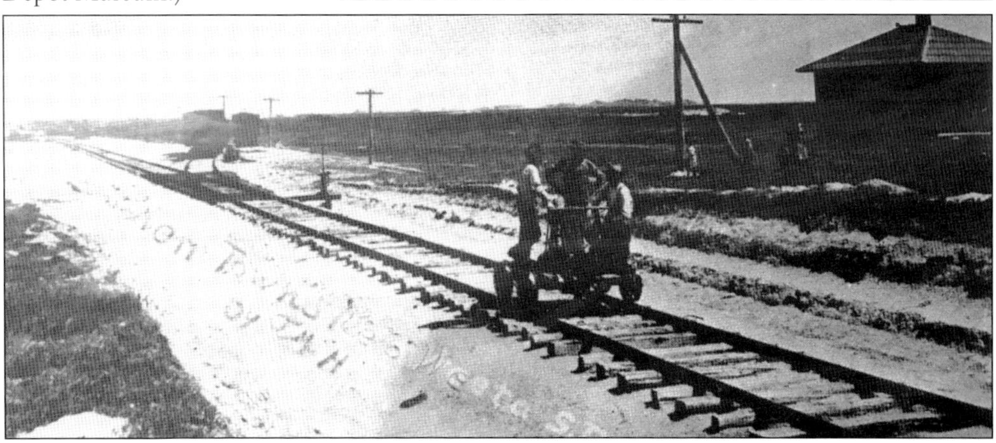

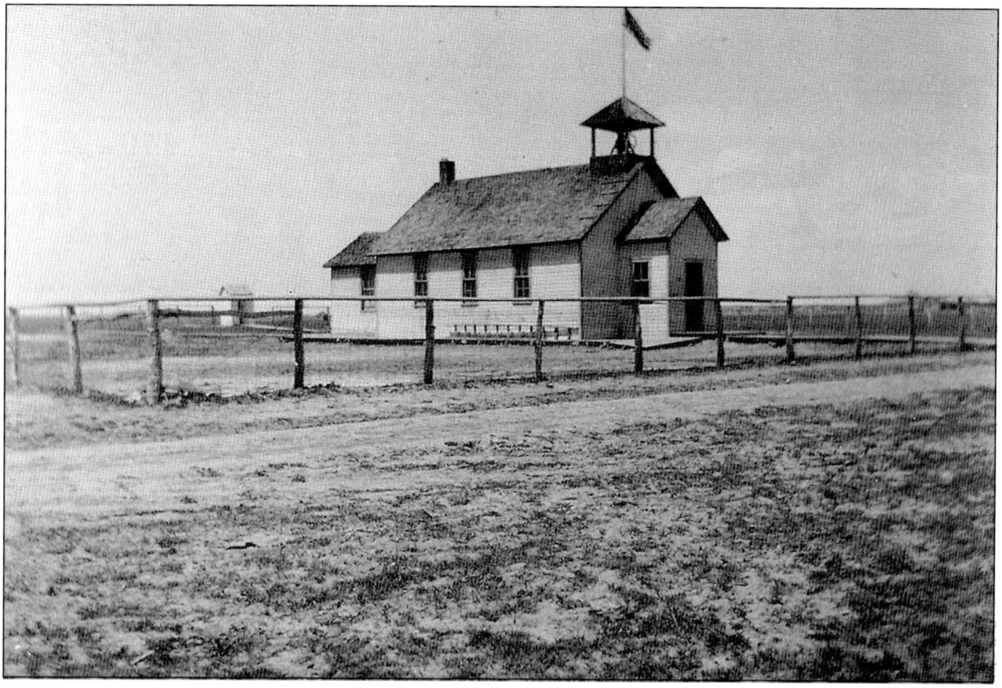

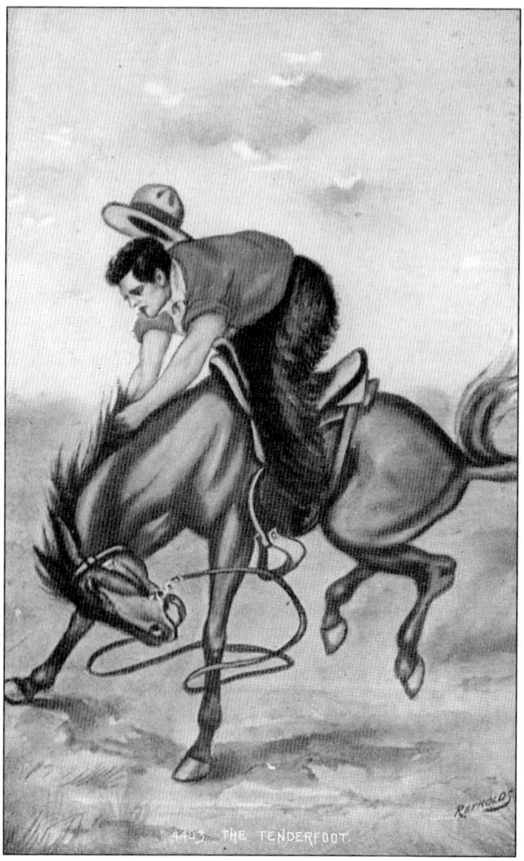

Located on the north end of Main Street, the school provided ample room for 40 students. It included three large classrooms, a large hall, and full basement. The school employed one high school teacher and two grade school teachers. The superintendant lived in two rooms in the basement. A long barn was provided to house the students' saddle horses during the day. School activities such as plays and debates were held in the nearby town hall. Entitled "The Tenderfoot," the postcard at left was not indicative of the region's populace. Riding a horse was paramount to living in the West. Not only was a horse necessary for transportation and gathering and working cattle, they also provided entertainment. Rodeos and roping events were held to show off hard-earned skills. Children either walked to school or rode horses. (Above, courtesy of Bernard and Barbara Herber; left, author's collection.)

The Christian church held the first church services in Weta. When J.C. McReynolds organized the Methodist church pictured at right, the Christian church was absorbed into it. The Methodist church was constructed in 1914, but drought conditions caused it to be sold. Rev. Thomas J. McNaboe, a Catholic priest from Kadoka, offered services to the towns along the railroad between Murdo and Rapid City, including Okaton, Stamford, Belvidere, Interior, Imlay, Caputa, Scenic, Farmingdale, and Weta. He came to Weta about once a month. The reverend traveled with a table and two large suitcases so he could improvise an altar wherever he offered services, often in a homesteader's shack. The Catholic church pictured below was built in 1918. Some years later, it was struck by lightning and burned. (Both, courtesy of Bernard and Barbara Herber.)

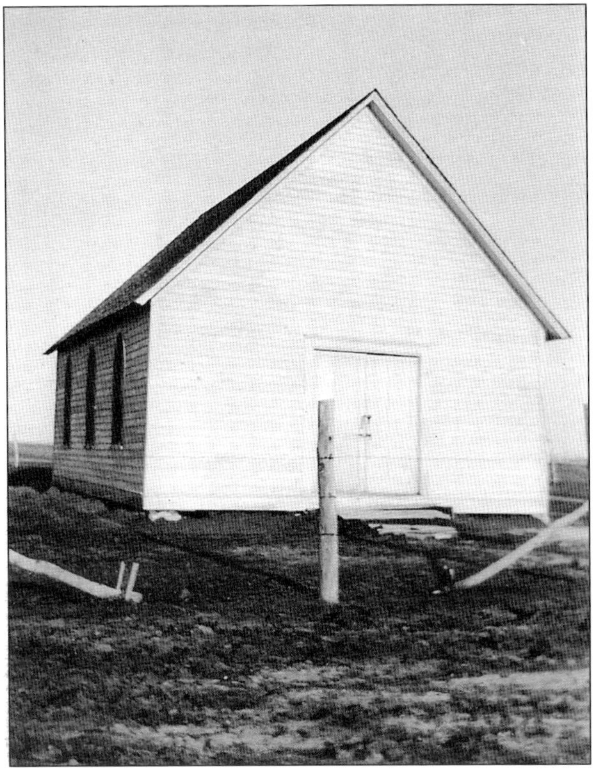

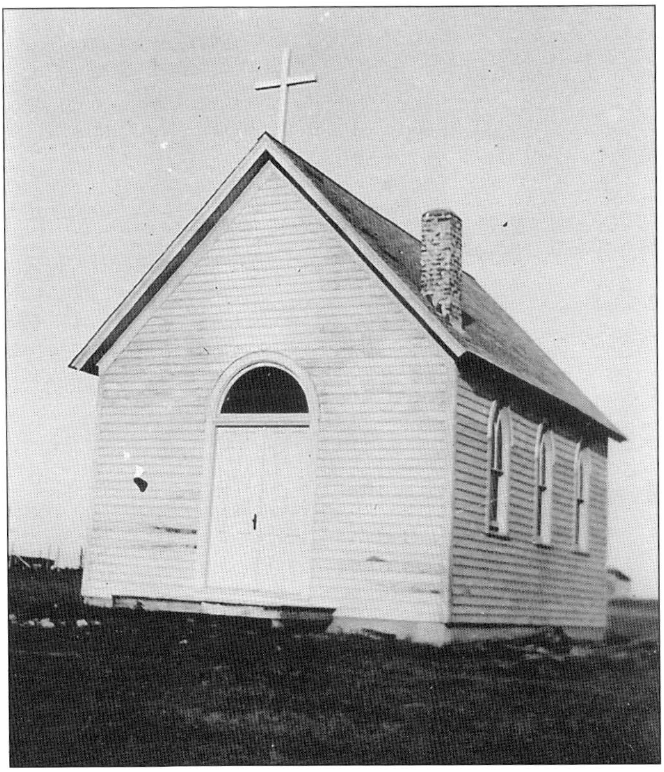

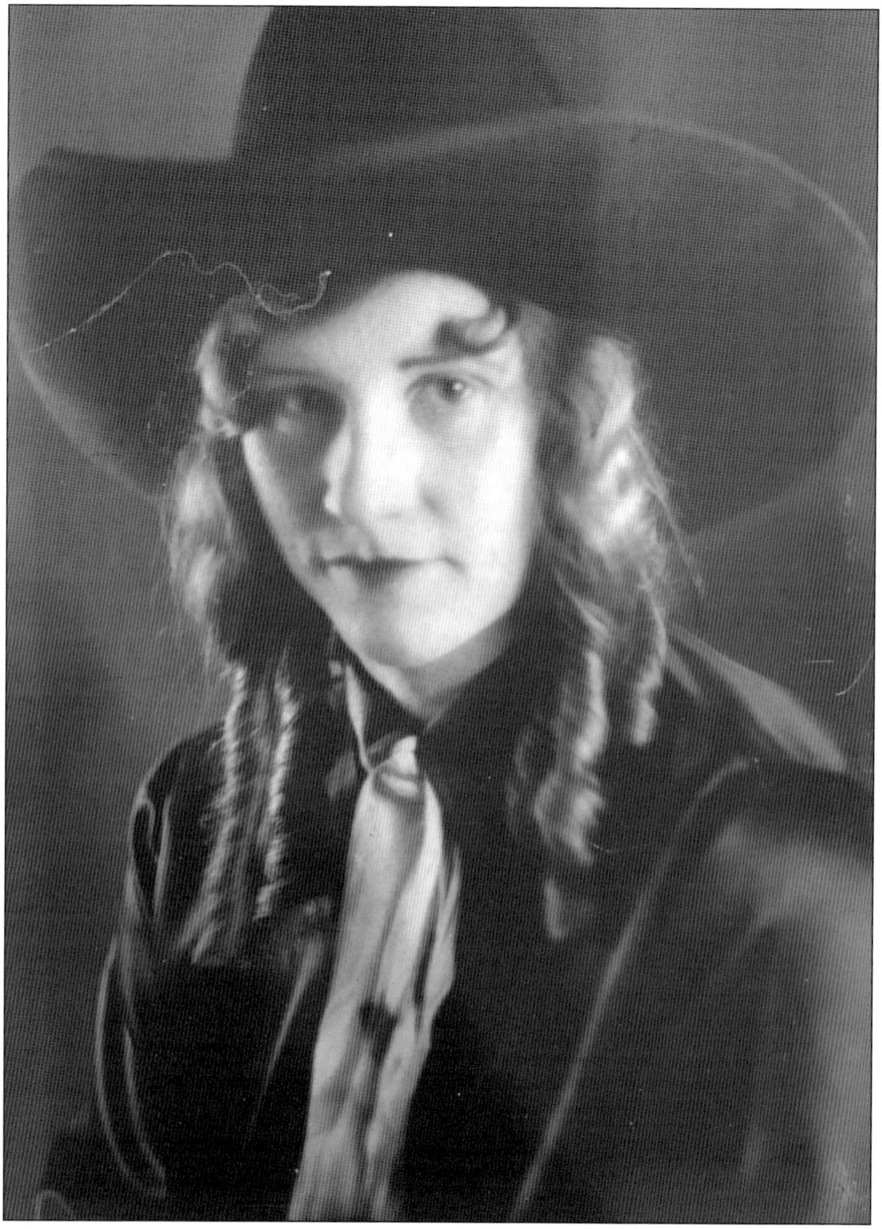

Pictured is Madge Runyan, the daughter of Walt and Viola Runyan of Weta. The Runyans operated a show troupe and put on Western shows in South Dakota, Nebraska, and Iowa. They also purchased land at the foot of Chamberlain Pass west of Kadoka across from the Sugar Loaf landmark. Walt constructed a set of buildings and a half-mile racetrack where all sorts of races were run, providing entertainment for the neighborhood. The daughters rode in races, mounted quadrilles, and also did trick riding. Madge drove in the chariot races. The family traveled one year with the 101 Ranch Show. Madge began riding the rodeo circuit when she was 16 but a series of misfortunes caused her to retire. Her sister Grayce rode broncs at 16, became world champion in 1926, and went on to win five championships. Other early national rodeo champions from the area were Eddie Seidler and Earl (Hans) Thode. The region continues to produce many rodeo champions.

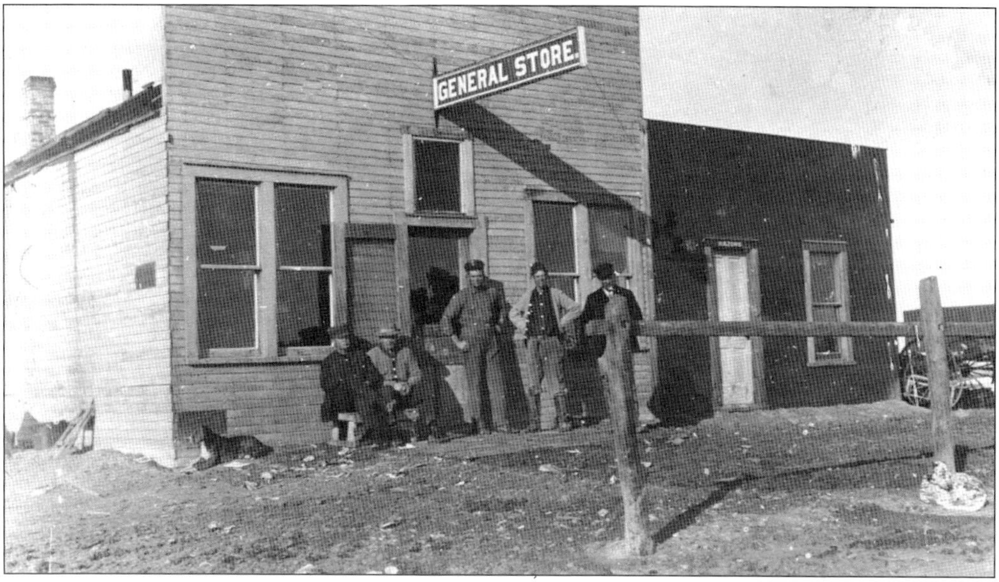

After Weta, the next stop for the train was Interior and then Conata. The Conata Post Office was established in 1908 and closed in 1954. The Dust Bowl of the 1930s drove many away, and when the railroad left in the 1950s, so did the residents. Two spinster sisters, Harriet and Be DeHaan, owned one of two general stores in Conata. The reservoir site marks the town. (Courtesy of Lawrence and Betty Kruse.)

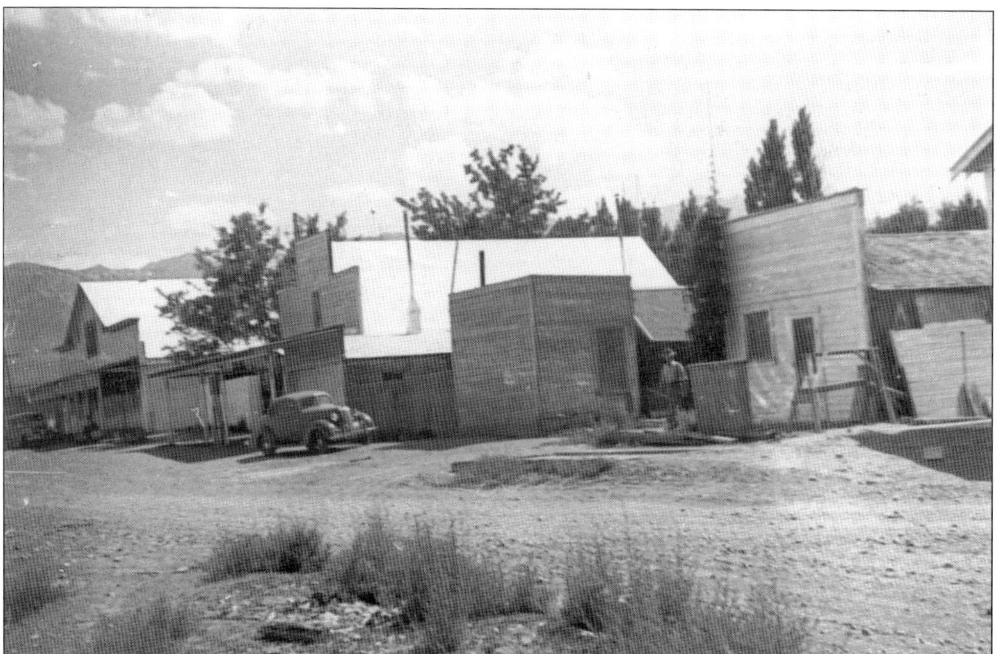

Imlay, another stop on the railroad, provided a set of corrals and loading chutes for the ranchers who trailed cattle to be shipped to market. It was a small town, consisting of a general store, a pool hall, a post office, and a dance hall. However, a murder rocked this small frontier town for a time. (Courtesy of the South Dakota State Historical Society.)

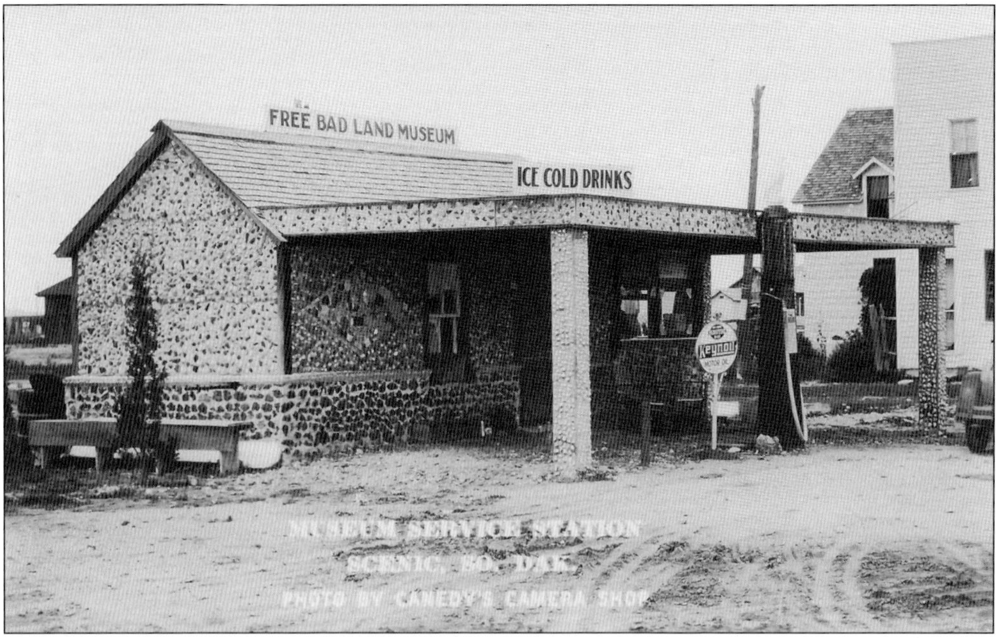

The above 1920s image shows Scenic, South Dakota's, museum and gas station constructed of native rock. The museum was known for its Badlands fossils and Indian artifacts. It also provided guide services to visitors. Below, baculite ovalus and placenticeras, a sample of Badlands fossils, are pictured. Seventy-five million years ago, the Badlands was a shallow inland sea during the Cretaceous Period, laying the foundation known as the Pierre Shale. Ammonites are found in these ancient marine deposits. Concretions must be carefully split open and prepared to reveal the ammonite. Instead of being coiled, baculites are straight and elongated.

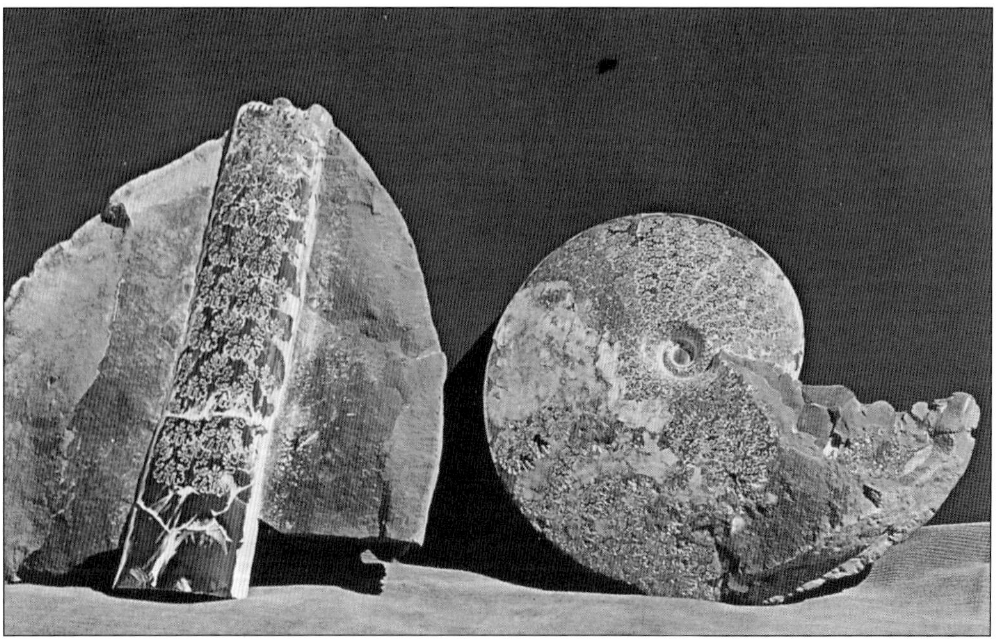

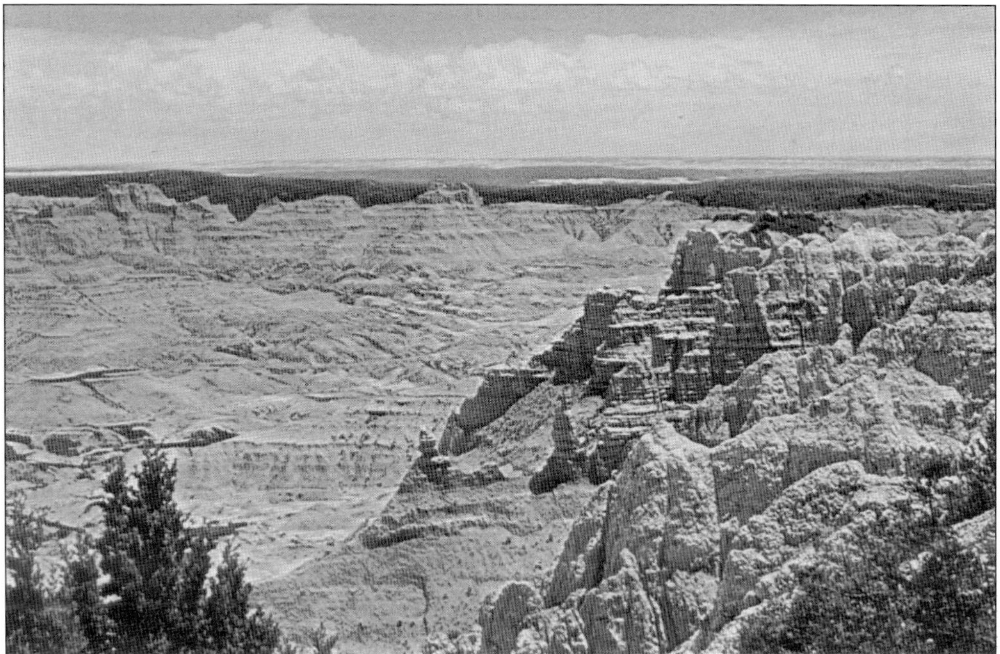

Sheep Mountain, South Dakota Photo by William W. Dunmire

The spectacular scenery of Sheep Mountain, located in the South Unit of the Badlands, is pictured here. Considered to be a beautiful area with its plunging canyons, it is located south of Scenic near the Stronghold Unit, which is co-managed with the Oglala Lakota Sioux. Established in 1906 as a railroad and cow town, Scenic was unincorporated and located just off Highway 44 below Sheep Mountain. The mountain is topped with a large grass mesa.

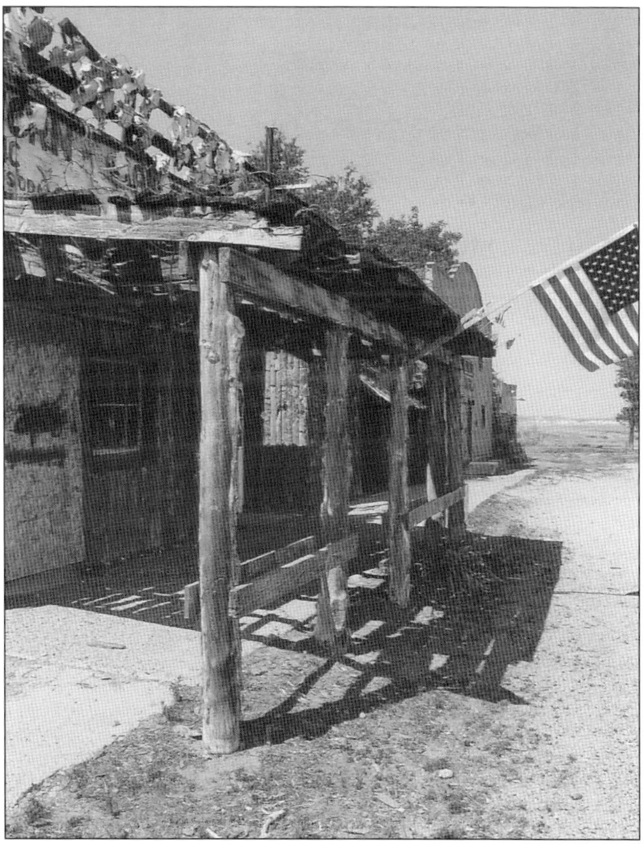

A side view of the Longhorn Saloon shows the front of the Scenic Community Hall, one of the original buildings, which has long been unoccupied. Practically all of the original stores have been moved off, burned, or torn down. Rustic-style buildings took their place, but even these now sit unoccupied.

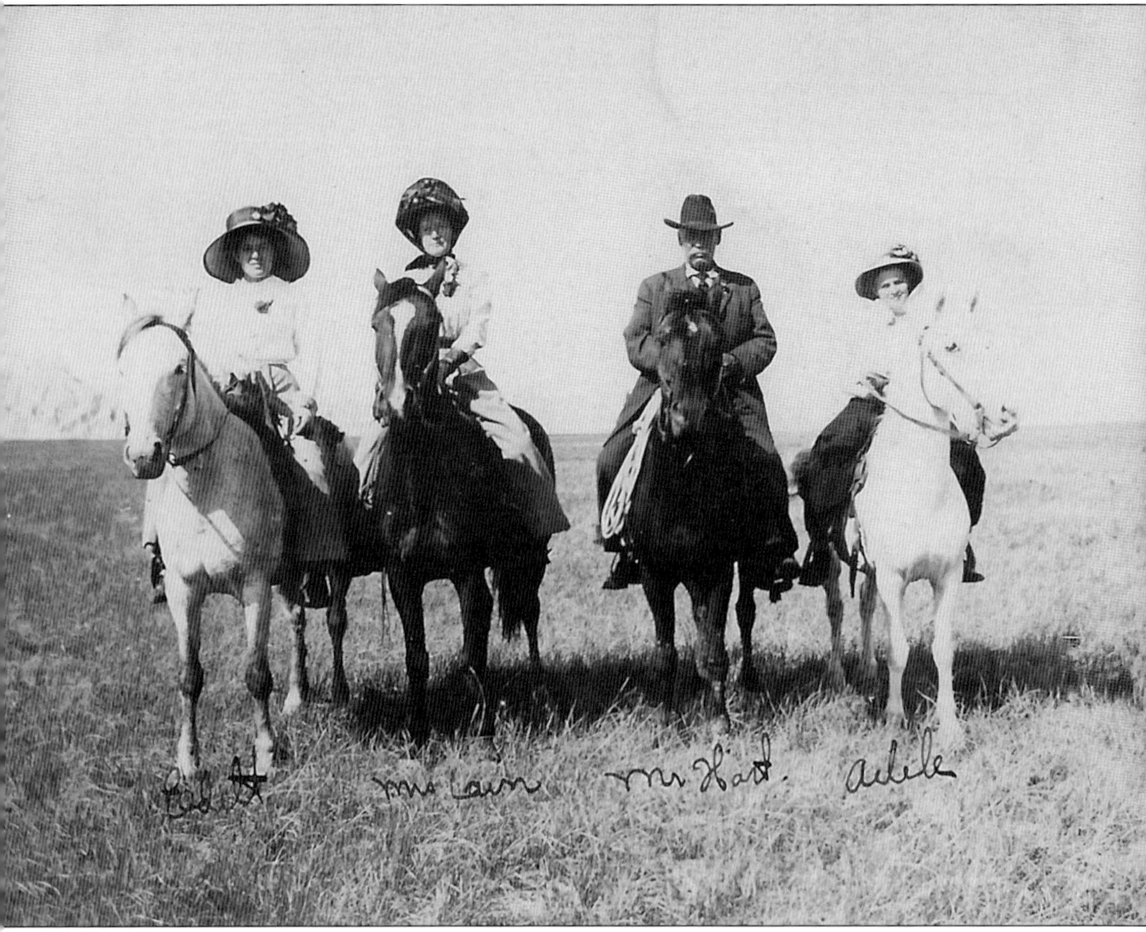

One of the women riders pictured on this postcard mailed from Quinn, South Dakota, in July 1910 penned a message to a man named Fred on the reverse: "Here is a cute picture of a bunch of Western Bums," she writes. "Can you tell my smiling face on it." The foursome was apparently riding near the Badlands, as a portion of them can be seen in the distance on the left. The man identified as Mr. Hart is Frank Hart, a legendary cowpuncher and bronc rider who won two world championships. He was also involved with the Interior Round-ups as a participant and judge. He and his wife, Tenny, settled three miles west of Scenic on a ranch. The train often dropped off passengers at the ranch to enjoy picnics and Fourth of July celebrations and then picked them up on its return trip. Frank's father, John Hart, was an early cattleman living on Spring Creek.

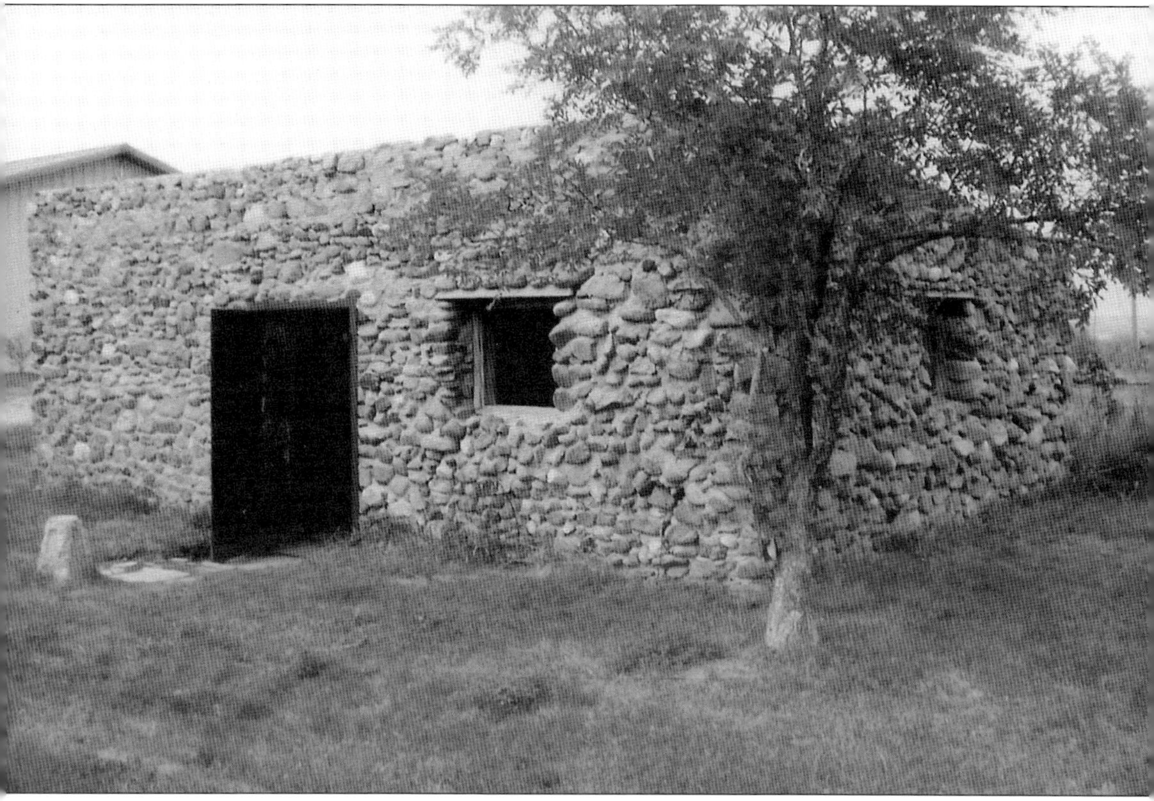

The Great Depression caused many Scenic businesses to shut down and the population to dwindle. When rodeo star Twila Merrill and her husband, Bud, bought the 12-acre town in the 1960s at the urging of her father, only the post office lease, the Longhorn Fuel and Food convenience store, Longhorn Bar and Museum, two houses, and two jails went along with it. Most of the original town had disappeared. An additional 34 acres surrounding the town was also in the deal. The historic stone jail, pictured, was built from local rock. When Twila's health failed, she put the town up for sale. A church from the Philippines purchased the town in 2011, but no one has moved in other than a caretaker. A museum housed in a church, a post office, and a gas station are all that remain in operation.

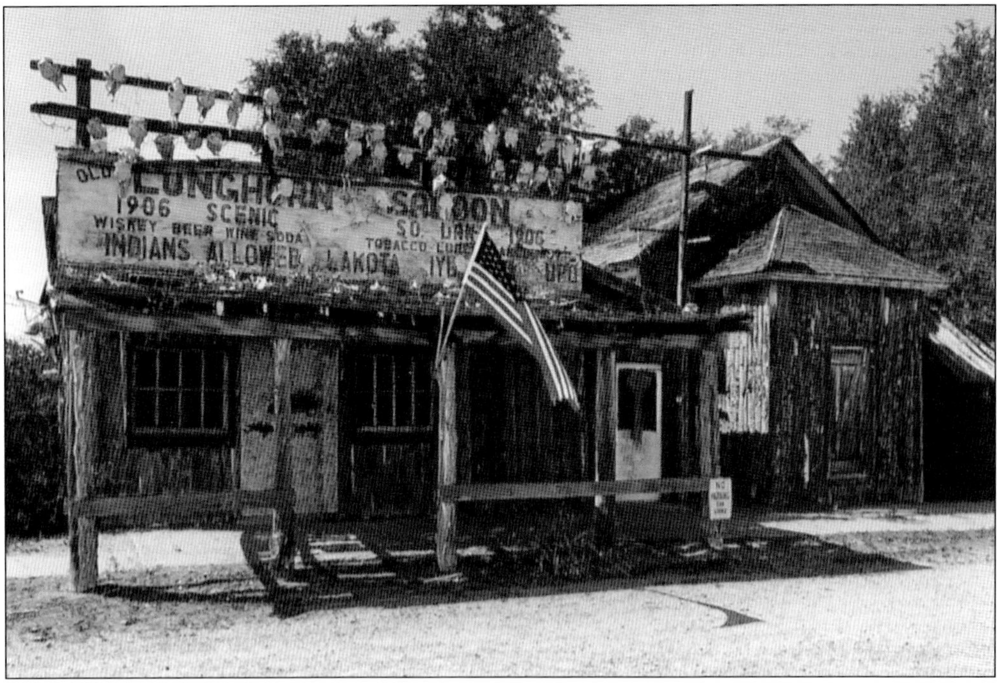

A lot of history and living happened before Scenic became a ghost town. The town, which could be rough and tough at times, sits on the western edge of the Badlands and joined civilization with a bank, a grocery store, two churches, a hotel, and a high school. The Longhorn Saloon, which is pictured here lined with cattle skulls, was a popular landmark. Sawdust covered the floor, and oil barrels with metal tractor seats became the bar stools. A barber chair sat in the middle of the floor in case anyone needed a haircut. Brands from various ranches were painted on ceiling tiles, adding a tribute to the past. The Longhorn Store was built near the saloon.

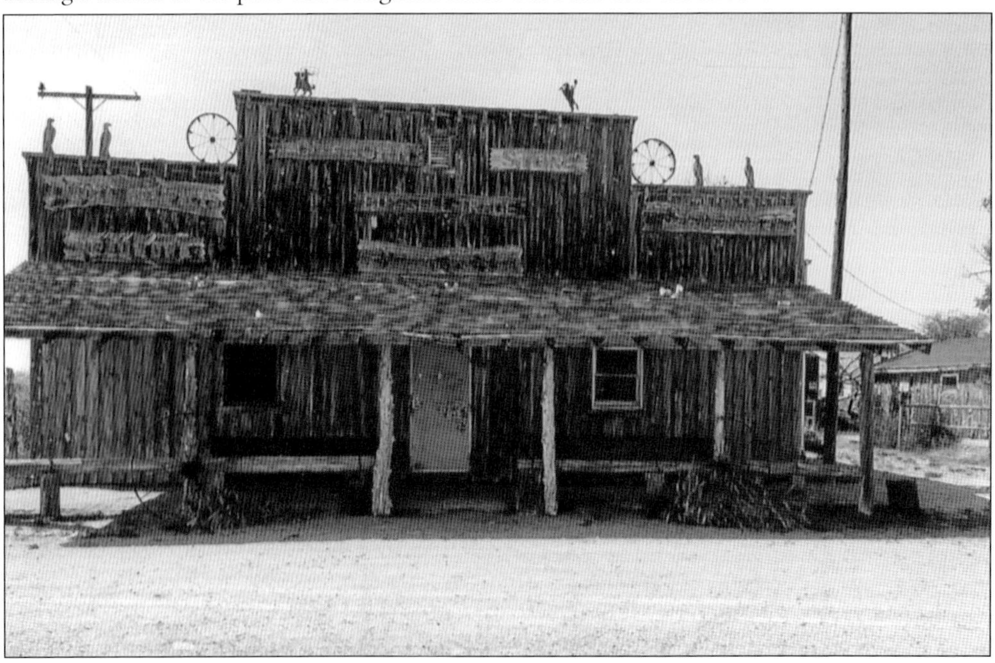

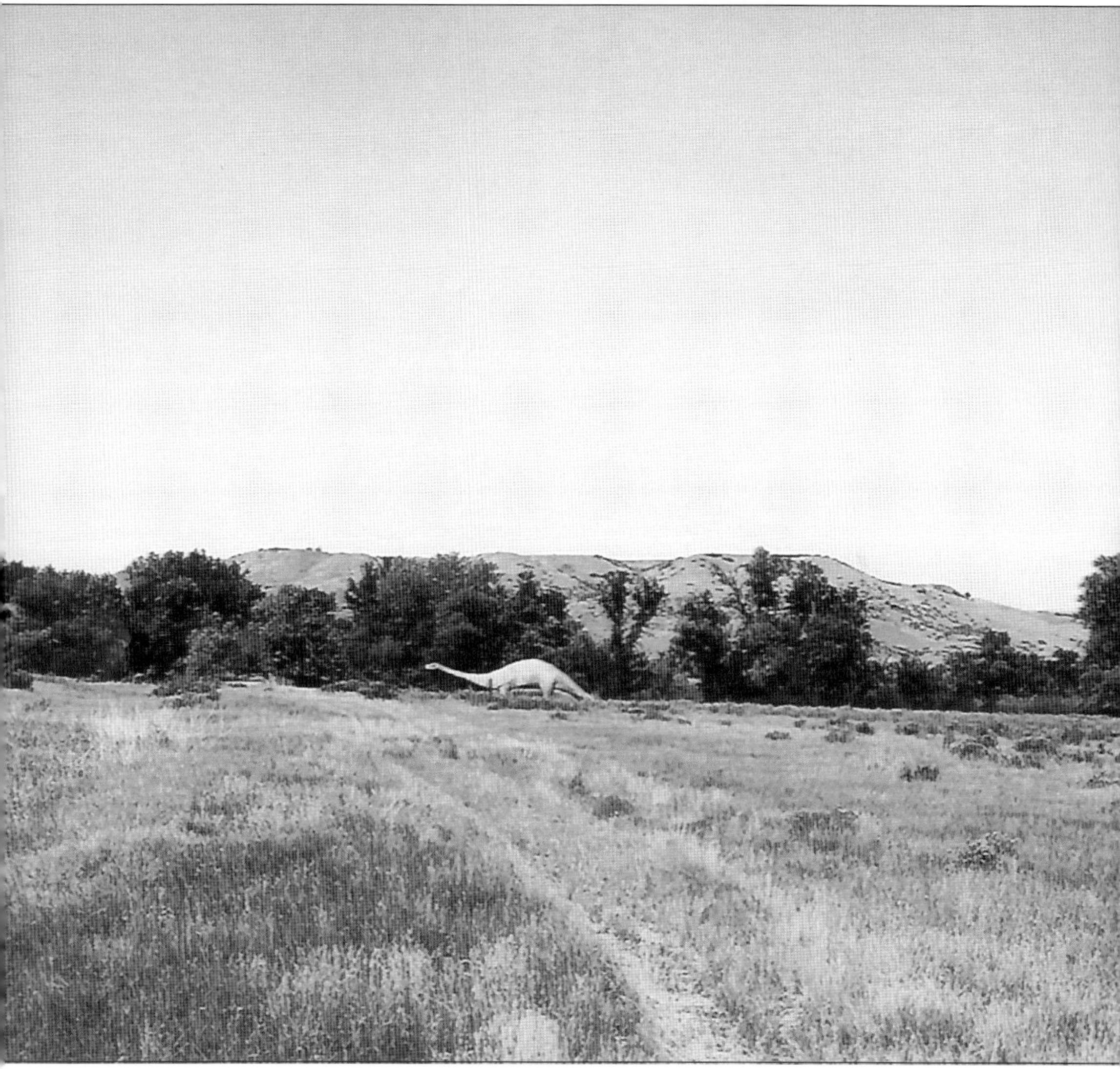

Creston was the next stop on the railroad west of Scenic. It was located on the west bank of the Cheyenne River at the mouth of Rapid Creek. Established early in 1884, Creston served settlers in the area by providing a store and post office. The post office was established in 1886 and remained in operation until 1946. The dinosaur built in 1933 was hoped to lure motorists off the highway to the Creston general store. There were 30 to 40 people living in Creston at that time. The old road that was built near the dinosaur and the remains of the bridge crossing the Cheyenne River are visible here. During the late 1990s, a chapter of the American Society of Civil Engineers at the South Dakota School of Mines and Technology refurbished the former roadside dinosaur attraction, which was in a serious state of deterioration. A few foundations from the former Creston still exist. The next stops on the Chicago, Milwaukee & St. Paul Railroad were Farmingdale, Caputa, and Rapid City.

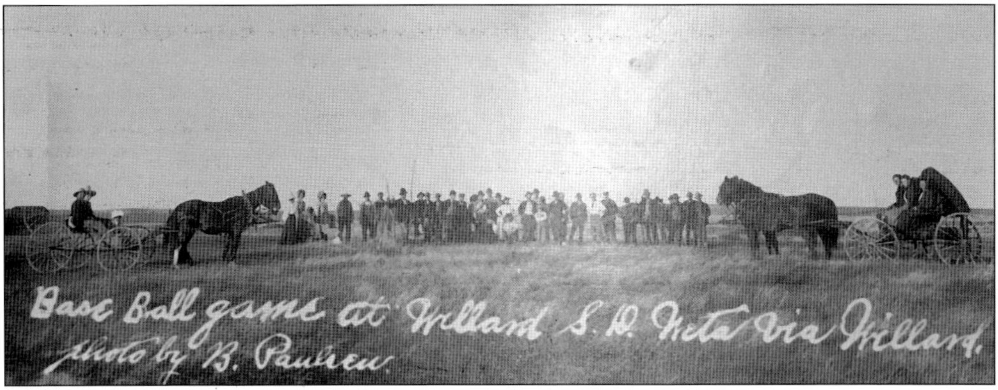

West of Kadoka on the upper prairie, Willard and Weta meet for a baseball game. Baseball was a popular pastime in the area, and it was not unusual for baseball scores to make the front page of the newspaper. In 1906, Allen and Amy Spaurs came to their claim 12 miles west of Kadoka, where they ran a post office and general store called Willard. Neither Willard nor Weta exist anymore. (Courtesy of the Kadoka Depot Museum.)

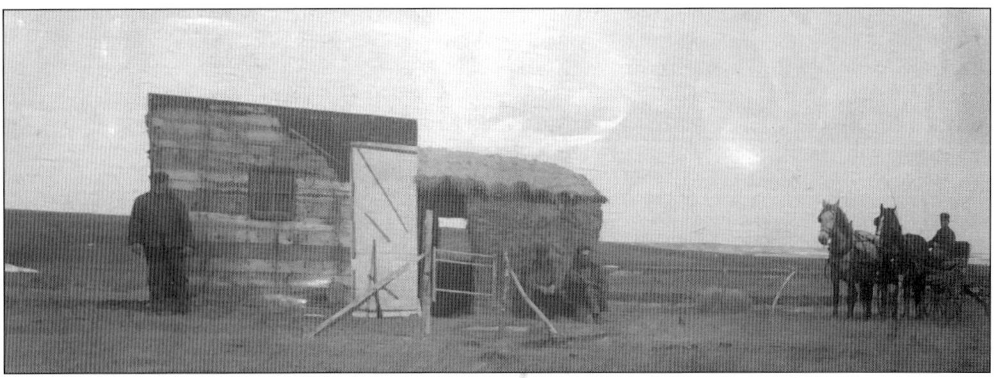

Unmarried women and widows were able to file on homestead claims. Anna Boock Paulsen was one of them. Before she married, she homesteaded on 40 acres near Willard. She married Barney Paulsen in 1910 and lived on her claim. Barney was a photographer who took pictures of the area. When he died, Anna went to live with her sister Alma and brothers at the Pearl Hotel in Kadoka. (Courtesy of the Kadoka Depot Museum.)

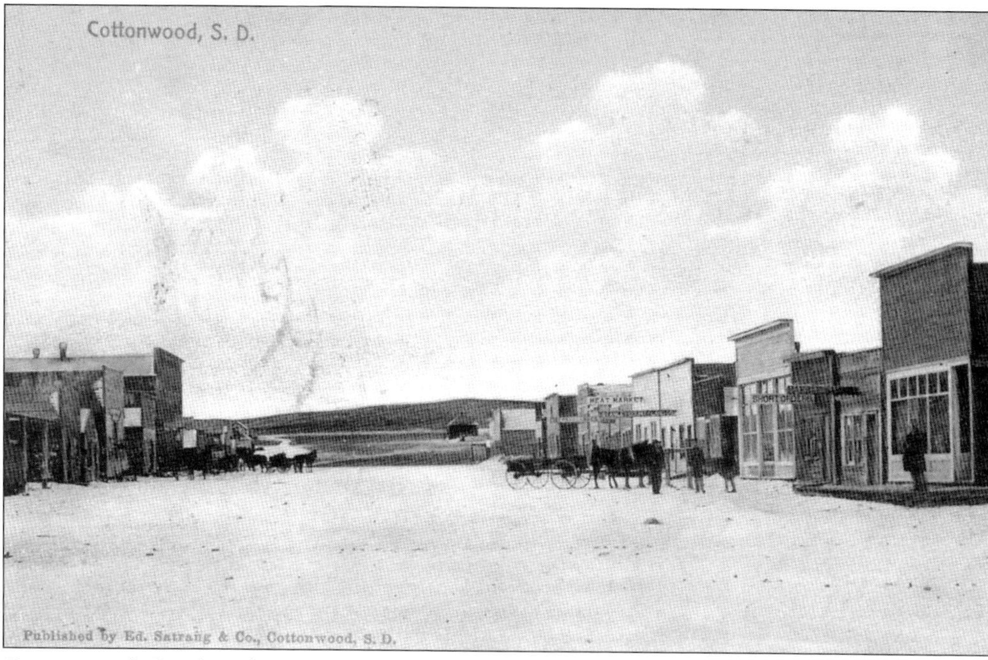

Cottonwood, South Dakota, is in the northwest part of Jackson County, north of the Badlands. The Cottonwood Post Office was established in 1906, and the Chicago & Northwestern Railroad came through around 1907. Cottonwood became an important trading center to early residents. The population reached 400 at one time. Businesses were numerous and included hardware stores, grocery stores, a bank, restaurants, a blacksmith shop, two lumberyards, cream stations, filling stations, saloons, and others. Two fires in the 1930s destroyed many businesses, and the town never recovered. The depot operated until the 1950s. Today, Cottonwood could be classified as a ghost town, although several families make their home there. Several buildings still stand. The church at right probably dates to around 1906. At that time, itinerant clergy traveled to churches on horseback or by team and wagon.

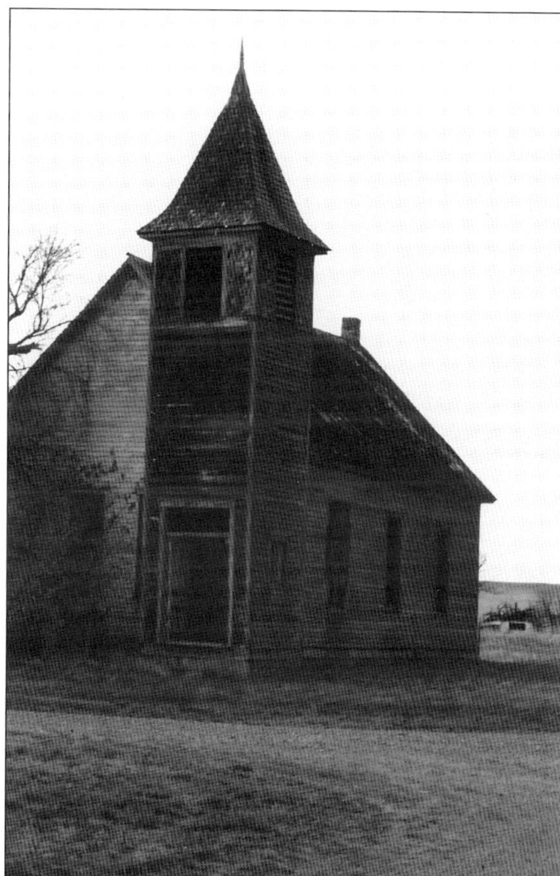

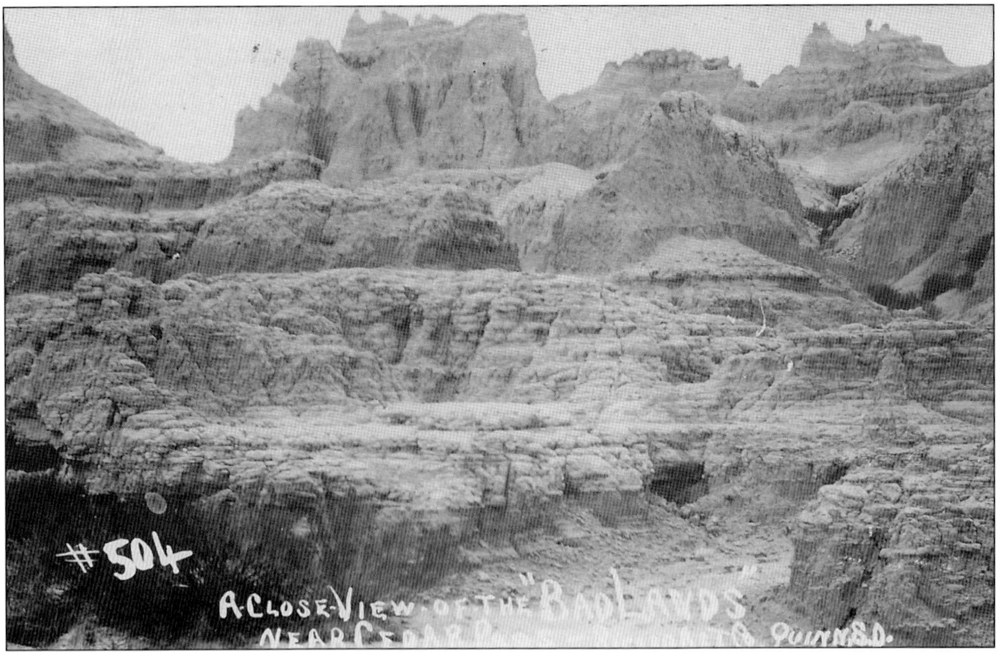

This view near Cedar Pass was produced by the Ricard Art Company in Quinn, South Dakota. Herman Ricard opened an art studio in Quinn. The sender of the postcard tells his friend that he had been working out in the country the last week, threshing and hauling the tank wagon. The card is dated August 5, 1909.

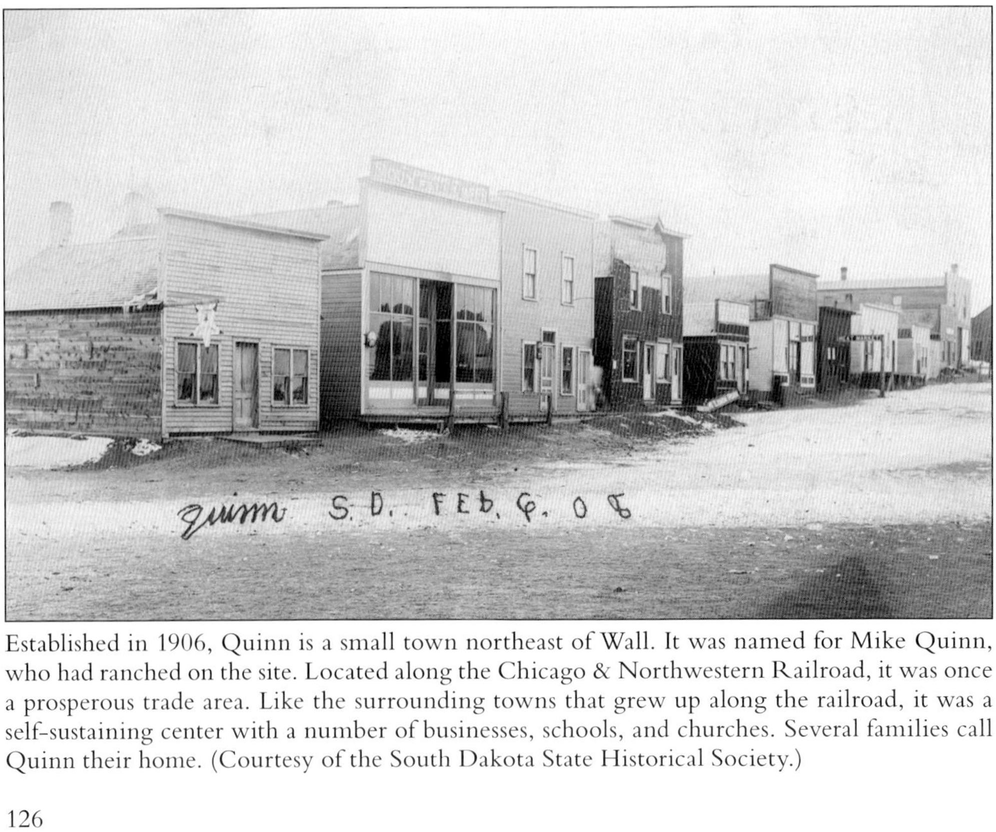

Established in 1906, Quinn is a small town northeast of Wall. It was named for Mike Quinn, who had ranched on the site. Located along the Chicago & Northwestern Railroad, it was once a prosperous trade area. Like the surrounding towns that grew up along the railroad, it was a self-sustaining center with a number of businesses, schools, and churches. Several families call Quinn their home. (Courtesy of the South Dakota State Historical Society.)

Bibliography

American Legion Auxiliary, Carrol McDonald Unit. *Eastern Pennington County Memories.* Wall, SD.

Burnham, Philip. *Song of Dewey Beard, Last Survivor of the Little Bighorn.* Lincoln, NE: University of Nebraska Press, 2014.

Cerney, Jan. *Badlands National Park.* Charleston, SC: Arcadia Publishing, 2004.

Hall, Philip. *Reflections of the Badlands.* Freeman, SD: Pine Hill Press, 1997.

Hauk, Joy Keve. *Badlands, Its Life and Landscape.* Interior, SD: Badlands Natural History Association, 1968.

History Book Committee of Kadoka Centennial Committee. *Jackson Washabaugh County History, 1889–1989, v. 2.* Pierre, SD: State Publishing Company, 1989.

Jackson-Washabaugh County Historical Society. *Jackson-Washabaugh Counties, 1915–1965, v. 1.* Pierre, SD: State Publishing Company, 1966.

Lewis, Mary Solon. *Interior, the Badland Town and Stories of Badland Homesteaders.* Wasta, SD: Lewis Publishing, 2016.

Mattison, Ray H., and Robert A. Grom. *History of Badlands National Monument.* Interior, SD: Badlands National History Association, 1968.

Shuler, Jay. *The Revelation Called the Badlands, Building a National Park, 1909–1939.* Interior, SD: Badlands Natural History Association, 1989.

www.indianz.com